A NIDA graduate, Merridy Eastman has performed in a swag of productions for the Melbourne and Sydney Theatre companies and spent several summers leaping about botanical gardens across Australia bringing Shakespeare to the masses. As well as being an ex-*Playschool* presenter, Merridy has had major roles in many television shows including *Neighbours*, *Blue Heelers*, *Always Greener*, and has recently joined the cast of Channel Seven's *Packed to the Rafters*. She is the author of the best-selling *There's a Bear in There* and *Ridiculous Expectations*, contributing writer for *Breast Wishes* the musical, and consequently featured in Penguin's anthology *Thanks for the Mammaries*.

how *now* brown frau

how *now* brown frau

merridy eastman

ALLEN&UNWIN

Published by Allen & Unwin in 2011

Allen & Unwin
Sydney, Melbourne, Auckland, London

83 Alexander Street
Crows Nest NSW 2065
Australia
Phone: (61 2) 8425 0100
Fax: (61 2) 9906 2218
Email: info@allenandunwin.com
Web: www.allenandunwin.com

Cataloguing-in-Publication details are available
from the National Library of Australia
www.trove.nla.gov.au

ISBN 978 1 74175 975 4

Set in 11/13.5 pt Bembo by Bookhouse, Sydney
Printed and bound in Australia by McPherson's Printing Group

10 9 8 7 6 5 4 3 2 1

The paper in this book is FSC certified.
FSC promotes environmentally responsible,
socially beneficial and economically viable
management of the world's forests.

For all my dear friends in Munich: Rowena, Dagmar, Jane and Lara for all the love, laughter and Knusprige Ente. *For dear Lisa, Valerie, Shoma, Christine and John for their much valued friendships and nutritious company always.*

And for Maxine Ryder, talented sculptress, fantastic tour guide, my beautiful smiling mate who looks good in any hat and deserves a gallery of her own.

And—Action!

Right. This was it. There was no turning back now, I thought, glancing again at the tall German sitting by my side as we sped down the A92 towards Munich. Here began my new life in Bavaria, with a man I'd met eight months earlier on a jetty in Lymington.

'Your thing is on inside out,' he'd said then, gently touching the sleeve of my cardigan.

Backlit as he was by the sun, all I could see was that he was tall, attractive, in his early forties, and had impressively straight teeth, but the voice was as clear as it was deep, and the accent, I felt sure, was French.

'Bavarian? Really?'

Geography had never been my strong point, but even I knew Bavaria wasn't in France.

If anyone had told me that at forty-two, in the year 2004, I'd be packing up my life in Sydney and relocating to Bavaria, I'd have called them a taxi. 'Brave' was the word my friends kept using, at least to my face. And I must admit, given I spoke no German and knew nothing whatsoever about Munich, except that it had hosted the 1972 Olympic Games and was home to the Oktoberfest, perhaps they were right. But brave wasn't the word to describe how I felt those last few weeks when I'd woken up at 4 am in a cold sweat with respiratory problems. Every actor knows only too well the recurring nightmare in which they find themselves naked on stage in front of an audience, having forgotten all their lines. Imagine how much worse that nightmare is when that stage is in Düsseldorf and all your cues are in German.

'Schlafmutzi!' Tom yelled, making me jump, as he released my hand and put his foot to the floor.

It wasn't quite the same mellifluous tone I'd heard on the jetty the previous summer, but we weren't by the seaside now. We were twenty kilometres north-east of Munich, and owing to an unusually late March snowfall, everything was white, from the endless fields on our left, to the forests on our right and to the alps in the distance. Only the autobahn, due to snow ploughs, salt scatterers and endless traffic, was devoid of snow, enabling the Bavarians in their good German cars with winter tyres to go very, very fast.

'Volldepp!' Tom shouted as he drove so close to the car in front that my right foot frantically searched for a brake pedal.

Curse these Europeans with their steering wheels and pedals on the passenger side. They were hard enough to adjust to without jetlag.

'Amateur, oder?' Tom shouted at the expressionless driver as we passed, and then squeezed my knee as he caught my shell-shocked expression. 'Sorry, my love. You ok?'

I told Tom that it wasn't his temper that worried me so much as overtaking another car on the left while simultaneously breaking the sound barrier. If I'd overtaken on the wrong side of the road while driving two hundred and twenty kilometres an hour back home, I'd have ended up weaving baskets at Silverwater Women's Correctional Centre.

It had been an unlikely place for a German and an Australian to meet up, the small Dorset town of Lymington on the south coast of England. But due to London experiencing one of its worst heatwaves on record last summer, my younger brother Max had wanted to escape from his small flat in Turnham Green and celebrate his fortieth birthday somewhere near the sea. And thanks to her BBC connections, my older sister Georgina was able to secure just the thing, a seaside cottage belonging to one of her colleagues.

'Angela. You know. Angela the newsreader. Nose-job Angela. Left her hubby for Miss Ireland.'

Even before she'd moved to London and become a seasoned journalist, my sister had a knack for summing people up with just a few short, punchy facts. 'Beethoven. Composer. Deaf as a post. Bipolar.' Or 'Frida Kahlo. Mexican painter. Impaled in a trolley accident. Monobrow.'

So who else was coming to our younger brother's seaside celebration? I'd asked.

The usual suspects, George said, rounding up various other expat friends of ours who'd made London their home, plus a visitor from out of town called Tom.

'German. Tall. Into water sports. Not your type at all.'

Really? If I was determined to do one thing that summer in London it was to try something new, take a few risks, change direction and start all over again. Sometimes a girl has to admit, especially when she's had a love life like mine, *I think I'm on the wrong train.* After yet another relationship had limped its way to the knacker's yard the previous year, at the age of forty-one the thought had crossed my mind that mine was a train for people who'd missed other trains, a train that took truly unnecessary detours, and a train that had occasionally doubled as a paddy wagon. But a publisher's invitation to come to London and publicise my first book had put an end to all that. Just weeks before I met Tom, I'd made a pledge to myself. From now on I was only going to date someone if he was genuinely interested in me, entirely available, and stone cold sober. And there he was, standing on the jetty in a seaside town called Lymington. Within a week, Tom had not only taken the trouble to read my book, but had asked me out on three dates in a row. Within two weeks he'd declared his love, and within three months, having stayed in each other's homes in Munich and Sydney, Tom and I were engaged to be married. The only catch was that one of us had to move from one hemisphere to the other.

As Tom slowed down to 180, I finally relaxed enough to recall my last frantic weeks in Australia. Having finished performing in a Noel Coward play at the Opera House, I'd flown south to Hobart to hug my dear shrinking parents one last time, loaded up my Sydney friends with pot plants, cutlery and picture frames, let out my little flat in Paddington, and sold my car and all my furniture through the *Wentworth Courier*, until the only remaining possessions I had left were now tightly compressed into two suitcases in the back of Tom's Volvo. Oh yes, and I'd had my amniocentesis test to make sure the baby was fine.

'And is he?'

'Yes,' I answered my beaming fiancé. 'He's lovely.'

Tom took my hand and held it to his chest, and kept it there as he overtook the driver on our right, shouting through his window. 'Voll Trottel!'

Even my trusty agent agreed it was a good idea to pack up and go. With at least twenty talented actresses over forty on her books all going for the same guest role on *McLeod's Daughters* and one margarine commercial, Sally looked at me as if I'd won a raffle.

'Go to Germany,' she said. 'Have a baby. You're missing out on bugger-all here. Unless . . .' Sally madly tapped on her computer keyboard. 'Have you already done an *All Saints,* darl?'

I'd hoped Sally had deleted my appearance on *All Saints* from her computer.

'Oh yes,' she murmured, frowning at her screen. 'The mother of a ballerina with halitosis.'

'Scoliosis.'

We nodded sagely. My performance on *All Saints* was at the very bottom of my guest role barrel.

'Go to Germany.'

But shouldn't I at least stay home to have the baby near English-speaking doctors, surrounded by a network of close friends and family? I asked my dependably honest friend.

'Look, darl,' Bev said, heaving another plastic bag of soiled disposable nappies towards her back door, 'for the first sleepless year of motherhood you may as well be living in a cave on a hill in Kazakhstan.'

Bev flipped back the wheelie bin lid, and as the flying nappy bag hit the bottom with a dull thud we were both nearly asphyxiated in a toxic cloud.

'Go to Malta. Be with Rolf.'

'Munich, and it's Tom.'

'Whatever.'

But the most surprising response to my announcement had come from my parents, or 'the Ancient Ruins', as my mother preferred to call herself and my father now they were approaching eighty. Rox and Dad had already seen their other two children leave Australia to pursue careers in London. And here was their one remaining child, just as she miraculously became pregnant with their first grandchild, off to live in Bavaria. It was the biggest bombshell I'd dropped on them since I told them I'd got a weekend job working in a brothel—'As the *receptionist!*'

But despite me putting ten thousand miles between us at such a benchmark moment in our lives, my parents could not have been happier. I could tell by the way they'd both flung their arms around Tom when I'd brought him home for Christmas, as if a passing ship had finally seen their flare.

'You dear, dear man,' my mother had murmured into his cashmere jumper in the hallway, while my father ran to the CD player to put on Mozart's *Die Zauberflöte*.

It didn't really hit me that I'd left one country to go live in another until a few hours earlier when I landed in Vienna. No busy international airport should be this quiet I thought as I watched the world pass by with the sound turned down. Just twenty-three hours earlier I'd sat at Gate 39 in Mascot as parting lovers practically copulated before me, overexcited toddlers escaped from their stressed mothers and crashed into postcard stands, besotted grandparents played one last game of peekaboo with their grandchildren, and families had complete meltdowns over postponed flights, misplaced passports and overweight luggage. But Vienna's muted soundtrack was nothing compared with the total silence on my packed flight to Munich. And by the time I stood at the baggage carousel at Franz Josef Strauss airport an hour later, I was fighting off a full scale panic attack. The only places this quiet back home were churches, libraries and ashrams.

Two years, I reminded myself.

'Just give it a go for a couple of years,' Tom had suggested over various romantic dinners during our whirlwind courtship. 'And then we'll see how you feel. If you don't like Munich, we don't have to stay there.'

I knew that I would always remember these words, but the question was, would Tom?

But as he deliberately took the scenic route through the wide majestic avenues of his hometown, I soon forgot my misgivings about the Bavarians and lost myself in Munich's historic architecture again. I'd fallen in love with Ludwigstrasse six weeks earlier when Tom had flown me over to 'test the water'. Giving a person two weeks to decide whether or not to relocate to Germany was a bit like asking someone to blow into a bassoon before signing up with the Berlin Philharmonic, and yet here I was, smiling nervously as I took my seat in the wind section. Although I still had serious doubts about living in a town where the commuters sat in silence, where the pedestrians berated you for crossing against the lights, and where the traditional meal was *Schweinshaxe* (roasted pork knuckle) and *Semmelknödl* (dumplings made out of stale bread rolls), I did love the idea of living in an ancient city in the heart of Europe. Whenever I felt homesick for Sydney's glittering harbour and myriad bays and beaches, all I had to do was catch a bus into the city, or Munich's Altstadt, and I felt much better.

Having left the city behind with its skyline of steeples and domes, we were now heading south towards Harlaching. Although it was good to see everything was greener since my last visit at the close of winter, my heart sank as I noticed the pedestrians on various street corners, still waiting for the green light despite there being no traffic whatsoever. I was a jaywalker, a street bounder, a car dodger from the big city who could stand in the middle of George Street holding a takeaway latte at peak hour. How was I ever going to make this adjustment? But soon my butterflies alerted me to a bigger problem. Passing the endless rows of apartment blocks with their steep alpine rooftops, I recognised Tom's local shops in the distance, some glistening with the remnants of snow: the *Minimarkt*, or supermarket; *Bäckerei*, or bakery; *Metzgerei*, or butcher; and *Apotheke*, or chemist, all standing like a formidable panel waiting to test me. Just the thought of entering one of them and dealing with Germans who spoke German was enough to make my palms sweat.

'Here we are,' Tom said, turning left into his quiet little street and pulling up outside the large, white, three-storey house that had been in his family for three generations.

And there was dear old Herr Müller, Tom's lovable if demented uncle who lived in the ground floor apartment, just as we'd left him six weeks earlier, in gloves, scarf and coat, sweeping the neat garden path into submission. His wife, Frau Müller, stood just as we'd left her too, stooped over a rogue leaf by the letterbox, wincing as she picked it up, then rubbing her back with an air of unappreciated martyrdom. Never in my life had I witnessed two people with so much time on their hands or with such a fear of leaves.

'Hallo, Herr Müller,' I said, delighted that the old man had shuffled over to open the gate.

'Grüß Gott,' he answered hoarsely, shaking my hand and offering the customary Bavarian greeting, pronounced *Grooss Gott*. 'Sie sind die Putzi, oder?'

'Nein, Papa!' his wife growled as she waddled forward, angry with her husband for confusing me with their Hungarian cleaning lady.

I was *die Freundin von Tommy*, she said, snatching the broom from his hand, *die aus Australien kommt*. Without greeting me, Frau Müller apologised for her husband's Alzheimer's and with her eyes on my feet, waited for me to pass so she could sweep up any dirt I'd brought with me from Australia.

'Ahrooooooooo . . . ooh!' rose a mournful cry from the other side of the Müllers' frosted glass door as we entered the building.

I'd seen some unusual breeds of dog in Munich during my last visit, but the Müllers' skinny white dog looked less like a canine than a sick albino deer and had a ghostly howl to match. I wondered what he'd suffered in his short dog life, and clearly I wasn't the only one. Other dogs from around the neighbourhood would pause at the front gate to observe the wretched beast howling on the path with their heads cocked to one side. 'Fritz? Is that *you?'* they seemed to be saying. 'What the hell happened, man?'

'Where are you going?' a voice hissed from behind when I was halfway up the stairs to Tom's apartment. 'Shoes!'

Oh, that's right. I was now living among a people who considered the wearing of outdoor shoes inside unhygienic, yet they allowed their dogs on public transport and into restaurants. And now I was expected to climb down the steep spiral stairway to change my shoes in the *Schuhkeller*, a miserable cave lined with shelves full of shoes.

'I don't have any Hausschuhe!' I shouted down to my German fiancé, secretly delighted I'd left my old slippers in a skip back in Sydney. 'So I'll just have to walk around in my socks.'

'You have Hausschuhe here,' the deep voice insisted from the basement. 'I bought some for you.'

I froze like a statue. He *what*?

'I bought Hausschuhe for you, and some good winter boots.'

No one had chosen my shoes for me since I was ten.

'How?'

'Online.'

I stared at the brass horseshoe stuck on the stairwell wall in front of me. Was this a German thing? Did men buy their girlfriends shoes, online, without asking? How did Tom know my size, let alone what colours I liked? And *boots*?

'Merridy!' the voice called urgently from below.

Before my runners spread the black plague throughout the house, I ran down to the basement, past the laundry, the ancient toilet, the dusty wine cellar, the vintage ski closet, the boiler room, and a mysterious room with a dungeon door, always locked. A few minutes later, coming out of the shoe room in a pair of amazingly comfortable black suede *Hausschuhe,* I paused at the locked gothic door and turned to Tom.

'What's in there?'

'That's my aunt's sewing room.'

I looked at him.

'Who locks up a sewing room?'

Tom put his arm around me and kissed my forehead.

'My aunt.'

By the time we reached our landing on the first floor, I knew by the giggling that Tom's affectionate, diminutive neighbour was waiting to welcome me. Gretchen lived in the granny flat above us, and despite us being unable to utter one sentence in each other's language, it was fair to say that Gretchen and I loved each other.

'Grüß' Dich!' she cried when I reached the top of the stairs, enveloping me in her small but powerful arms.

When they weren't off wine tasting in Süd Tirol, Gretchen and her petite Russian girlfriend spent their weekends doing energetic things like rock climbing, abseiling and taking part in kickboxing championships, and she had hugs to prove it.

'Hi, Gretchen!' I gasped in her crushing embrace. 'Look! Hausschuhe!' I cried, breaking away and pointing to my new feet. 'From Tommy!'

'Schön!' Gretchen cried, nodding approvingly at my shoes, and then pointed proudly at her own. 'Meine!'

I sighed wistfully at Gretchen's pretty Chinese slippers.

Unable to tolerate Gretchen and I cheering at each other's feet another minute, Tom interrupted to ask Gretchen something important, and after much nodding, he turned to me to translate.

'Gretchen says she'll water my plants while we're in Marquartstein.'

While we were *where*?

'In Marquartstein.'

Marquartstein?

'Where our holiday house is. At the foot of the alps. Where we're going this weekend.'

Really? It sounded terribly romantic.

'Where my family will be waiting for us.'

The old town

When Tom and I went on our first date the previous summer in London, we were both a little appalled by our lack of general knowledge. It was bad enough that I wasn't sure if Bavaria was actually part of Germany, but I couldn't believe that Tom had never heard of *The Sound of Music*. However, now I knew better. Bavaria was as much a part of Germany as Austria, where the von Trapp family came from, was not. And despite being neighbours who shared many things, including the same language and a fondness for *Lederhosen*, the Bavarians and Austrians did not appreciate being confused.

'They think we lack charm and are too direct,' Tom told me, 'and we think they could stop trying to be so charming and just be more honest.'

But Tom said he could understand my confusion about Bavaria's independence from the rest of his country. The Bavarians had always taken pride in having their own separate identity, he said, with their own traditions, culture, architecture, music, cuisine and even political parties. Having a stronger relationship with the land, Bavarians were proud, Tom said, of their peaceful rural villages, surrounding alps, lakes and forests. And they weren't at all surprised that Munich was consistently voted the city in which most Germans wished they could live. And why not? Tom asked. It had a stronger economy, was considered safer, cleaner, gentler, more ordered and, since the war, had been painstakingly restored.

Berlin might be considered the more exciting, fast-paced and edgier city, with more bars and cafés, a more vibrant arts scene and night-life, but it was also poorer, more crowded, dirtier, with lots of traffic, chaos, street buskers and graffiti. The more Tom talked about Berlin, the more I wished we lived there.

'Ah, but from Berlin,' he reminded me, pulling me towards him, 'we can't just get in the car and drive across to France, Austria, Switzerland and on to Italy.'

Now my Bavarian fiancé was talking. According to Tom, we could have breakfast in Munich, be in Salzburg for morning tea and reach Venice by sunset. And then there were the Alps, that magnificent sweep of snow-capped mountains in the distance that stretched along the Bavarian/Austrian border, down to Switzerland and into Italy and France. As a twelve year old playing one of the von Trapp children in the Theatre Royal production of *The Sound of Music* in Hobart, I'd finish the show every night ascending a large, papier-mâché alp with my fellow actors to the swelling chorus of 'Climb Ev'ry Mountain'. But now that I could see the real thing from our balcony, I knew that no amount of papier-mâché could take its place, and that any family attempting to cross that terrain in socks, sandals and full Austrian eisteddfod costume would never have been seen again, not even by a lonely goatherd.

Before the impending official welcoming ceremony with Tom's family in Marquartstein, an event that stirred butterflies in my stomach every time I thought of it, Tom kept us busy with a daily schedule of sightseeing based on the compact travel guide he'd given me back in London.

'So what would you like to see today?' he'd ask, as if testing me over our breakfast of rye bread, cheese, sliced ham and salami. 'Olympiapark? The Deutsches Museum? The Hofbräuhaus?'

But my answer was always the same and Tom knew it. With its history of kings, queens, plagues and monks, I just couldn't get enough of Munich's Altstadt. I loved walking through the old city streets where every ancient building, be it a gothic church, a neo-classical theatre, an ancient brewery or a Renaissance palace, had a story to tell, some of them dating back from a thousand years ago when the city had been founded by Benedictine monks.

'That's why it's called *Münch-en*.'

But Tom didn't need to tell me that. Nor did he have to tell me who the guy on the horse was on the Wittelsbacher Brücke, as we crossed the Isar River on our way to the city.

'Otto I, Duke of Bavaria,' I said, pointing to the statue, 'the first of the Wittelsbach dynasty that ruled Bavaria from 1180 until the end of the First World War.'

'How did you know that?'

I blamed the BBC. Ever since my parents had insisted we stop doing our homework and come downstairs to watch Keith Michell in *The Six Wives of Henry VIII*, I'd developed an insatiable appetite for history.

Having parked in the inner-city borough called the Glockenbachviertel, arm in arm, Tom and I would cross the busy Sonnenstrasse and approach Sendlinger Tor, south of the city. This was my favourite and oldest of the three remaining medieval gates to the Altstadt. Through the sweeping arched entrance of this great, red brick wall with flanking towers, one covered with ivy, I could glimpse the Old City waiting for us on the other side. The two other medieval gates, both within twenty minutes' walking distance, were Karlstor towards the west and Isartor towards the east. Although both gates had medieval towers and pointed archways, neither of them looked as ancient as Sendlinger Tor with its crumbly red bricks. In fact the grey plastered and painted finish on Karlstor made it look so much like a theatrical set, I half expected to see actors in medieval costumes appear on its turrets, blowing trumpets.

Every day, Tom and I would walk through the ancient entrance, and then wander down my favourite street in Munich, Sendlingerstrasse, as historic as it was narrow, that led to the centre of the city. First stop was always the famous Asamkirche. Built by the two Asam brothers, Cosmas and Egid, this small baroque church was originally, and somewhat unbelievably, the brothers' private chapel. Standing in the doorway I would often join other speechless tourists taking in the gilded opulence before me.

'Holy vestibule,' I muttered.

It looked like the Palace of Versailles crammed into one room. Every inch of its rosy marble walls was richly decorated with stuccowork, gilt statues of cherubs and angels, oil paintings, frescoes, sculptures of saints, and even a grim reaper. Marble columns of pale blue and gold twisted their way to a ceiling on which a lavishly painted fresco depicting heaven was trimmed with gold. Even the ornate church pulpit, like a miniature grotto, was so elaborately decorated with silver and gold leaf, framed by marble cherubs, angels and an animal with horns, that the only words I could imagine anyone saying from it were, 'Could someone please take my photo?'

After staggering out into the daylight, Tom would take my hand and continue down Sendlingerstrasse until we reached Munich's famous city centre, Marienplatz, through which thousands of tourists passed every hour, according to Tom. Having begun its life as a marketplace, this constantly busy city square had witnessed everything from celebrations and tournaments to plagues and executions. And looming over the entire piazza was the neo-gothic town hall, or Neues Rathaus. Despite its ancient looking façade dripping with sculptures of dragons and saints from local legend and history, the Neues Rathaus was actually built towards the end of the nineteenth century. And even though it housed Munich's lord mayor, had six inner courtyards and the famous Ratskeller restaurant in the basement, the real drawcard of this building was its clock tower. If it was approaching 11 am, I'd take my place among the thousands assembling in the city square too, and wait for the clock to come to life. As the sound of forty-three ancient bells hammered out a little tune, a dozen mechanical copper figures began rotating, first on the upper stage as they performed a stiff but charming jousting match. No sooner had they exited left than a troop of 'barrel makers' entered on the stage below to dance the famous *Schäfflertanz,* originally performed in 1517 to prove to Munich's townspeople that the plague was finally over.

As Tom had witnessed this delightful ritual since childhood, he'd often take this opportunity to go buy himself a *Butterbrezn* from Rischart's Bäckerei, but for this girl who'd grown up with nothing more exciting than the animated clock in Hobart's Cat and Fiddle arcade, I found Munich's Glockenspiel enchanting.

From Marienplatz we were just metres away from Munich's oldest church, the Gothic/Romanesque St Peterskirche. Having been burnt down, bombed and reconstructed many times in its life, the Alte Peter, or Old Peter, had a Renaissance steeple, a tower with eight clocks, an interior lined with murals and a stunningly ornate and detailed gold Baroque high altar. Another notable feature of this church, apart from the stunning 360 degree view of Munich from the steeple lookout once we'd climbed the three hundred steps, was the famous relic kept below. Joining a small group in the second chapel, I once eavesdropped on their tour guide as she expounded upon the jewel studded skeleton resting on a cushion inside the glass coffin before us. St Mundita had been beheaded by the Romans in 305 AD, and since her martyrdom, according to the guide, had become the patron saint for single women. For a moment we all stood staring back at her ghoulish glass eyes and jewel encrusted mouth in her skeletal remains, until a lanky Texan woman to my left broke the silence: 'Well, that's encouraging,' she drawled.

Skipping the baroque beauty and ancient relics of St Peterskirche, Tom and I often walked straight into Munich's colourful and fragrant central marketplace instead. Every day thousands of tourists and locals gathered around this Viktualienmarkt's *Maibaum*, or maypole, to browse through its outdoor stalls selling fresh flowers, fruit and vegetables, including some that I'd never seen.

'Spargelzeit!' Tom announced, as I examined the thick white sticks in crates next to the radishes. 'It's asparagus season!'

At first I thought he was joking, but apparently the Germans consider this vegetable a real delicacy. Instead of growing their asparagus above the soil, turning it green with the sun like we do, the Germans deliberately grow theirs below, Tom explained, giving it a sweeter flavour and a tenderer stalk. And every year from April to June, *Spargel* is eaten as a main course, usually in servings of six, covered in melted butter or Hollandaise sauce, often with ham and boiled potatoes. I was just about to touch one of the white stalks when the young man standing next to me was reprimanded for doing the same.

'Rühr's nicht an!' the buxom seller roared from behind her eggplants, reminding me of a blue heeler I'd once encountered in the back of a ute.

Americans, Tom whispered as he gently led me away, had a disgusting habit of touching fruit and vegetables before buying them.

I nodded. So did we, but I'd just given up. Forever.

On the other side of Marienplatz, past all the restaurants full of Bavarians eating *Spargel*, stood one of Munich's largest churches, the Frauenkirche, meaning Church of Our Lady. This enormous gothic church was mostly famous for its two towers. In fact it was impossible to imagine Munich without their two onion-shaped domes silhouetted in the city's skyline. According to Tom, this was due to stringent historical preservation laws forbidding anyone to either build above the domes themselves, or to obstruct the view of the domes from anywhere else in the city.

'That's why we have no skyscrapers,' he'd say with a smile, giving me a kiss.

And it was true. In a city with a population of 1.3 million people, the only buildings that scraped the sky here had steeples, domes and ancient clock towers.

'Shall we grab some lunch on the way to the palace?'

Tom knew that a trip into Munich's Altstadt was never complete for me without a leisurely stroll down Residenzstrasse to Max-Joseph-Platz, the centre of Munich's elegant quarter. Looking out over the square from behind its Corinthian columns was the Nationaltheater where many of Wagner's operas were first performed. But right next door was Munich's Residenz, palatial home to various Bavarian monarchs, including the Wittelsbach dynasty, from 1385 right up until the end of the First World War. I was originally intrigued by how much the palace exterior resembled a theatrical set, until Tom explained that due to a lack of funds after the war, instead of restoring the original frontage, local artists had been paid to paint a fake stucco façade. But inside more than one hundred and thirty rooms had been painstakingly restored to their original state, including a royal chapel, an antiquarium, a rococo theatre, a grotto, a mirrored cabinet, fountains and various galleries as well as ten courtyards.

And then, if Tom didn't wish to visit his old friend Katrin, it was on to my favourite place in Munich, Odeonsplatz. If it wasn't too cold, I'd sit on the stone steps of the majestic Feldherrnhalle, a Florentine temple built by Ludwig I to honour the heroes of Bavaria, and, flanked by two magnificent stone lions, enjoy the view. Looking out on Odeonsplatz, Ludwigstrasse stretched out before me: to my right was the palace Hofgarten and to my left the Theatinerkirche, a Roman baroque church, yellow on the outside, white on the inside, with two matching bell towers. But if Tom wanted to visit Katrin, we often strolled down Maximilianstrasse, otherwise known as the Golden Mile, past the Bayerisches Staatsschauspiel theatre, past shops such as Dolce & Gabbana, Versace, Louis Vuitton, Dior, Chanel, Escada, Bulgari, and so on until we reached the elegant doorway with spiral stairs leading up to Katrin's boutique art gallery.

'Do you mind?' Tom would ask, kissing my hand as we ascended.

'Of course not,' I'd say, hoping Tom's old friend Katrin might have stepped out for lunch. But one look at the way Katrin's fashionable clothes hung from her angular frame and it was clear that this was a woman with better things to do than eat lunch. With her blond ringlets falling down from clips on each side of her thin face, Katrin reminded me of a pedigree poodle, a poodle with an expensive collection of cashmere cardigans, tight designer jeans and Italian shoes, that also ran an art gallery. Having watched them warmly greet each other, I'd stand there while Katrin entertained Tom with one scandalous story after another, usually involving the arduous attentions of some new admirer, a besotted ex, or a blind date, until I relieved Tom of his duties as translator and perused her current exhibition instead. For the next twenty minutes I'd examine every dull painting in Katrin's spartan gallery until Tom could ignore my yawns no longer.

'Katrin was just asking if we'd like to go to a gallery opening next Tuesday!' he'd cry, holding out his hand to me.

But I knew by the way Katrin smiled sadly at my RM Williams boots that she'd done no such thing. Nor did her dinner invitations ever include me. Katrin and Tom had a long history of attending art gallery openings, or else making salads for each other, Katrin's apparently swimming in vinegar.

'Merridy can't stand vinegar,' Tom had once told her, trying to include me in their conversation.

'Nein?' Katrin asked, as if I had a medical condition. 'You don't like Essig?'

'Can't stand the stuff,' I confessed.

'Well, I love it,' she announced, beaming at Tom. 'I can never have enough, kann ich, Tommy?'

I was surprised she didn't bathe in it, I told Tom as I stomped down the stairs afterwards.

Tom thought I was being mean, but I knew a territorial poodle when I met one.

'Woman can't keep her clothes on!' I continued as we reached the footpath. 'If she's not skinny-dipping with one fellow, or doing naked yoga, another's spying on her getting dressed at the gym!'

But what could I do? Katrin was part of my fiancé's life, a life I now shared with him in Munich. Other friends of Tom's couldn't have been kinder to me. Despite being an ex-girlfriend, Betty never felt the need to plant the image of herself naked in Tom's consciousness every time they met, and then there was Peter, Günther, Alexander, Birgit, Veni and Andreas, who'd all gone out of their way to make me feel welcome. If this beautiful ancient city was going to become my home for the next two years or so, I often thought as I sat on the steps of the Feldherrnhalle in Odeonsplatz, I was going to have to deal with bigger challenges than Katrin. Three in the next year alone if I counted German lessons, married life and, looming largest of all, motherhood. But before facing any of these major challenges was the one directly ahead of me. In a small alpine village called Marquartstein, in their holiday house surrounded by snow, my new German family was waiting to meet me.

Marquartstein

As we drove south from Munich through the Bavarian countryside, I couldn't help noticing how many old farmhouses and inns had painted frescoes on their facades.

'Lüftlmalerei,' Tom said, 'meaning air paintings, first became fashionable about two hundred years ago.'

Although some had chosen to paint fancy decorative windowsills with shutters around the frames, giving their houses a very theatrical appearance, others preferred life-size scenes from the bible, or from hunting, nature, or anything meaningful to the Bavarian way of life. Agriculture was especially popular, featuring cornfields, milkmaids, cows, a rustic looking horse and cart, or perhaps a chap in *Lederhosen* playing some sort of lute. Tom said if I wanted to see some serious *Lüftlmalerei*, one day we'd drive further south to a village called Oberammergau. Not only did Oberammergau have the most illustrated houses in Germany, but once every ten years, between May and October, people came from all over the world to see this little village perform the Passion Play, something they'd been doing ever since God had miraculously saved them from the bubonic plague back in 1633. I didn't know what was more extraordinary, a show that had been running for nearly four centuries, or the fact that half the village, over two thousand locals, took part in it. Only those born in the village, or who'd lived there at least twenty years, were allowed to participate, Tom said, and in order to achieve the most authentic look for the play, for a whole year beforehand all the men would cease shaving and cutting their hair. If this wasn't community theatre at its best, I thought as we passed a house painted with shepherds, what was?

Even Tom had to suspend his road rage as we followed a horse and cart through the charming village of Marquartstein on this fresh spring morning. Passing one large *Landhaus* after another with wooden shutters and window boxes full of tumbling lobelia and petunias, I felt as if a childhood wish had been granted and I'd been magically transported into a picturesque toy village. Even the locals, some of them in their traditional *Lederhosen* and *Dirndl* with woollen jackets, looked as though they'd been wound up that morning by an enormous child who any second might step over the surrounding alps to adjust a sheep here, or stick a maypole there. But by the time Tom finally pulled up at our destination I was under no such quaint illusions as to my surroundings. I stood by the car looking at the very real, dark wooden house with its sloping alpine roof looming before us, and searched for a crucifix. Having counted so many during the one hour car trip from Munich, stuck on farmhouse gates, on doors, on letterboxes, and one protruding from the ground at a bus stop, I'd gathered that here, *auf dem Land,* we were indeed among believers.

'Are your parents practising Catholics, Tommy?' I asked as we walked up the noisy gravel driveway.

Tom shrugged. 'Not really.'

Having met Herr *und* Frau Baumgartner on my last visit to Munich when they invited us to their elegant city apartment for afternoon tea, I already knew them to be kind, gentle, quietly spoken people who'd made up for their lack of English with an unbelievable selection of creamy cakes. And if it had been a shock to discover their son wanted to marry his pregnant girlfriend, a forty-one year old actress from Australia who'd written a book about working in a brothel (as the receptionist), they hadn't let on at all. In fact, I was rather touched by Frau Baumgartner constantly diving into her small English dictionary to look up words, and Herr Baumgartner's attempt to communicate with me by placing various clay animals from his vintage menagerie next to my plate.

'Schaf,' he'd said. 'Baaa.'

•

While we waited at the large wooden door with no crucifix, I took a few deep breaths. Although the first queasy trimester of my pregnancy had ended a month ago, the thought of meeting my entire extended German family over brunch had brought it back with a vengeance.

'And none of them speak English?' I asked again, trying to sound breezy.

Tom picked a ball of lint off my coat. 'I think my mother can speak a little. And my sister Ulrika too, but they probably won't.' Tom had already warned me that Germans like to do things really well or not at all.

'And would the Müllers be coming too?' I asked.

God no, Tom scoffed. Herr Baumgartner and his sister Frau Müller hadn't spoken in decades.

I was about to ask why when the large door creaked open.

'Grüß' Dich, Merridy,' Frau Baumgartner greeted me, pulling me into the warm but dark hallway and kissing me gently on both cheeks.

With her fuzzy dyed reddish hair framing her sensitive, pale face, and layers of woollen clothes under an apron tied around her slim waist, Tom's mother reminded me of my favourite Raggedy Ann doll, before I'd left her too close to our old oil heater.

'Grüß Sie, Frau Baumgartner,' I answered.

Although my future mother-in-law could call me *du, dich* or Merridy, until she gave me permission I had to address her with the more formal *Sie,* or else Frau Baumgartner. I thought of my fellow Tasmanian Mary Donaldson up the road in Denmark, who possibly wasn't allowed to call Queen Margrethe II Margie yet either.

'Shoes!' Tom reminded me.

And I wondered if Prince Frederik made Mary take her shoes off too, every time they entered the palace.

'Bitte, kommen,' Frau Baumgartner beckoned, before furtively groping for a doorhandle in the wall behind her, reminding me of the car accident some forty years earlier that had left her with permanent double vision.

In my socked feet, I followed Tom's mother into a cosy combined living/dining room decorated to the hilt with traditional Bavarian ornaments. To my left was a small galley kitchen, and to my right a breathtaking view of the surrounding alps through the French windows. But straight ahead, waiting to greet me like a formal welcoming committee in front of the dining table, were my smiling, neatly dressed in-laws.

'Hallo,' I said, nervously offering my hand and the only German I knew, apart from *Kindergarten, Zeitgeist* and *Schadenfreude.*

'Grüß Gott, Merridy,' they each replied quietly, gently passing me down the line like a new pet rabbit, kissing me lightly on both cheeks, except for the ten year old Leopold, who briskly shook my hand.

'Frohe Ostern,' Frau Baumgartner added, and after holding her little yellow dictionary up to her nose, peeped over with the translation. 'Heppy—Istar.'

Looking behind us I now noticed the coffee table in the lounge area was covered with baskets full of shiny Easter eggs and hand-painted boiled eggs in little straw nests. Even the rustic candle chandelier in the middle of the room was dripping with delicately decorated eggshells hanging from lacy ribbons.

After a short exchange with his mother, Tom turned to me to explain the absence of his aunt and uncle. Due to 'fern', he said, Onkel Norbert had had to take Tante Ilsa back to Munich straight after breakfast.

Oh, what a pity. Was she allergic to foliage?

'Föhn,' Tom repeated, and spelt it for me. 'It's when dry air falls from the alps causing the low pressure system to collide with the high pressure system, giving some people headaches. Migraines even.'

Really? Because of some wind coming down an alp Tante Ilsa had to lie down in a dark room with an icepack on her forehead? I looked at Frau Baumgartner, who was now holding the side of her face as if someone had hit her.

'Föhn always sets off my mother's neuralgia,' Tom explained.

I'd never heard of such a thing. It was like discovering dense fog could make some people flatulent.

Forbidden to help the three generations of Baumgartner women, including Ulrika's young daughter Claudine, carry food from the galley kitchen to the dining area, and not able to join the men in conversation on the L-shaped sofa, I stood for a moment at the French windows to take in the view. The picturesque landscape outside reminded me of a doll my mother had given me when I was home sick with bronchial asthma. The doll might have been made in Taiwan, but she wore the dress of the Black Forest district and had three large red pompoms on her hat. And best of all, when you twisted her wooden base, she played Schubert's *Heidenröslein,* a song my musical father knew by heart and would sing from every room of the house for the rest of the day.

Röslein, Röslein, Röslein rot, Röslein auf der Heiden.

'Alpen,' a hoarse voice uttered by my side.

Herr Baumgartner weakly gestured beyond the soft green paddocks towards the surrounding alps.

'Yes,' I agreed with him. 'Beautiful.'

'Schnee,' he added, and with his shaky fingers mimed snow falling.

'Yes, snow on the—tips,' I confirmed. 'Cold out there, but lovely and warm in here!'

'Kachelofen,' Herr Baumgartner said, and pointed to the large ceramic woodfire stove in the corner. 'Holz. Feuer. Warm.'

'Lovely.'

The old man and I both nodded at the *Kachelofen* until his daughter came to our rescue.

'Mittagessen!' Ulrika announced, instructing her children to take their places.

With my back to the view, I was seated at the end of a long dinner table handsomely set for eight or—Christ!—nine, if you counted the huge four foot wooden crucifix hanging on the wall opposite. Not religious? I'd never seen such a large effigy of Jesus outside of a cathedral. I was still staring at his bloodied feet and gaping chest wound when a hand touched my arm, making me jump.

'Oh!' I cried. 'Pretzels!' and thanked Ulrika as I took one from her basket.

'Brezn,' Tom corrected me. 'Only Americans call them pretzels.'

Whatever they were called I was intrigued, I told Ulrika, by the huge popularity of this shiny, looped white bread covered in rock salt that everyone, including toddlers, seemed to enjoy eating dry from a paper bag. In Australia, we just didn't eat bread on its own.

'Have you one with butter eaten, Merridy?' Ulrika asked, and I nodded enthusiastically as she told me, in her halting English, about the delicious combination of bread and butter.

It was easy to forget that just six weeks earlier the stylish Ulrika had given birth to her third child, Oliver, now asleep in a bassinet on the couch. But Leopold and Claudine never forgot their baby brother, and it was touching to see how often they skipped over to check on him before returning to their places and smiling at me from ear to ear. The children's warmth was in stark contrast to their police commissioner father Horst, who sat under Christ's feet and studied me as if he was still on duty.

'Nein, Mama! Nein, nein! Mein Gott . . .'

Ignoring the protests of her son, Frau Baumgartner managed to carry the pot of hot water to the middle of the table without scalding anyone, and we sat in silence as Tom's father used tongs to carefully distribute one *Weisswurst* from within to each plate.

'Yes please,' I told Ulrika, who spooned some very wet potato salad onto my plate between the smooth, fat, white veal sausage and my *Brezn*.

'Guten,' Horst said.

'Guten,' everyone repeated, picking up their cutlery.

Given that Jesus was practically sitting at the table, I was surpised we weren't saying grace, and was just about to chop the head off my sausage when Tom stopped me.

'Let me cut it for you.'

Somewhat irritated at the suggestion that I couldn't cut my own sausage, I watched as my Bavarian fiancé, like a skilled surgeon, made a shallow incision down the length of my *Weisswurst* before delicately peeling back the transparent membrane on both sides with his knife.

'You don't eat the skin,' he explained, planting a kiss on my cheek, my cheek that was now burning under the bemused gaze of the rest of the table.

While I sat there eating the rich, spongy sausage, I took in my surroundings. To my left was the open lounge area, but to my right was a wall literally covered with Bavarian relics. Hanging beside a smaller crucifix in the far corner were several painted plates depicting hunting scenes. Next to them, a mounted stag's head protruded from the wall with a stuffed owl perched on one of his antlers. Although someone had placed spectacles on the stag's nose, the comic effect was somewhat nullified by the flanking antique hunting rifles. Closest to me and standing in the corner to my right was a tall, ornately hand-painted wooden cupboard. Accidentally fall back on those cupboard doors, I thought to myself, looking up at the beer jugs, oil lamps, antique sewing machine, stuffed hawk and piano accordion all perched on the top, and you wouldn't stand a chance.

'You ok?' Tom asked.

Realising I had the whole family's attention, I took advantage and asked how many people lived in Marquartstein.

They all looked at each other. *Drei Tausend? Drei Tausend Einwohner in Marquartstein, Papa? Zwei oder drei?*

'About three thousand,' Tom finally conceded, patting my knee.

And while they continued discussing the population and economic prosperity of rural Bavaria without me, it occurred to me that my past record for charming the pants off the families of new boyfriends had actually been rather good. Sustaining long-lasting relationships might have proven a challenge, but for impression made on the parents I usually got an A. Deprived of the ability to express myself, however, it was impossible to establish any rapport with the Baumgartners at all. And although

Tom was considerate enough to translate an anecdote here or explain his family's mirth there, I began to feel more and more like the family pet, cared for but invisible.

Forbidden again to help the women clear our plates and bring out the marble cake, I remained at the table with Tom's father, who stared blankly out at his beloved alps while his son and son-in-law discussed the latest Audi.

'You like Kamille Tee?' Frau Baumgartner asked, returning to the table with a large brown teapot.

A little disappointed that camomile tea was all that was on offer, I nodded, and then watched in disbelief as Tom's mother stirred five teaspoons of white sugar into the pot.

'Milch?' she asked, about to pour milk into my sweetened herbal tea.

I shook my head and watched helplessly as she poured milk into the others' cups.

'You ok?' Tom asked, as he did every twenty minutes or so, to check that I was still coping.

I nodded. Although I'd never seen people drink herbal tea with milk and sugar before, I was acquainted with the convenient blind spot covering the area occupied by an outsider at the table. I thought of all the people I too had smiled at warmly before ignoring them. That Chinese exchange student in Year 10, the Czechoslovakian conductor my sister once dated, and a deaf actor from Queensland who for some reason ended up joining us for a Christmas lunch. I knew it was a bore having to translate every anecdote, how it broke the flow of conversation, ruined comic timing and, worst of all, encouraged unwanted dependency. But having now found myself on the receiving end of this wretched deal, I badly wanted to turn back the clock and apologise to Chenguang, Tomak and the deaf guy from Bundaberg.

'Merridy, schau!' Ulrika sang, waking me from my reverie. 'I bring something for you.'

'Oh!' I said, following her gesture towards a stack of baby magazines called *Eltern* sitting on the coffee table.

'You will need them soon, yes?'

'Yes indeed!' I answered, laughing until I caught her husband's eye.

From the end of the table, Horst squinted at me as if he could already see me in my nightie, putting out his wife's German baby magazines with the recycling.

'Lernt die Merridy schon Deutsch?'

It was the first time the policeman had acknowledged me verbally since we'd met at the line-up before lunch.

'Noch nicht,' Tom answered.

'Noch nicht?'

For a few minutes I watched in silence as the two men had a somewhat heated discussion about my plans to enrol in a German language school in the city, until finally Horst addressed me directly.

'I'm just saying, Merridy, that Tom should speak to you only in German.' Horst popped a chocolate Easter egg in his mouth. 'This the *best* way for you to learn.'

For a moment I sat motionless, stunned by my future brother-in-law's somewhat brutal welcome, not to mention impressive command of English.

Promising Tom that I could find our quarters on my own, I left them all listening to Horst's amusing anecdote about Hansi Beisswanger's *Weisheitszahn*, whatever that was, and made my way back to the hallway and down the poorly lit spiral staircase to our chilly room below. Having felt my way along the long, cold corridor, I finally reached the doorway, groped inside for the switch, flicked it on and gasped. Not sure how many more deer antlers, antique guns and dead birds I could take, I shuffled over to one of three single beds against the wall, sat between a stuffed grebe and an elk, and had a bit of a cry. What the hell was I doing here? 'Tom should only speak to you in German.' I wished I could turn the tables on my future brother-in-law. I wanted badly to drop Horst in the middle of Tanzania, four months pregnant, without a word of African under his belt, and see how he felt, sitting around the campfire eating goat with his girlfriend's Masai tribe when brother Olekorinko suggested he be spoken to only in Maa.

'What are you doing in here?' Tom asked at the door five minutes later.

It was just the question I'd been asking myself, I answered, blowing my nose.

'But what did you expect?' he said, sitting next to me and rocking me in his arms. 'Of course it's going to be difficult. Of course you won't understand them. Of course it's going to take time.'

I looked into my fiancé's eyes. How could I tell him how archaic I found it all, the *Grüß Gotts*, the formal *Sie*, the unhealthy diet of bread and sausage, the truly disturbing number of deer antlers, crucifixes and dead birds. How depressing I found his aunt and uncle's fear of leaves, everyone's fear of shoes, of crossing empty streets, of talking on the train, and his family's reluctance to speak English with me, in case they made a mistake. How could I explain that at every turn since arriving in Bavaria, everything I saw, smelt, tasted, experienced failed to impress, attract or inspire me, except, of course, the old city. I kept catching myself wishing Tom was French, Italian, Spanish . . . Portuguese even.

'My dear love,' he said, pulling me up to my feet and kissing me. 'You'll see. It will get better. Just you wait.'

I was on the phone, telling my parents in Tasmania about my weekend at Marquartstein. I told them about the sweet tea, the painted eggs and the cake we ate for breakfast in the shape of an *Oster* lamb. I told them about our walk along the Chiemsee nearby, the largest lake in Bavaria, and eating at a Bavarian restaurant in the village, and about the *Föhn*, that had sent Tante Ilsa home with a headache. And knowing how much they enjoyed such things, I described the villagers in their Trachten, or traditional *Lederhosen* and *Dirndls*, celebrating Easter, and how to my actor's ear the Bavarian dialect sounded Scottish.

'Well isn't that interesting?' my mother began. 'I daresay some of the Germanic tribes that migrated to Britannia in the fifth century would have ended up in the Highlands, which *might* explain *some* phonetic similarities.'

Although she could call a portable fan-heater a 'hot blowy box', sometimes Rox's general knowledge could surprise like a freak wave. None of us would ever forget her answer during a game of Trivial Pursuit when asked where *panini* came from: 'Well that depends, Honeybee. Are you talking about the white bread that comes from Italy or the ancient Indian Sanskrit grammarian, because he came from Peshawar.'

Not wanting to upset them, I left the worst till last.

'You'll pick up German in your own time, don't you worry about Hornet.'

'Horst.'

'And then just think what it will be like to understand a Mozart opera,' my father petitioned.

'Or see a Brecht play performed in his native tongue,' my mother added.

'To be able to understand every word Hitler and Goebbels were saying from those podiums,' my father said.

For a moment my father's words hung in the air.

'She doesn't want to understand Nazis!' my mother shouted.

'Yes she does!' he protested. 'Everyone does. It's fascinating!'

'Never mind Goebbels, Honeybee,' Rox continued soothingly. 'Just think what fun it will be to be a student again, learning German with other young people, some possibly in the same boat as you.'

Before saying goodbye I asked my father, just for old times' sake, if he could still remember the Schübert song my musical doll used to play before I overwound her.

'Sah ein Knab ein Röslein stehn,' he sang, 'Röslein auf der Heiden.'

Dad may not have been Irish, but you never had to ask him twice to sing a song or recite a poem.

'War so jung und morgenschön,
'Lief er schnell, es nah zu sehn,
'Sahs mit vielen Freuden.

'Röslein, Röslein, Röslein rot,

'Röslein auf der Heiden.'

After we'd said goodbye, I listened to the exchange between my parents as they made several unsuccessful attempts to hang up.

'I wish I could sing like you, Bug.'

'You could if you stopped telling yourself you can't.'

'You always say that, but you know very well I sound like a cat stuck in a drain . . .'

My fellow aliens

I found it very hard to say *Grüß Gott.* The Bavarians might have grown accustomed to greeting each other with this blessing made popular by the Catholic church in the eighteenth century, but whenever I said 'May God greet you,' I felt as if I belonged to a commune that studied the bible in the mountains without electricity. I'd been approached by them at Central Station back in Sydney, usually in pairs. 'God's blessings be upon you,' they'd say, handing me a smiley badge and a pamphlet.

'But we say it out of habit,' Tom said, 'whether we believe in God or not.'

Whether Bavarians believed in *Gott* or not, they definitely believed in *Grüße.* Instead of sending love, regards or best wishes, they were forever sending each other greetings.

'Grüße an deiner Mutter.'

'Grüße an ihren Familien.'

And sometimes beautiful greetings.

'Schöne Grüße an Bettina.'

Even when I was on the phone to my parents in Tasmania, Tom would call out from the couch, 'Greetings!'

Grüß Gott was the formal way Bavarians, including neighbours, greeted each other in the street, or when entering a shop or a waiting room, or when being introduced. But Tom and his friends used the less formal *Grüß' Dich*, meaning 'Greetings to you', often the precursor to a question that always puzzled me: *Alles in Ordnung?* Back home, 'Is everything in order?' just wasn't a question one asked unless one was talking to a power of attorney or a tax accountant. But in Germany, *Ordnung* was a priority, something for everyone to strive for on a daily basis. As was precision, because the other word I heard a hundred times a day was *Genau*, meaning 'exactly'. Or *Klar*, meaning 'clear'. Fascinated by their discourse, I sometimes tried to imagine what it would sound like if Australians greeted each other the Bavarian way.

'God's greetings to you, Macca. How's the family? Everything in order?'

'Greetings to you too, Davo. Yes, everything's clear, thanks. You coming to our barbecue on Sunday?'

'Exactly.'

'At fourteen hundred hours?'

'All is clear.'

'Beautiful greetings to Deidre.'

'Same to Trish.'

Not surprisingly, whenever Tom left me at home on my own, especially during those first weeks in Munich, I always felt a little apprehensive about answering the front door, or anything else for that matter.

'Pick it up!' he'd cry whenever our cordless phone rang and I was nearest.

'Can't!'

'It's easy!'

'You!'

'Just say it!'

'No!'

'Why not?'

'It sounds rude!'

'It's not rude! It's the way we all answer the phone! Try it!'

Finally, grabbing the thing with a vice-like grip, I'd tremulously answer: 'Baumgartner.'

Even though I wasn't yet formally a Baumgartner, as I was answering a phone in a Baumgartner's residence, Tom said I had to say Baumgartner.

Why couldn't I just say hallo?

'Because we don't say hallo.'

No, they didn't. And nor did they speak English, despite Tom's assurances that they would. *Nein!* several voices had emitted down the phone when I'd asked. Even our cheerful plumber Herr Lackmann had shaken his head as he passed me on his way down to our *Keller,* as if the very question, *Können Sie Englisch sprechen?*, had stolen his vocal cords.

'Don't worry,' Tom said, kissing me goodbye one Monday morning. 'Just say *Grüß Gott, Frau Grebo,* and give her the thirty euros by the phone. She won't speak to you anyway, her German's atrocious. But she's a good cleaner!'

Having heard the doorbell an hour later I bounced down our stairs to let in the Baumgartners' Bosnian *Putzifrau.*

Standing on the other side of the glass door was a short, middle aged woman with messy dark hair and a wide smile, wearing a dress over her trousers. In her right hand she held a bucket full of cleaning agents, and in her left, her handbag.

'Grüß Gott, Frau Gre—'

'I love you!' she greeted me loudly from the porch.

Even the men working on cars at the *Tankstelle* across the road looked up from their bonnets as I quickly showed in our surprisingly effusive cleaning lady.

'You English, yes?' she continued, following me up the stairs with her bucket rattling.

That's right.

'My English!' She pulled me around to face her. 'I love you! Yes?'

'Very good,' I told Frau Grebo.

'Ich bin Senka,' she said, breathless as she offered me her hand on the landing. 'Aus Spit.'

'Ich bin Merridy, aus Sydney,' I told her, shaking her hand. 'Viel weit. Down unter.'

Senka squinted up at me. 'Sie sprechen nicht so gut Deutsch.'

'Nein,' I nodded, agreeing with her.

Senka took a step forward as if about to whisper something of great importance.

'I . . . *LOVE* you!' she shouted in my face, and roared laughing as she walked in through our front door, turned right into our bathroom, put down her buckets and lifted the lid of our toilet.

I'd heard of getting straight to work, but this was incredible.

An hour later, I was sitting at our dining table, happily writing to the industrious sounds of Senka scrubbing, polishing and hoovering her way through every room of our apartment, when the vacuum cleaner droned to a halt.

'Du!' the voice shouted, and I looked towards our bedroom.

Shouldn't she use the formal *Sie*? I thought to myself.

'DU!' the voice roared, making me jump out of my chair and run to our room.

A sweaty Senka stood next to our king sized bed, hands on hips, waiting for me.

'Schau!' she said.

I obediently watched as she threw Tom's doona onto his side, beat it to death with her hands, spread it out evenly, and then folded it up twice until it was a raised, neat block of smooth bedding.

'Und hier!' she said, pushing me out of the way to do the same on my side, until our large bed with its two doonas neatly folded on top had given the whole room an instant facelift.

I'd deliberately not bothered making the bed the traditional German way. It had been my silent protest about having to sleep under separate doonas, which was, I felt sure, a plot to discourage the national birthrate. Senka must have read my mind.

'Baby kommt?' she asked, pointing at my stomach.

My mother-in-law had already told her, no doubt.

I nodded. 'A boy.'

Senka smiled from ear to ear. 'Und nächstes Jahr, girl!'

Oh, I didn't think so, I told her, leaving her to her work. Given that I was already over forty, it was a bit like promising someone who'd just won the lottery that they'd win again next year as well.

I'd just made us both a cup of tea when I was summoned again.

'DU!'

This time I followed the voice to our second bathroom.

'Schau,' Senka commanded, pointing inside the toilet.

Oh dear, what was it? Gingerly I peered over the rim to see nothing but sparkling clean porcelain.

'Komisch, oder?' Senka whispered conspiratorially, gesturing with disapproval at the design of the toilet itself. 'Deutsche Toiletten.'

If *komisch* meant strange, curious, freaky, I had to agree with her. Since arriving in Germany, I too had taken an instant dislike to the older German toilets with their large, elevated shelf that sat just inches below one's posterior. It was just a closer relationship with ablutions than anyone but a gastroenterologist would desire, surely.

'Ja, komisch,' I said.

I waited to hear if she had anything more to say, but as Senka began spraying under the seat, I realised she'd made her point and I was free to go.

Just before Senka left, having disinfected even the phone, we had one more clumsy attempt at a conversation.

'Was gut in Australien?' she asked, standing at the door with her bucket and handbag. 'Bananas? Pineapple? Bier?'

I nodded. 'Bananas und pineapple. And yes, beer too.'

'Oh ja. Mein Mann, he *love* Bier! Viel viel viel . . .'

I nodded. 'In Australia too. Men drink viel beer. Big problem.'

'Mein Mann big problem!'

'Oh . . . ja . . .'

Senka and I paused, both of us perhaps recalling occasions that had involved men and too much beer, until she stepped onto the landing, pointed to my stomach and shouted.

'Your boy love bananas!'

'I hope so.'

'I go now.'

'Danke for gut cleaning!'

'I love you!'

•

I'd already heard that Turks made up the largest ethnic minority in Germany, but I gathered by the conversations I overheard on the street, and often these were the only conversations audible, that Munich was also home to thousands of migrants from all over Eastern Europe. I saw hardworking women like Senka falling asleep on the train reading their magazines written in the Cyrillic alphabet. And whenever I walked past a building site, the voices of workers shouting over the noise of heavy machinery were decidedly more Slavic than German. All the Baumgartners' friends seemed to have a *Putzifrau* called Nadezhda or Dubravka, or a handyman called Yavuz or Berk. To rebuild its economy after the war, Tom explained, Germany had opened its doors to immigrants willing to do manual labour for low wages, including women needed to work in factories making clothes or assembling electronics. But recently, with a Turkish population of nearly four million and an unemployment rate of over ten percent, the issue of ethnic minorities had become contentious in Germany. Not so much in Munich, Tom said, as in the former East Germany, where unemployment had soared since reunification, and where the far right and neo-Nazis made sure that the Turks, the Asians and any other *Ausländer* felt most unwelcome.

'See?' he said. 'Aren't you glad you live in Munich?'

I learnt more about migrants in Munich when I woke up thirsty one morning at five o'clock. The sun hadn't risen yet, and I was standing at our kitchen window with my glass of water, looking at the tram stop on the corner. Soon the first empty *Strassenbahn* of the day would rattle past on its way to the city, and Harlaching's early commuters would stand at the lights as dawn broke, even in the absence of traffic, waiting for permission to walk. I was just about to go back to bed when something moved under the street light on the footpath below. Jumping back into the darkness, I waited for a moment before daring to take another peek at him. Not only was he now standing at our front gate, but he waved!

'Tom! Tom!' I whispered, shaking my fiancé's shoulder a moment later. 'There's a large man standing at our front gate and, Tommy!—he waved at me!'

'It's prob'ly Pavel,' Tom groaned, turning away.

Pavel? Who was Pavel? Pavel the friendly psycho from the local asylum? Pavel who liked to lick people?

'Pavel from Poland . . . Pavel looking for work . . . I'll talk to him later.'

What kind of job did this Pavel think we might have that needed doing at five o'clock in the morning?

'Pavel always does this,' Tom croaked. 'He likes to get in early . . .'

Pavel didn't have a key, did he? 'Cause I didn't want to wake up in another hour to find him sitting on the end of our bed giving me a pedicure either.

'Komm gleich!' Tom shouted out the kitchen window to Pavel two hours later, and then resumed drinking his coffee while I finished interrogating him.

Every spring Pavel drove all the way from Warsaw, where he lived with his family, to Munich where he'd try to find work. Not the brightest of fellows, or the most skilled, Pavel was nonetheless a good worker, as strong as an ox, could lift heavy things, cut down trees, demolish walls, and paint. He'd certainly done his share of painting, I said, looking down at the ghostly vision smiling up at me. Pavel's overalls and coat were so rock hard with plaster and paint, he could have stood on a box in Marienplatz, tossed his cap on the ground and made a fortune as one of those irritating statues. But why Munich? I asked. Surely Berlin was closer.

Tom shrugged. 'He likes it here. Munich's friendlier, safer, there's more work. He can camp in the Feldmanns' garage around the corner and go door to door looking for work.'

Their *garage*?

'He never parks directly outside. At least Pavel's clever enough not to do that.'

Never mind where he parked, did the garage have heating? A shower? Cooking facilities?

Tom looked at me. 'It's a *garage,* Merridy. That's why Pavel only comes in spring.'

I watched Pavel from our window, flapping his arms to keep warm, waving cheerfully at the *Tankstelle* men arriving for work across the road. He was even early for spring.

'Mind you,' Tom muttered, putting on his coat to go downstairs, 'last year he was here till November finishing the Lichtenöckers' fence.' He returned to kiss me. 'I don't know how he survived that one.'

'Can't you go knock on his rollerdoor?' I'd ask Tom whenever Pavel was in town. 'Couldn't he do a bit of weeding in the garden? Shell a few peas? Darn a few socks or something?'

We weren't a charity, Tom reminded me. He wasn't going to 'create' jobs for Pavel just because his Australian fiancée wasn't used to living in a country with up to one million illegal migrants. So behind Tom's back, I once gave Pavel a fiver. I couldn't help it. On my way back from the bathroom one rainy morning, having heard someone coughing outside, I peered out the window and there he was, looking up through the drizzle, smiling and nodding. I could have thrown a stick into the street and Pavel would have brought it back between his teeth.

'Pavel!' I whispered down to him, my head almost freezing in the cold morning air.

'Hallo!' Pavel whispered back. 'Der Tom's Frau. Gut Frau.'

After ten years of doing odd jobs in Munich, Pavel's German was about as good as mine.

'Der Tom—schlafen—Pavel,' I whispered, miming sleeping. 'Can you come later? Später?'

'Ja ja! Kein problem.'

As the smiling giant turned to leave, I read the thermometer that Tom had stuck on the wall next to the window. Three degrees Celsius.

'Pavel!' I called after him. 'Wait! I wake him for you, yes?'

'Komm später,' Pavel said, waving.

'NO, PAVEL! DON'T GO BACK TO GARAGE!'

Pavel smiled at me over our rubbish bins, and tipped his cap.

'JUST STOP, WILL YOU?'

I ran into our lounge room, found my bag and ran back to the kitchen window.

'Here!' I said, scrunching up a five euro note and throwing it down to him.

As he made his way along our street in the drizzle, Pavel kept turning around to thank me for the small, crumpled note in his hand, and I kept waving. Hopefully he'd find a job before he reached the Feldmanns' concrete bunker, perhaps chopping more wood for the Luchsingers at number thirty-two.

Much less heartbreaking were the legal immigrants I met through Tom's family, like Rutana from Thailand, Frau Baumgartner's beautician, who lived just a station away. When Frau Baumgartner offered me a salon gift voucher, I didn't have the heart to tell her that I never visited beauticians, pedicurists or manicurists. I knew they provided services that a lot of women considered treats, but I just wasn't one of them. If I wanted good skin, I went to bed early. Good nails? Stop biting them for a week. And feet? I forgot I had them most of the time. But as Frau Baumgartner had been kind enough to give me a voucher, I was more than happy to go and meet another outsider who'd made this Bavarian city her home.

'Frau Baumgartner's English lady! Yes?'

Wearing rubber gloves, the diminutive, bubbly Rutana hastily made me feel welcome, before quickly returning to her client in the next room. For a few minutes I sat in Rutana's waiting area, which consisted of one chair in a narrow hallway opposite a cuckoo clock and a statue of Buddha, listening to the conversation going on next door. Frau Baumgartner may have described her beautician's German as *schrecklich*, even after thirty years, but Rutana sounded fine to me, not even pausing for breath when she reappeared a moment later, escorting her elderly client to the door.

'Sorry me so long!' Rutana cried, showing me into her 'salon'. 'But Frau Ringlmann always talk talk talk!'

And while Rutana chatted nonstop, deftly disposing of soiled tissues and wet towels, I took off my boots and passed an eye over the shelves full of cosmetics and lotions.

'What you wan', darli'?' she asked, suddenly facing me. 'I can do your face, your nail, or your fee'.'

Rutana caught me staring at the long, coiled hose on the top shelf.

'Or I can do Einlaufmittel!' she cried. 'How you say—anal?'

Enema, I told Rutana. Not anal. Enema. If she went around telling people she did anal, she was offering them an entirely different service. I told Rutana a facial would be just fine.

As I lay back on her white, imitation leather, reclining beautician's chair with a bib tucked under my chin and a showercap on my head, I tried not to panic as Rutana plastered my face with cream. I'd never known a person to ask so many questions, find everything so funny, or be so unconditionally generous. By the time she'd finished massaging the moisturiser into my forehead, cheeks and chin, I had places to stay all over the world, whether it was with her ninety-nine year old mum in Lampang, her brother in Singapore, her twin sister in Banda Aceh, or her aunt in Perth.

'You got long neck,' she told me, massaging the cream into my throat. 'Lady before you—no neck. I say, *Where your neck, Frau Ringlmann?* And she laugh. She German but she laugh.'

I knew what was coming next.

'How you find de Germans, darli'?'

I told Rutana that I liked them well enough, but was still getting used to a certain reserve and stiffness.

'Oh I *know*!' Rutana interrupted as she wiped the goo off my face. 'They 'orrible! I Buddhist, so I no like say bad thing 'bout nothing, but Germans is 'orrible and mean and cranky people, darli'!'

If she really thought so, why was she still here? I asked.

'I marry German!' Rutana sighed as she threw a hot towel over my face. 'But after five year I leave. He depressant. Rutana too happy for depressant. I stay for business, darli'. I have lotta lotta ladies, an dey love Rutana. Rutana make dem laugh.'

So were there many Thais living in Germany? I asked, changing the subject.

'Oh sure!' Rutana cried, now massaging what felt like sand

mixed with honey into my forehead. 'Lotsa girl. They come here and work very hard, so can send money home. Hey!'

What? I opened my eyes, and was almost blinded by the sting of exfoliant.

'You want girl? I send you girl from Thailand, darli'!' she cried. 'She clean your floor, she wash, she cook, she shop, an' when baby come she take care of baby!'

Well, even if we could afford such a person, I told Rutana, we didn't have room for her.

'You no need room, darli'!' Rutana shouted. 'She live under table. You pay her two hundred a week, an' she work like slave for you!'

Rutana was serious.

'I serus! I know plenty Asian ladies live under table! But you must say she friend, not slave, or they send her back again.'

Right.

While Rutana went to answer her phone, I lay there with what felt like cement on my face, imagining Tom and me sitting at our dining table every night as Boon-Nam snored at our feet, exhausted from doing the ironing. But the image of Boon-Nam's protruding legs had reminded me of a real problem Rutana might be able to help me with. And when she returned I asked her, where on earth did women get their legs waxed in Munich? Back home the beauticians did it, but here they all just shrugged at me as if to say, *Vax? Vas ist Vax?*

'Me!' Rutana shouted. 'I wax your legs for you, darli'! I got wax here . . . somewhere . . .'

I opened one eye to see Rutana scanning the far corners of her laboratory for wax. 'An' I sure I remember how to do it.'

I didn't like the word *remember.* Not when we were talking about pouring hot wax onto my bare skin. So changing the subject again, I asked Rutana about something else I was missing from home.

'You don't need Thai restaurant, darli'! You come to Rutana! You like Pad Thai?'

Sure.

'You come my place, darli'. I cook you Pad Thai and wack your lex.'

I left Rutana's with armfuls of presents, including moisturisers, soaps, Thai sweets made from coconut and almonds, and two dvds.

'You like Julia Robert?' Rutana had asked at the door in such a way it would have been cruel to say no. 'She so funny in *Pretty Woman*!'

Yes, who knew how hilarious and romantic prostitution could be until *Pretty Woman.*

'Here *Runaway Bride*,' she said, handing me the dvds, 'and *Evita.* Julia Robert not in *Evita.* That Madonna.'

Rutana was delighted to hear I hadn't seen either film.

'I made you beautifu', darli', like Julia Robert!' she cried from her doorway, waving as I got into her tiny lift.

'Thank you so much, Rutana!' I called back, holding up my bag of goodies.

It wasn't until I noticed the somewhat bewildered expressions inside our *Minimarkt* on the way home that I suspected Rutana had gone to town with the rouge and the lipstick, my free bonus for being 'such nice lady'. And once I was home, I knew for sure. The person staring back at me from our bathroom mirror wasn't Julia Roberts so much as Ronald McDonald.

'Oh, they do not live under a table!' Tom protested over lunch when I told him about Rutana's offer to find us a cheap Thai maid.

But how would Tom know? Perhaps this had been Rutana's own introduction to life in Germany. Perhaps her first home had four legs. After all, Pavel's was a garage. As I watched the Tolstoyan labourer pushing yet another wheelbarrow full of rocks from the Ohrenschall's garden along the footpath below, it occurred to me that if travel broadened the mind it could also be a very levelling experience. Our circumstances might have been vastly different but, whether they were here legally or not, these migrants and I had one thing in common. We were fellow aliens, away from our friends and families, trying to find our way in Germany. And whenever I saw them sitting on the U-Bahn with their calloused hands and tool belts, I felt glad of their company, warmed by their smiles and less alone in Bavaria.

Surfing in Bavaria

It may have been seven degrees Celsius, but on this chilly, damp, winterish Saturday morning in late April my Bavarian fiancé woke up with surfing on his mind. And so having packed his wetsuit, rubber boots, goggles, towel, video camera, tripod, thermos, lunch and, unbelievably, his surfboard into the back of the car, Tom drove us two kilometres down the road to a boat landing area called the *Floßlände* on the Isarkanal in Thalkirchen. Curious to see him surf in a city without a beach, I'd agreed to come along in my thermal underwear, three layers of clothes, beanie and duffle coat to record the event on video.

As Tom and I made our way along a trail from the car park through a forest of almost leafless trees, the sound of rushing water grew louder and louder until at last we reached a grassy clearing.

Having exchanged greetings with various friendly youths setting up tents, waxing their boards and changing into their wetsuits on the grass, I followed Tom to the bank of the canal. Standing on the edge, I felt the drop in temperature as the water rushed past our feet at a ferocious speed. Following its journey under the small arched bridge to our left, I looked up to read the large sign hung from the rails. *GROSSSTADTSURFER, e.V 2000,* or as Tom translated, City Surfers Club, registered in 2000. And beneath the sign was the reason we were here, a permanent frothing, foaming 'standing wave' made by a small ramp in the canal floor. On this man-made wave about a metre high and stretching seven metres from one bank to the other, I was going to witness some 'serious inland surfing'.

'Hallo, Thomas!' someone called.

Tom had already told me about Andi, the tall, handsome, tanned man with a blond ponytail striding towards us, and I was still struggling to believe it. When he wasn't working as an ambulance paramedic, building a hospital in Sudan, test driving BMW motorcycles on the Canary Islands or improving conditions for the monkeys at the zoo next door, Andi, who also had a black belt in karate, ran Munich's City Surfers Club. While the two men greeted each other with manly hugs and firm pats to the upper arm, I wondered if Andi could also speak English.

'Nein,' he answered, with a dazzling smile as he shook my hand. 'Sorry.'

He didn't have to be sorry for anything. On top of everything else, Andi looked like the Earl of Greystoke.

Half an hour later, surrounded by young people wearing wetsuits under their overcoats, I sat on Andi's fold-up chair protecting my front row position on the bank. I may not have been able to feel my toes, but after living among the elderly folk who shuffled along the swept pavements of Harlaching, I found the sight of piercings and dreadlocks exhilarating. Looking across the water to Tom and his friends, shivering in their wetsuits on the bank opposite as they waited in line with their surfboards, I had to admire their determination. Back home, I had friends who didn't go to Bondi all summer simply because they lived in the western suburbs, but here were people who lived three hundred kilometres from the nearest coastline and yet they'd left their warm homes on a cold morning, surfboards underarm, and made their way to a canal in a forest to do a bit of surfing.

So far about ten young German men and one teenage girl had taken a turn to stand on the water's edge, throw his or her board into the surf and then, to my amazement, jump on top of it. I thought this impossible feat alone deserved rapturous applause, but even more impressive was how long they stayed on their board before falling into the icy five degree water. Although it was alarming to watch one after another disappear under the bridge like helpless victims in a flood, Tom had assured me that the current delivered them around the corner to the *Floßlände*, where they could climb up the bank, down the hill and take their place in the queue for seconds.

My stomach was doing cartwheels. As Tom stood at the head of the queue in his black wetsuit, ready to toss his board in before him, I was still struggling to master his fancy video camera with its high definition and powerful zoom.

'Bastard!' I cried in frustration when my fiancé finally moved into place and all I could see through the lens was black.

'Schutzkappe auf,' a baritone voice said in my ear.

I looked to my left to see a handsome, soaking wet man wrapped in a beach towel.

'Schutzkappe,' he repeated, pointing to the lens cap on Tom's video recorder. 'Auf.'

'Thanks!' I said, taking the cap off. 'Danke!'

Manfred spoke perfect English and was very delighted to discover that Tom had not only got himself a girlfriend, but one from Australia.

'Sie kommt aus Australien!' he shouted, pointing me out to some wet friends watching from the bridge. 'Tommy's Freundin.'

Manfred's wet friends all waved and smiled as if I might have Qantas tickets in my pockets.

'What are you doing here?' one shouted back.

'Look!' another cried out, pointing to something directly behind us. 'We already made a home for you!'

The last thing I expected to see in the middle of a Bavarian forest by a canal on a cold morning was a Fosters beer tent.

'They're our sponsors,' Manfred explained.

I was so busy watching the two attractive girls in Fosters hats handing out cans in such unusual circumstances, I almost missed Tom's first leap into the foaming surf with his board.

'He's very good,' Manfred assured me, nodding at Tom.

Having found the video record button just in time, Manfred and I watched eagerly as Tom tossed his board into the surf and then, to my amazement, leapt on top of it. I nearly burst with pride as I filmed him, wobbling at the knees as he smiled triumphantly, until suddenly his board shot out from underneath, sending him backwards into the wave feet last. Holding my breath, I searched the choppy water for any sign of life until up bobbed Tom's face, still smiling. Zooming in for a close-up, I managed to follow the head as it was carried under the bridge and then disappeared out of shot like a floating coconut.

'The great thing about Thomas,' Manfred said with a smile, 'is he never gives up.'

Back at home, curled up together on our blue sofa and drinking hot chocolate while watching my out-of-focus, unsteady, and at times violent recording of the day's events, I grilled my Bavarian boyfriend about this thirty year river surfing phenomenon in Munich. If I wanted to see some real inland surfing, Tom said, we should go to the Eisbach, right on the edge of the Englischer Garten in the city, where Manfred and his friends often surfed on a larger, more dangerous wave. Throughout the year tourists would gather on Prinzregentenstrasse to watch these intrepid surfers take turns in the choppy water below. Tom had seen Manfred surfing there even when there was snow on the ground. Sometimes they even rigged up some generator-powered lights and surfed there at night.

Was that allowed?

'It's not exactly encouraged,' Tom said, 'but it's not illegal like open Isar surfing.'

Open Isar surfing was only possible a few times a year when, due to heavy rainfall, a torrent of water from the alps came thundering through Munich. When the water crossed under the Wittelsbacherbrücke in the city, a natural wave created by the uneven riverbed provided hardcore surfers with a challenge they just couldn't resist. That is until the police arrived to give them a warning, Tom said, much to the disappointment of the crowd gathered above.

I knew it was foolish to try to explain river surfing to them over the phone, but I'd hoped the little film I'd sent as an attachment with my email might have done all the talking for me.

'No, Honeybee,' my mother contradicted me a second time. 'All we've got here is a lovely photo of dear Tommy looking very smart, standing up in a canoe.'

He wasn't standing in a canoe, he was surfing on a surfboard, and if they just pressed the little arrow at the bottom left of frame, he'd move!

'Oh, he can't be surfing, love!' my father's resonant ABC radio announcer voice boomed into my ear. 'It's not Tom at the beach. It's Tom looking very handsome, fully clothed, under a bridge, standing on a—'

'A canoe!' Rox cried out again.

'It's not a bloody canoe! And he's not fully clothed,' I shouted at them. 'Tom is wearing a wetsuit because it's winter and he's river surfing on an artificial wave under a bridge down at the Floßlände on the Isar River.'

The silence from Tasmania actually gave me hope. My parents were often silent when digesting complex information. But when my mother finally spoke again, all hope was dashed.

'And you say he's *river dancing,* Honeybee?'

'Not river dancing! River surfing!'

Another silence.

'Right,' my mother said at last. 'Your father's back with our glasses now.'

'Yes. We've both got them on,' my father echoed, 'and ah!—you're right! He *is* wearing a wetsuit!'

See.

'Isn't he lovely and slim, your Tommy?'

'Now press the little arrow at the bottom left of the screen!' I nearly screamed at them. 'The little arrow is the play button, you see? So press it. Press it now!'

A silence.

'Have you pressed it?'

I could hear both of them muttering.

'Completely black.'

'That's funny.'

What? What was funny?

'Whole screen's gone completely black, Honeybee,' my mother said at last. 'I think your photo of Tommy river dancing in a canoe was just too much for our computer.'

Tom may not have surfed the dangerous wave under the Wittelsbacherbrücke in the city, but I sent the little film of my Bavarian fiancé to everyone I knew. He might have fallen into the icy water after only a second before his head sailed down the Isar like a lost ball, and my dear friend Lee, whose husband surfed at Manly every morning, may have laughed for days on end, but I was incredibly proud of my German river surfer.

Ich bin Merridy

By 1 May there were small signs that spring, instead of an extended winter, had finally arrived in Bavaria. Tom and I were now woken up every morning by a chorus of noisy birds singing outside our windows, and I was delighted to discover the stark pine trees at our back fence were not only turning green, but were home to a colony of red, black and brown squirrels. Inspired by all this industry going on in our garden, I'd prepared to start something too. Today, I was going to enrol at one of the more affordable German language schools in the city.

I was sitting on the third floor of Inlingua Sprachschule, waiting to take the test that would determine which level of Deutsch I should begin the following Monday.

'And have you learnt German before?' the friendly German receptionist asked the pretty Indian girl before me.

Sheepishly, the girl confessed she'd picked up a little over a working holiday, but that was all. Then she was given some papers and shown into a nearby classroom to do the test.

'I'm a beginner too,' I told the receptionist when it was my turn.

'So you've never learnt German at all?' she asked, smiling.

'Well, yes,' I confessed bashfully. 'When I was at school—just for a year.'

'Really?' she cried, pulling out another set of test papers from a drawer. 'You might just surprise yourself, you know. People often do.'

And so off I went, almost skipping with optimism into another empty classroom to do my German test. Maybe the receptionist was right. Maybe those German lessons with Mrs Frost in 1975 would all come flooding back to me.

Five minutes later, I sat at my white laminated desk with my head in my hands, suppressing a strong desire to wail. The only thing I could remember from my time with Mrs Frost was my slide project on Beethoven, and the word *Autobus.* Page after page, one sentence after another tormented me with their missing words.

Hallo, ich ______ Hans.

Six letters. I was tempted to write 'killed'.

Peter ist gross, aber Ludwig ist ____.

Dead.

Barbara spielt Cello. Sie ist eine ________.

Show-off.

Thirty miserable minutes later, I didn't so much skip back to the front desk as crawl.

'And if you feel Level Two is too slow for you, Vajra,' the receptionist was saying to the Indian, 'just let us know and we will put you up to Level Three, ok?'

Picked up a little over the holidays? I watched as Vajra swung her lying ponytail over her shoulder and floated down the stairs with her Level Two books under her arm.

'And how did you go?' the receptionist asked, turning her sunny smile towards me.

Reluctantly, I handed over my crumpled papers.

Ten minutes later, she emerged from her office looking a little tired, dishevelled even.

'I think,' she said quietly, 'we'll put you in the Beginners Course.'

As Tom and I stood in front of the *Fahrscheinautomat,* or self-serve ticket machine, at our local train station on Monday morning,

I tried not to be intimidated by all the buttons, slots, screen and instructions in German.

'You don't want the Einzelfahrkarten,' Tom said, pointing to one of the fifty buttons, 'because they're too expensive. Same goes for the Tageskarten. Either get a Streifenkarten and use two stripes travelling between two zones, or better still a Monatskarte.'

A *Monatskarte,* Tom explained, leading me to another *Fahrscheinautomat* nearby, was definitely the better option, until he discovered you could only pay for them with an *ez-Karte,* whatever that was.

'Well, don't they have a ticket-seller here?' I asked, searching the walls for a booth.

Tom looked at me as if I'd asked where the dancers got changed.

'Ticket-seller? There's no ticket-seller! You buy your tickets from a Fahrscheinautomat and if you haven't got change or an EC-Karte you get them from the Zeitungskiosk.'

Well, of course you did, I muttered to myself as Tom ran off. Anyone knew that. And if you didn't have a spare Fritzenburger, you could try putting a Glockenstein or two into a Schnurk.

'Quick!' he called back from the escalator. 'There's one upstairs.'

At the newsagency kiosk on the street upstairs I listened intently to Tom's incomprehensible exchange with the dour looking beehived woman behind the counter.

'You see?' he said as we ran back down the second escalator. 'You just have to ask for Eine Monatskarte, Innenraum or zwei Ringe, ok?'

'And what do I do with it?' I asked, clutching the tiny piece of paper with a bit of black print on it that had cost us forty euros for a month's travel.

'Put it somewhere safe,' Tom said as the 8.46 train pulled in at the platform two seconds late, 'in case the Kontrolleure get on.'

'The *who*?' I asked, following the other silent commuters into a carriage.

'The Kontrolleure,' Tom whispered from the platform.

'What do they do?'

'Shh!' my German fiancé hissed, annoyed by my volume. 'They board trains at random asking to see tickets. You'll know it's them when they show you their Ausweis.'

Their *what*? The *Kontrolleure* would show me their *what-ice*? But it was too late. With a beeping alarm and recorded instruction to *Bitte zurück bleiben,* the carriage doors shut, separating me from my only lifeline here in Munich. I waved goodbye until the train was abruptly sucked into the black tunnel, and then turned to face my fellow passengers looking out their black windows. Clutching my *Monatskarte*, I sat in a seat by the door like a frightened rabbit, waiting for the *Kontrolleure* to come on and show me their *Aus-heiss. Haus-ice. House mice.*

Seven minutes later, amazed that no one had asked to see my ticket at all, I ascended the escalator from Sendlinger Tor into the warm sunshine and noise of city traffic. One of the best things about Inlingua Sprachschule was that the escalator from the station below delivered me directly to its front entrance. After walking through the gates I followed the path until I was in a large courtyard, made my way through the youthful crowd gathered under the oak trees, climbed two flights of spiral stairs and walked into Room 207, a bright, clean classroom on the second floor. Through the windows, the tops of the magnificent trees in the courtyard waved gently in the breeze. A dozen white desks were arranged in a horseshoe shaped row around three desks in the middle, all facing the teacher's desk centre stage. And sitting in the middle of the row, leaning his chair against the back wall, sat a fit looking fellow with tattooed biceps and a buzz cut, wearing a Tooheys beer T-shirt.

'Hi,' I said, claiming one of the desks by the windows and unpacking my two shiny green textbooks that had set me back sixty-three euros.

Slowly, he took the pen from his mouth and looked my way. 'G'day.'

'Where you from then?'

'Sydney.'

He didn't ask where I was from. Like two dogs meeting in a park, Tooheys and I sensed at first sniff that we lacked compatibility. Thankfully the silence was soon broken when three beautiful young creatures chewing gum, giggling and speaking Spanish almost fell into the room. I'd never seen so much tousled hair or such scant clothing since my last holiday at Byron Bay. Despite the chill in the air, each one wore a tiny mini-skirt and a cut-off top revealing a flat, tanned stomach, complete with pierced belly-button. Even Tooheys was having trouble keeping up his indifference as they plonked themselves down at the three central desks in front of us, noisily unpacking their books, tiny phones and cigarettes. To show them I had nothing but admiration for their youthful exuberance, long tanned limbs and sexy outfits, I smiled warmly at them, and to show me they couldn't have cared if I'd jumped out the window, they totally ignored me.

A few more stragglers arrived, including a plump Asian girl wearing pigtails and a tight yellow knit dress, a smiling man in brown who looked like the Amitabha Buddha, and a woman wearing jeans and a bright pink hijab that covered her hair. A tall, handsome young man of Middle Eastern appearance loped across the room until, distracted by the Spanish girls, he collided with the teacher's desk in the middle.

'Sorry!' he said, rubbing his thigh, happy to have made them laugh.

The door opened again and this time all of us, even the Spanish chorus, did a double-take. *Why on earth would pop star Robbie Williams be taking German lessons in Munich?* As if used to having this effect on people, the young man feigned oblivion and busied himself unpacking his things at the desk by the door. We were still shamelessly gawking at him when the door opened again and this time even Robbie stopped to stare. A statuesque blonde wearing high heels, thick make-up, a lime green beret and a leopard skin top tucked into tight blue jeans made her way along our row of desks. As she plonked her purple suede bag on the table next to mine, took her beret off and shook her hair extensions, none of us could wait to go home and tell our partners—our class wasn't just transcultural, we even had a transsexual.

Sitting in a cloud of her perfume, I waited until my classmates resumed their chatter before introducing myself. Her name was Natalya and she was from Omsk, Russia.

'Whir dey from?' she asked, raising one heavily drawn eyebrow at the noisy chorus giggling in front of us.

'Spain?' I offered.

But I gathered by her cold glare over my shoulder that something else had displeased Natalya even more, and I turned just in time to see our tall swarthy friend two seats away wake from his trance and attempt a yawn. Distracted by a squeaking sound, the room fell silent again as we all watched the doorknob rotate left, then right, then left again. Hopefully this would not be our teacher. Finally it opened to reveal an enormous hairy man in bicycle gear standing in the doorway, smiling in wonder at his own achievement.

'Hola,' the giant announced in a husky voice.

'Hola,' a few mumbled back at him, except the Spanish girls, who put their hands over their mouths and slid off their chairs in hysterics.

Baring his few remaining teeth, our large classmate made his way along our row, stepping on bags and dragging cardigans off chairs until finally he stopped at the desk between me and my tall dark friend. It was courageous, I thought, to have left the house that morning wearing blindingly bright yellow bicycle shorts and a red singlet. I watched as he sat down, emptied his carry bag of books onto the table, took in his new surroundings and finally looked at me.

'Hola.'

'Have you just ridden here?' I asked, gesturing to his huge fluorescent legs.

The giant was about to answer when he was suddenly rendered insensible by the sight of my Russian neighbour. I waited until he recovered enough consciousness to recall my question.

'Hola,' he said again, and smiled.

And that's when I noticed the cotton wool, stuffed deep into his left ear.

At five minutes past nine, she arrived.

'Hallo! Hallo!' sang a petite middle-aged woman with short hair as she darted to the centre of the room.

Beaming at the nervous class before her, our sprightly teacher placed her books, mobile phone and a packet of cigarettes on the table in front of her. She couldn't have been more exuberant if she'd jumped out of a cake.

'Ok!' she announced, clapping her hands together. 'Ichh binnn,' she pointed to herself, 'Frrrrau Schhhhmeck!'

And with that announcement, Frau Schmeck broke into such an enthusiastic smile we could see her tonsils.

'Und Sie sind—?' She cast a mischievous look around the room, sending everyone's heart rate through the ceiling until she landed on me.

'Merridy,' I answered, going crimson under her intense gaze.

'Sie sind?' Frau Schmeck repeated, cupping her hand to her ear as if she hadn't quite heard.

'Merr-i-dy,' I repeated, like I'd done my whole life.

Frau Schmeck dropped her smile and shook her head, as if my name was Deb and we all knew it.

'Ich binnnn—' she said, waving me in like an orchestra conductor. 'Ich binnnn—?'

Finally I got it. 'Ich bin Merridy.'

'Gut!'

I felt like lighting up a cigarette.

'Und woher—' Her mischievous eyes searched the room for her next victim. '—kommen Sie?' She pointed euphorically at Tooheys.

'Australia,' he answered flatly, like it was the dullest pit on earth.

'Ich komme aus—?'

'Ich komme aus Australia.'

'*Ouss-trah-lienn!*' Frau Schmeck enunciated for the class, working her lips and baring her teeth. She went to the board and wrote *Australien.* 'Ich komme aus *Ous-traaah-liennnn*!'

Just a few minutes into the lesson and there was no doubt in my mind. With her agile body, dramatic hand movements, strong voice and expressive face, Frau Schmeck had worked on stage. I'd have put money on it.

'Und Sie?' she asked, suddenly turning on Robbie Williams.

Everyone sat on the edge of their seat, poised for the unlocking of a mystery.

The young man looked back at her with wide eyes.

'Woher kommen Sie?' she asked him.

You could have heard a pin drop.

'Ow gawd!' he howled, throwing his hands up to his face. 'I'm completely hungover, but here goes!'

His name was Adrian, not Robbie, and he was from Wapping. And *ja*, Adrian admitted in his Cockney accent, he could already speak *ein bisschen Deutsch*. 'Mein boyfriend bought me ein computer course,' he explained, and then, looking around the room, let out a laugh like a machine gun.

'Und ist ihre Freund einer Deutsch?' Frau Schmeck asked.

'Gawd yes!' Another burst of automatic fire. 'He's a flight attendant with Lufthansa.'

'Kein Englisch!' Frau Schmeck cried.

'Shit! Sorry! I mean *Ooh Scheisse*!'

Adrian no longer reminded anyone of Robbie Williams so much as Frankie Howerd.

For the rest of the morning Frau Schmeck went through the class like a delirious cannon, firing unexpectedly at random students until we all knew how to introduce ourselves and say where we came from. All except one. For the third time our determined teacher focused on the giant sitting next to me and, with her best smile, tried again.

'Und Sie sind—? Ihre Namen ist—?'

We looked at our fellow student in his bright yellow bicycle shorts and prayed for a miracle.

'Ich bin,' he began doubtfully, 'Frau Schm—'

'NEIN!' she shouted. '*Ich* bin Frau Schmeck!' She jabbed herself fiercely in the chest. 'Wer sind Sie?'

'Ich—sind—Sie—'

'WHO ARE YOU?' the Russian beside me exploded.

'Kein Englisch, Natalya!'

'José!'

We all looked at the giant. José? Did he just say his name was José?

'Sí, José,' José said again, and smiled as if all we'd had to do was ask. 'Hola.'

And so for the rest of the week the fifteen of us would sit all morning with furrowed brows learning not just how to introduce each other, but the name and gender of various objects. At ten thirty Frau Schmeck would announce it was time for our *Unterbrechung*, or break, and sighing with relief we'd switch on our mobile phones and head for the stairs like we'd been splitting the atom all morning. Sometimes I'd have to stop on the stairwell and guard my pregnant stomach until the stampede from all the other classes, desperate for coffee and cigarettes, had passed. Once outside I'd hold my breath as I made my way through their cigarette smoke, counting the languages I could hear until I reached the footpath. And passing other pregnant tummies, I soon realised I wasn't the only one from another country to have fallen in love with a German last summer. Although most seemed happy with their new circumstances, a few looked somewhat bewildered, as if the last thing they could remember was some nice backpacker offering to buy them a drink in a bar.

Having heard the rumble of fifty hungry foreign students approaching, the women in brown uniforms at the *Bäckerei* next door would visibly stiffen in preparation for an onslaught of totally incomprehensible requests. Taking the lead, the older women would step forward to show their juniors how to take a firm lead with *Ausländer*, or foreigners.

'*Brezn!*' they'd tell us firmly, extending our lesson as they pointed to the pretzels. 'Obstquark' at the tubs of fruit and sweet curd. 'Schinken und Käsesemmeln' at the ham and cheese rolls. And, of course, 'Do-nut!' With his *Rosinenschnecke* (snail pastry) and my *heisse Schokolade* (hot chocolate) Adrian and I would stand on the footpath outside where he'd regale me with the latest episode of his turbulent love life.

Adrian never asked about my life with Tom, and as Tom never threw my clothes out onto the street, we possibly did seem a little dull. One day he did enquire how my pregnancy was going, but just as I began to tell him I was due for my first German ultrasound, Adrian held his hand up and warned me he fainted at the sight of blood, and that childbirth stories made him want to throw up. Despite Adrian's delicate stomach and lack of curiosity about others, I found his refusal to curb his exuberance on the quiet streets of Munich refreshing. I also appreciated his superior knowledge on subjects I knew little about. Natalya, for example, was definitely not a transsexual. According to Adrian, she was just a big-boned girl with a very eighties wardrobe and I clearly needed to watch more Eurovision song contests.

'Last week's was the best ever!' he cried. 'Ruslana from the Ukraine. Hair down to here, boots up to here, and dressed as a sexy cavewoman. Utterly *brilliant*!'

Although Adrian had tagged me as his coffee break companion, I also enjoyed the company of others in my class. I liked Mahvash, an earnest woman from Iran, even if she did insist on calling me 'Merinda'; Renaldo, a bubbly young Argentinian working for Siemens; and Nam-Hong, a gentle chap from South Korea. As Nam-Hong spoke no English whatsoever, we did a lot of nodding and smiling. *Me too*, we said, pointing to our tired eyes, our unfinished homework or our rumbling stomachs. And then there was Mustafa, our tall, handsome class clown, who always brought in a bag of Turkish shortbread, and whose unrequited love for the three Spanish women was our daily entertainment.

Even though he hadn't met my fellow students, Tom enjoyed their company too. As I regaled him in the kitchen with stories of my morning at Inlingua, I could sense the weight lifting from his shoulders. Being my soul source of comfort and communication, translator and carer couldn't have been easy. Doing my paperwork alone must have made Tom rethink his marriage proposal. If he wasn't on the phone to his health insurance company to discuss my *Krankenversicherung*, he was filling out papers from the *Kreisverwaltungsreferat* to secure my residency. Or else he sat at his laptop searching the internet for a local marriage celebrant, a professional translator, an obstetrician and the right venue for our *Hochzeitsfeier.*

'What's a Hochzeitsfeier?' I asked.

Tom pulled me towards him and kissed me.

'Wedding reception!'

My big fat German wedding reception!

I stood with Tom and Frau Klöffel, the *Geschäftsfürerin* or manageress of the restaurant on the majestic balcony of the palatial Maximilianeum, admiring the view of the city before us.

'Frau Klöffel just said it was originally built by King Maximilian II in the mid 1800s as a residence for gifted students,' Tom said.

'Talk about good student accommodation!' I told Frau Klöffel.

The Maximilianeum restaurant manager blinked back at me.

'I mean, I wouldn't have minded a small room in a neo-Renaissance palace when I was a student.'

Somewhat nervously, Tom translated for me, but Frau Klöffel was clearly not amused. 'Es ist kein Schloss,' she corrected me. 'Es ist das Bayerische Parliament.'

Well, it looked like a palace, I whispered to Tom while our guide turned to deal with a passing colleague.

'You heard her,' Tom hissed back. 'It's not a palace. It's where the Bavarian parliament sits.'

'Right,' I said, pointing to the fountain below, 'then we must remind our wedding guests not to bring their bathers.'

But Tom was already gone, obeying the command to follow.

'Frau Klöffel says we could even have a band,' he translated over his shoulder as she led us back through the grand receiving hall towards the restaurant.

A band? From the moment we drove towards the shiny gold building reflecting the sun at the end of Maximilianstrasse,

I knew there would be no band. Others might have thrown their wedding receptions on the Maximilianeum balcony, in its opulent restaurant or on its picturesque grounds with a band, or even a string quartet, but they most probably had names like Baron Ludwig Von Liechtenstein and Adelheid Habsburg Hanover-hof.

At Frau Klöffel's invitation, we sat down at an elegant table by the windows in the restaurant to discuss catering options. The room was empty except for two portly gentlemen sitting in a corner, possibly the Ministers for Transport and Education. Finally realising that I spoke no German at all, Frau Klöffel drummed her polished fingernails on the table and looked around the room as if searching for toys to keep a child entertained.

'Vould you like to see our vedding pictures?' she asked, pointing to a polished antique table in the middle of the room.

'Oh, yes,' I said, noticing the large album on the table next to the vase of lilies. 'That would be wonderful!'

Frau Klöffel and I looked at each other until I realised she was waiting for me to go.

'Right then.'

Leaving them discussing Thai spring rolls versus *Nürnberger Bratwürste*, I went over to the table and, bending under the enormous flower arrangement, looked through the photos of other people's wedding receptions: other people who could afford jazz bands, string quartets, make-up artists and professional wedding photographers to capture them for posterity in their ivory silk taffeta dresses and Armani tuxedos.

All the way home in the car, Tom debated the pros and cons of finger food versus a buffet bar, prosecco versus French champagne, until, noticing my silence, he squeezed my leg and told me not to worry about the expense. But it wasn't Frau Klöffel's impending quote for a wedding reception at the Maximilianeum that had rendered me mute. It was the photo album.

'Why?'

'Oh, I don't know, maybe the lack of *pregnant brides* in it?'

We drove past the Ostfriedhof, the enormous cemetery that took up several blocks, in silence. In all his enthusiasm, Tom had forgotten that by the day we got married, his July bride might look a little different. But I hadn't, and felt miserable. On my own wedding day I wouldn't be able to dance without feeling like a walrus in a dress, or to drink alcohol, and despite Frau Schmeck's best efforts, I wouldn't be able to understand my own wedding guests. Speaking of which, how many was Tom thinking of inviting?

'Hallo, Herr Müller,' I said, striding past the old man standing on our garden path in his pyjamas, holding a dinner fork in his hand.

I was halfway down the stairs to the *Keller* when I heard Tom's breathless voice behind me.

'What about we make it just one hundred guests then?'

I pushed open the door to the shoe room.

'A lot of them will speak English, you know,' he continued, running behind me, 'and don't forget your family will be there.'

Holding one shoe, I spun around to glare at him.

'My family?' I asked, the tears beginning to well. 'You mean all *two* of them?'

Tom knew very well that the only members of my family who could be on hand for my wedding day were my younger brother Max, a freelance actor and drama teacher, and my older sister Georgina, a financial correspondent for the BBC, both of whom lived in London. Although I was delighted they were coming to support me on my big day, just recently they both seemed to be entering a bit of a transition period. Around about the same time I announced I was pregnant, George had decided to lose weight and, having joined her gym across the road in Shepherds Bush, began ringing me every week to ask if I was 'fat yet'.

'Well, I gotta tell you, little thing,' she'd sing down the phone while her camera crew set up outside Northern Rock, 'the weight's just *dropping* off me and men are falling from the skies. Apparently I look fabulous!'

I rang my brother to complain. Was I being paranoid, or was our sister turning our respective expanding and shrinking bodies into some kind of competition in time for my own wedding day?

'Oh, I think that's being a bit ungenerous, darls,' Max said, reminding me of all the wise priests he'd played on stage over the years. 'You're getting married, George is on a health kick, why not just be happy for each other?'

He was right of course. Poor Max. It hadn't been easy growing up with two weight-obsessed sisters. And right now, Max had bigger problems of his own to deal with. None of us could believe the rotten timing. Just as my marriage was coming together, our brother's had come to an end.

'But you are coming, aren't you, Max?'

'Yeah, darl,' he sighed. 'Wouldn't miss it for quids, even though it's right in the middle of my tour.'

In the midst of his own 'hero's journey', Max had agreed to do a regional tour of his one-man show based on Homer's *Odyssey*.

'But I think I can fly over between Grimsby and Hastings.'

Dear Max.

'Hang on,' he said. 'George says she wants a quick word.'

'Hi, little thing,' my sister's voice sang down the phone. 'Are you fat yet? *You can still fit into jeans?* Fuckity-fuck! What's wrong with you?'

Not able to afford two trips to Europe in one year, my parents had decided to forgo our wedding and come over to meet their first grandchild a few months later instead.

'But don't you worry,' my father bellowed down the phone, 'we're going to celebrate your wedding at July's book discussion group. Ida's bringing the champagne and Val's making a fruit cake specially for the occasion.'

'Pity we'll be discussing *Angela's* bloody *Ashes*,' my mother groaned. 'Three hundred and sixty pages of alcoholism, poverty, starvation and babies dying all over the place. I suggested Gertrude Stein's *Life of Alice B Toklas*, but oh no, instead of enjoying the company of two highly gifted, feisty, fairly well-endowed Jewish lesbians, we have to celebrate your wedding in the squalid filth of a hovel somewhere in Limerick.'

Never mind, I told my mother, trying to wrap up the conversation before we had the usual tense exchange about my wedding dress.

'And have you bought yourself some dainty, sylph-like bridal shoes?'

Damn. No, I groaned, and by mid July no one would mistake me for a sylph anyway.

'Well, you can easily cover it up, you know, with a bouquet, or clever bunching. What about an empire line dress, or something in the Grecian style?'

'Look!' I shouted down the phone. 'I'm not covering up anything, do you hear? I'm wearing my stretchy pink lace Sarah Jane dress and that's that!'

I hated yelling at my mother down the phone from a distance of ten thousand miles, but her image of me walking down the aisle like something out of a Van Eyck painting was more than I could bear.

Even before Frau Klöffel's quote arrived, Tom realised that a splashy wedding reception at a posh venue was perhaps not going to be the best idea for him and his pregnant Australian bride. As the days got warmer, Tom rang around his network of school friends and was pleased to discover his old friend Jörg was now the *Bürgermeister*, or mayor, of Grünwald, our neighbouring municipality and home to Munich's aristocracy. Not only would Jörg be delighted to marry us in the local town hall there, but Tom had even more good news.

'The Grünwald Rathaus is just up the road from Fritzi Oberhauser's restaurant, the perfect venue for our post wedding lunch!'

Faced with Tom's irresistible enthusiasm for traditional Bavarian restaurants, I surrendered to his bear hug like a rag doll. Celebrating my wedding over a plate of *Schweinshaxe mit Sauerkraut und Knödel* wasn't quite the romantic wedding reception I'd hoped for, but nor had I imagined I'd marry a man who owned a pair of suede shorts with braces either. Face it, Merridy, I said to myself. You now live in Bavaria. Sometimes you just have to go with the flow or, as the Germans say, *mit dem Strom schwimmen.*

'Hallo, Fritzi?' Tom shouted euphorically down the phone, still leading me around our kitchen in a waltz. 'Hier ist der Tommy!' He kissed my cheek then waltzed out of the room with the cordless phone. 'Tommy Baumgartner! . . .'

What a pity we hadn't bumped into each other on the streets of Taroona all those years ago in Hobart, me and Mary Donaldson, I thought as Tom left me in our kitchen looking at photos of her royal wedding splashed all over the front page of the *Süddeutsche Zeitung*. Just think of the long phone calls we could be enjoying now, comparing the Baumgartners to the Glücksburgs, the text messages we could exchange, whingeing about Danish grammar and German prepositions. What a journey it had been for both of us, we'd have to agree, from playing on the streets of Hobart to walking down aisles, one in Copenhagen, the other in Munich, to marry our respective princes, Mary's in front of a hundred and eighty million people and mine in the Grünwald Rathaus, six months up the duff. Oh Mary, I thought, eyeing her pearl duchess satin dress lined with silk organza, what a big year it was turning out to be for both us girls from Tassie.

You're not wearing that!

It was my father-in-law's seventy-fourth birthday and so as day follows night, we were off to have dinner in a Bavarian restaurant. Tante Clara and Onkel Gustaf would be there, Ulrika and Horst had driven down from Coburg with the kids, Tante Zelda was coming as usual, and someone called Zabo was going to perform magic tricks between courses.

'He's an old friend of my father's,' Tom chuckled from our bedroom doorway. 'He used to dress up as a magician when we were children and do really bad—What are you doing?'

I stopped pulling on my black opaque pantihose and stood like a flamingo on one leg.

'What?'

'You're not wearing that.'

I looked down at my clothes. What was wrong with my black polyester-cotton skirt, black stockings and matching black wraparound top? Bloch's Ballet Shop had been dressing me for years and no one else had complained. Wrapped tight in jet black with high heels and diamante earrings, I looked quite elegant, didn't I?

'We're going to dinner, not a gymnastics class.'

Clearly Tom had never seen *Turning Point.* Or how my black crossover top could make me reach gracefully for the salt as if I was doing an arabesque from the waist up, but under Tom's withering gaze, my inner swan snuffed it.

At times like this, I felt alarmed by the width and depth of the chasm that opened between us. As I looked at my husband to be standing in the doorway, immaculate as ever in his Fiorelli micro blend grey suit, I felt embarrassed by my working actress's wardrobe. Just as well Tom had never seen me back in my drama school days, I thought, my colleagues and I sitting cross-legged on the floor in our black leggings and cut-off pullovers, forming a circle around an overflowing ashtray and half a flagon of riesling. Staring into Tom's pale blue woven silk tie, I doubted that he'd ever worn leggings in his life, let alone drunk from a flagon. But coming from such different backgrounds, Tom and I were bound to have developed different tastes in clothes. While he was growing up in *Lederhosen* and braces in Munich, I was running around in bathers and thongs in Queensland. And later, when he'd dressed smartly for lectures on Tourism and Hospitality, I'd dressed to roll around the floors of NIDA being a tumbleweed.

'Haven't you got a good outfit in there somewhere?' Tom asked, frowning at my clothes rack.

From the minute I'd arrived in Munich, I'd noticed how well people dressed. You couldn't miss it on the streets. Women in particular took great pride in looking chic, and the only men who wore shorts and thongs, according to Tom, were Australians over for Oktoberfest. So it was no surprise that my German fiancé was constantly frowning at my scuffed RM Williams boots, picking balls of wool off my cardie, or pointing to a speck on my jeans. And like Eliza Doolittle adjusting to a new society, I was learning a whole new set of rules. Tracksuit pants, for example, were not to be worn outdoors unless for the express purpose of exercising. The deliberately crumpled look no longer said 'lived-in chic' so much as 'homeless'. And never, under any circumstances, was I to answer the front door in my dressing gown. I learnt the latter just a week previously when I'd pursued Tom to our letterbox holding the cordless phone.

'It's for you!' I'd said, before he left me having a conversation with a German plumber.

'What are you *doing*?' Tom hissed.

I felt like Cherie Blair answering the front door of Number 10 in her nightie.

'Get back inside! Back! Back!'

I wondered if my fellow Tasmanian, Princess Mary up the road in Copenhagen, elicited the same response when she followed Frederik outside with the palace cordless. At least Frederik, with the paparazzi camped on his doorstep, had a good excuse. All we had was a couple of mechanics in dirty overalls from the garage opposite and the occasional granny pushing her shopping trolley. Did it really matter if a few strangers saw me at our front door in my white towelling dressing gown?

'Yes!' Tom answered, amazed I had to ask. 'Of course!'

This fear of being seen in night attire at least explained Tom's behaviour whenever our doorbell rang early in the morning. Like all our neighbours, Tom was fond of buying things from catalogues over the internet, including shoes, so it wasn't unusual to be woken up at 7 am by a delivery man holding a clipboard at our front gate. Nor was it unusual to watch Tom leap out of bed, grab the nearest pants and take off with his head already inside a pullover. It just didn't make sense to me to go to all this trouble for a complete stranger holding a packet of thermal underwear from Tchibo.

'Don't you have some good pants and a blouse?' Tom muttered, still trying to dress me for his father's birthday dinner.

I watched his disappointed gaze travel from my end of the clothes rack to his, as if now seriously considering lending me one of his good suits, until his eyes narrowed at something hanging at the far end. Oh dear, I thought, following his gaze. I'd meant to throw out the red polka-dot dress I'd bought for five quid at Camden Markets three years ago but still couldn't let go for sentimental reasons. I'd found the dress while attending a two week clowning workshop held in London by the famous Philippe Gaulier from Le Coq in Paris. With a list of protégés that included Roberto Benigni, Emma Thompson, Geoffrey Rush and Sacha Baron Cohen, Gaulier was regarded by many as the greatest teacher of clowning in the world today, a fact I reminded myself of whenever he'd turn to ask the rest of the class, 'Oo else 'ere fands Mer'dy uz ferny uz a twalet?'

At the beginning of the course, before sending us out to find costumes, Philippe allocated to each of us an archetype from which we should begin our journey of discovery. As I stood trembling before the class in my red plastic nose, our formidable teacher leant on his wooden staff and studied me through his round spectacles.

'Mini Murse!' he finally announced, and everyone cheered.

And so for nearly two weeks that summer, wearing the Mini Mouse red polka-dot dress, oversized tennis shoes and the glomesh purse I'd also found at the markets, I took off every morning from my sister's house in Shepherds Bush and caught the tube to Chalk Farm looking like I was on my way to a sheltered workshop. But I wasn't alone. Scattered on peak hour trains all over London, other clowns sat in their feather boas, army boots, ballet tutus and kilts, all too preoccupied with what daily torment lay ahead to feel remotely self-conscious about their choice of clothes. I looked at Tom, now squinting with disapproval at the garment hanging on the clothes rack, and wondered what he would have thought had he found himself sitting opposite such an eccentrically dressed creature on the tube. What would he have thought had someone whispered into his ear that he was looking at his future wife?

Long after Tom had gone downstairs to polish his Roberto Cavalli pointed-toe python shoes, I sat on our bed feeling ashamed of my reflection in the mirror. I tried not to think of her, but it was useless. Whenever Tom and I hit a bump in the road, up she popped the way ex-girlfriends do when one feels insecure. Although I'd never met Lisetta, I'd seen her winning smile in photos and had even secretly translated the handmade heart-shaped cards from Valentine days gone by. If I really wanted to torture myself, all I had to do was wait for Tom's Tuesday night volleyball, go to the living room cabinet, slide out the bottom drawer and study such mementos from their five year relationship. Why Tom still hadn't thrown these souvenirs out was a question I was saving for a bigger crisis.

'And one last piece of advice,' I'd declare from the doorway, holding a packed suitcase in one hand and a baby capsule in the other. 'Before you bring your *next* wife home, at least have the decency to remove *whatsername* from the bottom drawer over there!'

No doubt the petite blond businesswoman who ran her own PR company never had a problem dressing for Tom's father's birthday dinners. No doubt Lisetta had dozens of stylish outfits to choose from, instead of a maternity dress for her wedding day, a Logies gown and a costume for a clown workshop. I felt just like the wretched narrator in Daphne du Maurier's famous novel, married to the cool Maxim and haunted by the irreplaceable Rebecca. I might not have had the cold-hearted housekeeper Mrs Danvers reminding me I was trespassing on forbidden territory, but some days on German public transport, Mrs Danvers seemed to be everywhere.

It wasn't as if my parents hadn't brought us up to take special pride in our appearance, but whereas Tom's family liked to blend in, my family liked to stand out. I blamed Rox. A teacher-librarian by profession, our bohemian mother had always had a soft spot for clothing and jewellery with a bit of history, and had never been able to walk past an unusual textile or exotic print without cocking her head to one side and considering a dressmaker.

'The jacket material's from the Hmongs down at Salamanca Market,' she'd told me breathlessly last Christmas, 'courageous people from southern Laos displaced during the Indochina War. And *who knew* their exquisite embroidery would go so perfectly with my ancient Egyptian scarab beetle earrings?'

When Frau Baumgartner first saw a photo of my mother, she studied it for some time before handing it back to me with a warm smile.

'Deine Mutter ist sehr—artistisch.'

Too right. Pre-Raphaelite even, according to her friend, poet Gwen Harwood.

Encouraged by our artistic mother from an early age, therefore, my sister and I expressed ourselves through our clothes as well. Influenced by Fleetwood Mac, Georgina wore lots of Boho dresses with lace ribbons tied in her hair until Boney M came along and she made herself voluminous cheesecloth harem pants. Meanwhile, wearing enough eyeliner to sink a ship, I was more influenced by Blondie and once went to a party wearing a green plastic garbage bag tied at the waist with an enormous shiny red belt.

'You *are* funny,' was the only resistance we got from either of our parents, until I discovered gyms in the eighties and began wearing Nikes. This was the only item of clothing that could almost reduce Rox to tears.

'Why in God's name would you want to look like John Newcombe from the ankles down?'

And then there was our father with his impressive array of silk cravats. Dad always looked smart and handsome, but never more so than when he became Hobart's chief theatre critic. As he stood in theatre foyers in his black pants, matching polo neck and distinguished greying hair, I always thought my father cut a modish figure, although perhaps he could have lost the monocle. But in recent years, due to his bad circulation, Dad had been dressing much more for comfort, and to protect his knees from

Hobart's Antarctic winds Rox had bought him a pair of ski pants. Nothing could have pleased our father more. Not only did the noisy ski pants keep his knees warm but Dad swore, as he went around our house turning all the heaters off, they saved him money. However, if Tom believed tracksuit pants were strictly for exercise, it followed that he'd deem ski pants strictly for the slopes. So I was glad that by the time he met my father, Dad had moved onto the fleecies. Although a close cousin to the tracksuit, at least the fleecies were quieter than their predecessors and, not being made from herringbone fabric, Dad couldn't patch the holes with gaffer tape.

'Just leave him alone,' Rox said when I teased him about this at Salamanca one Christmas. It was selfless acts such as refusing to buy himself good thermal underwear, she reminded me, that had helped provide all three of us with a private school education.

An hour after my wardrobe crisis I sat in the popular downstairs Ratskeller restaurant and thanked the waitress for my glass of *Apfelschorle*, non-alcoholic apple cider. Having already wished Tom's father 'Alles Gute zum Geburtstag,' I was happy to be left out of the family's German conversation and study my new surroundings instead. Like so many other traditional Bavarian restaurants Tom's family patronised, this one made me feel as if I was in church too. It wasn't just the arched windows and vaulted ceiling painted with frescoes, or even the crucifixes. It was the wood. I was sitting on it, looking at it, and leaning against it. But at least the Ratskeller wasn't as cheerless as the converted ancient brewery my in-laws usually chose. No matter how often I sat inside the drafty Löwenbräukeller with its empty stage, looking up at its faded flags hanging from the ceiling, and no matter how often Tom promised me it transformed into a veritable party tent during Oktoberfest, I could never forget it had once been a favourite location for early Nazi Party meetings, and half expected Goebbels to appear at the podium.

'Ente,' the plump waitress in a *Dirndl* said, placing my duck before me.

As usual, everyone seemed to have ordered *Schweinshaxe* or *Schweinebraten* except me and, to my surprise, Tom. In an effort to kill himself before reaching fifty, Tom had ordered a thing called the *Grillwurst Schmankerl*, a large mountain of various sausages stacked high on a bed of potatoes, bacon and sauerkraut.

'How did your husband die?'

'Schmankerled.'

Despite Tom's concern, none of his family took a second look at my Morrissey wraparound black spandex dress, except my brother-in-law Horst, who eyed me from head to toe, spun me around and asked his wife if she could believe I was five months pregnant. My German might have been almost non-existent, but I had no trouble at all understanding the withering look Ulrika gave her husband. Quickly taking my place at the table, I found myself sitting opposite Tom's young niece, Claudine, who looked so smart and spotless in her beige skirt and crisp white blouse, I wondered if she and her friends ever dressed to emulate Shakira, Beyoncé and Britney, like so many teenage girls did back home. Although they didn't wear school uniforms in Germany, I was surprised at how unadventurously the girls dressed, save for their choice of earrings. It wasn't unusual to find myself on the U-Bahn sitting opposite a teenage schoolgirl wearing jeans, runners and a zipped up hoodie with a coloured chandelier dangling from each ear. It was a strange combination, but my inner fifteen year old completely understood.

Our empty plates were still being collected when all conversation was interrupted by the delicate dinging of spoon on glass summoning our attention. We looked up to see a frail, antiquated man before us, stooped behind a small, portable table covered in a red silk cloth.

'Damen und Herren,' he wheezed, barely audible over the noise of the busy kitchen behind him. 'Ich bin sehr—zeh—' We waited for his hacking cough to subside. '—Zabo, der Zauberer!'

'Zauberkünstler!' Tante Zelda mouthed across the table during the applause.

And as she wiggled her fingers in the air, I nodded back with all the excitement I could muster for a ninety year old magician.

While we all watched Zabo's trembling hands produce an endless string of silk handkerchiefs stuffed up his right sleeve, I decided that if the old man could just live until our desserts arrived, that would be miracle enough. But he did better than that. Long after I'd finished my *Strudel*, Zabo was still producing coins from the hidden crevices of his shaking palms, from behind Onkel Gustav's ear and one, to the delight of the children, from a handkerchief after he'd sneezed into it. Unfortunately, however, our magician couldn't make the heavy blanket of cigarette smoke disappear, and so, having finished our coffees and said goodbye, Tom and I left Zabo putting a blindfold on a giggling Tante Zelda.

It wasn't until we were in bed that I confronted Tom about the shadow he'd cast over my night. He should have noticed when he met me—I wasn't a businesswoman with a sports car and a fancy wardrobe like his other petite, well-groomed, businesswomen ex-girlfriends. I was an Australian actress and writer who once did a clown workshop, and if Tom didn't like it, he shouldn't marry me.

Tom laughed and pulled me in towards him. He knew all that, he said, kissing me. 'But I just think you should have some really nice clothes as well.'

I did have nice clothes. He just didn't like them.

For some reason Tom found this hilarious.

'I want you to go into town on Monday,' he said, suddenly serious. 'Take the card I gave you and, avoiding ballet shops, go buy yourself some beautiful, good quality outfits.'

No one had ever given me a credit card before, let alone shouted me a new wardrobe. And although half of me was still angry with Tom, the other half was already hotfooting it down Maximilianstrasse in Chanel with several shopping bags under each arm. I might even duck into Massimo Dutti in Theatinerstrasse, I told myself, where the model in the window wore a certain black stretch matte jersey knit dress that made her look so elegant, as if any second she might just surprise us all with a *grand jeté en tournant*.

What are you from job?

'It sounds angry, so I only speak it when I'm mad!'

Oscar Wilde, on speaking German

A few of us arrived for class at the beginning of our third week to find our tall, besotted Turk, Mustafa *aus* Ankara, leaning casually on Frau Schmeck's desk, flirting with the Spanish girls—or 'The Aguileras' as Adrian liked to call them.

'So many beautiful women!' Mustafa proclaimed as we made our way to our seats. 'And from all over the world! Venezuela, Finland, Russia, Japan . . . Australia!' he cried, hastily including me in his harem. 'You!—look so young for your age.'

I turned to face him.

'How old is you?'

'I'm forty-two, Mustafa.'

'And you don't look a bit!'

'Thank you.'

'No way you look dat old.'

Frau Schmeck danced into the room, smiling from ear to ear, dying to tell us more about doors, tables, bags and chairs. But she had no right to smile, not when we found out what Germans did to articles. As Frau Schmeck drew a graph on the board showing us the sixteen ways to say 'the', I thought my head was going to explode. Not only did every noun have a gender, but its article changed according to the grammatical case being used. So why Frau Schmeck didn't throw chalk at the three Spanish girls sitting in front of us, who continuously chatted in their native tongue throughout this minefield of articles and prepositions, was a mystery to all. Didn't they know marriages were at stake here, and that some of us would be tested at the next family gathering under a massive crucifix by a police commissioner from Coburg?

Using all her skills as an actress, Frau Schmeck explained to her class the conditions under which *Nominativ Artikels* changed to *Dativ Artikels.* For example, when something was placed next to a book, *das Buch, Nominativ Artikel,* became *dem Buch, Dativ*

Artikel. Never had the simple placing of one object near another been so painfully studied. Watching our faces as Frau Schmeck slowly placed her chalk inside the cupboard, under her bag, or on the floor, you'd think we were all recovering from serious head injuries. But it got worse. The following day our ambitious teacher introduced us to a third case, *Akkusativ,* that changed the *Artikel* yet again. If *Dativ* applied to the indirect object, Frau Schmeck explained, then *Akkusativ* applied to the direct. In other words, if I locked three noisy young women in a cupboard, the cupboard, being the indirect object, would be *Dativ, im Schrank.* However, if I then opened the door quickly to toss in something else, an enormous rat for example, the cupboard would become *Akkusativ, den Schrank,* and the girls would be upset. *Bestürzt.*

'It's my fault, Honeybee,' my mother sighed wistfully down the phone from Tasmania. 'I should have taught you Latin at home, like I did with your brother. Latin is the key to language, you know.'

Yes, I knew. I'd heard it all my life, along with 'We're sending you to the best private school in the southern hemisphere.'

'I did try to give you and Georgina a bit of French tutoring after school, but I don't suppose you remember.'

Au contraire. How could my sister and I ever forget *La Plume de ma Tante,* the thin, dark green textbook whose flimsy pages were yellow with age and wear from our mother's days at Abbotsleigh? The text may have been dull enough to drive a child to despair, but that was nothing compared to the effect our Australian accents had on our mother.

'Pluuume!' she'd shout, thumping the dining table.

'Ploom,' we'd repeat flatly.

'Pluuuummme!'

'Ploom!'

'*PLUUUME!*'

I might have ended up the only eighth grader who spoke French like Edith Piaf, but that still didn't save me from getting the dreaded 'Lower Pass'. Why had I found languages so hard? Why was schoolwork always such a struggle for me? Why didn't

Georgina and Max have to repeat the year too? Was I just thick or something?

'No, not at all,' my mother protested. 'You just—'

I waited on tenterhooks for some kind of explanation for my lack of academic success.

'You were just always more interested in putting things on your head.'

Here it was again, this image of my A-grade younger brother surrounded by his soccer and archery trophies, my class captain big sister wearing her debating team badge, and then me in the middle, balancing a mango on my noggin.

For the rest of the week, Frau Schmeck introduced us to the *Dativ Artikel* following the preposition *von*. I was the daughter *von meiner Mutter*, Tooheys was the brother *von seinem Bruder*, and Adrian was the boyfriend *von seinem bipolar flight attendant boyfriend Heinzi*. It was all going very well until Frau Schmeck asked José if he had a cousin. As if waking from a coma, our large friend from Brazil stared at Frau Schmeck, then at the blackboard behind her, down to his notes, then up again.

'Telefon?'

But before we could even check José's ears for cotton wool, the room came to life with bells, clarinets and the hypnotic beat of belly-dancing music.

'Sorry! Sorry! Sorry!' Mustafa cried, pulling a noisy mobile phone from his large canvas bag. 'Sorry everybody!' he cried, turning the exotic ring tone off.

Frau Schmeck glared at our student from Ankara. It was a strict rule that all mobile phones were to be switched off in class lest they interfere with navigation instruments while struggling to grasp complex German grammar.

'Musik,' Mustafa smiled sweetly, pointing to his dead phone. 'Von Türkei.'

Having exhausted all our living relatives, with great excitement Frau Schmeck moved on to another use of the word *von*.

'Natalya! Was sind Sie von Beruf?' she asked with a wicked smile.

What was a *Beruf*? we all wondered, turning to Natalya, whose expression made me want to grab her wrist and check for a pulse.

'Sind Sie eine *Tanzerin,* Natalya?' Frau Schmeck asked, making us all laugh at her hilarious mime of a go-go dancer. 'Oder sind Sie eine Ärtzin?' She ran over to Mustafa, and mimed listening to his breathing through a stethoscope. 'Was sind Sie, Natalya, *von Beruf*?'

What are you, Natalya, from job? The Germans sure had a strange way of asking what you did for a living, but we all leant forward with hands clasped, dying to hear Natalya's answer.

'Ich bin Architekt,' came the monotone answer in a thick Russian accent.

No one moved.

'Eine Architektin?' Frau Schmeck asked, trying not to sound astonished.

Natalya nodded. We looked at her spangly earrings, blonde hair extensions, purple bodice top with green hipster jeans and matching stilettos, trying to imagine a building back in Omsk that Natalya might have designed. It was much easier to imagine her putting foils in her sister's hair than sitting at a drafting table in an architect's office.

'Wie interessant!' Frau Schmeck cried, before hastily clapping her hands and moving on. 'Und José?'

But José was still staring in wonder at Mustafa's mobile phone as if half-naked, dancing women with bells on their toes lived within its magical metallic case.

'Nam-Hong?' she asked his neighbour instead.

Whenever Nam-Hong spoke, unsure if he was speaking Korean, English or German, we always looked to Frau Schmeck to see if he was making any sense at all. With an expression of intense concentration, Frau Schmeck would stand before him with her mouth open and hands reaching out as if ready to catch a large vase.

'Ein Mönch?' she repeated incredulously. 'Sind Sie ein *Mönch,* Nam-Hong? Wirklich?'

Nam-Hong nodded. He was definitely a *Murnk,* whatever that was.

'A monk!' someone said.

'Oh, monk!' we all cried.

'You dark horse!' Adrian exclaimed.

As it turned out, Nam-Hong had come to Munich to study theology, but before I could ask why a Korean monk would choose a university in Bavaria, I heard my name.

'Merridy?'

Oh no. Couldn't we hear more about Nam-Hong's monastery, or Natalya's design for a dance floor under the Kremlin? Should I do the usual detour and say I was a nanny?

'Ich bin eine—how do you say actress?'

'Eine Schauspielerin?' Frau Schmeck opened her mouth so wide, I thought I could see Sydney. 'Sind Sie wirklich eine Schauspielerin, Merridy?'

'Ja.' The time had come. 'You too?'

'Ja! Ja!' she cried, nodding fervently.

The class watched on as my teacher and I played Snap. I had worked mainly on stage in Melbourne and Sydney, and Frau Schmeck had worked with a company in Östereich, or Austria, where she came from. But our conversation was suddenly interrupted by a shrill scream from the other side of the room.

'Oh my God! You were on *Neighbours*!'

I knew I should have said nanny.

'She was on *Neighbours*!' Adrian yelled at the three Spanish girls.

'Kein Englisch, Adrian!'

'I can't believe you were on fucking *Neighbours*!'

'Qué es *Neboros*?' the Aguileras asked each other.

'Same television show as Kylie Minogue!' Adrian yelled at them, pointing at me as if I was a bag snatcher.

'Genug!' Frau Schmeck said, clapping her hands.

But it was too late. The leader of the Spanish pack looked at me for the first time, and even stopped chewing.

'You mudda von Kylie Minogue?' she asked in a husky, cigarette voice.

'Yes, that's right,' I told her, 'and my other daughter's Nicole Kidman. Any other women approaching forty you think I might have given birth to?'

'Kein Englisch!'

'I don't like Nicola Kidman,' Natalya told Mustafa. 'She cold.'

'Well, if that isn't the pot calling the kettle black,' Adrian retorted.

'OK!' our teacher yelled over the noise. 'KLEINE PAUSE!'

Ever since I read that due to *Neighbours* being screened twice a day some children in the UK had even developed Australian accents, I knew that the British response to this long-running soap opera was strangely enthusiastic to say the least. And although Adrian was annoyed that he couldn't remember my small role in more detail, I couldn't have felt more relieved. He could recall that young Brett had been seduced by a friend of his mum's, but luckily for me Adrian had forgotten that Cheryl's 'friend' was also her golfing partner, and that I'd therefore spent six months of the series wearing navy knickerbockers. In Adrian's hands, this kind of information could have turned my German course into one long summer of shame. As it was, by the time he'd finished interrogating me over my hot chocolate and his three cigarettes, I couldn't wait to get back to German grammar.

'Les?' Frau Schmeck asked Tooheys, who stopped leaning against the wall and took the pen out of his mouth.

'Ich bin ein Soldat.'

'Ein Soldat?'

For our benefit, Frau Schmeck stood at attention and saluted him.

'Sind Sie schon im *Krieg* gewessen?'

To translate *Krieg,* Frau Schmeck crouched behind her desk, then bobbed up to release the pin from a pretend hand grenade before lobbing it towards the windows. Determined not to find her antics amusing, Les nodded. He was in Timor, he told her, but not in combat. If he'd stayed in the army, Les continued, his cheeks going from pink to red to purple, he'd possibly be in Iraq right now.

'Iraqi?' Frau Schmeck repeated.

'Ja.'

Like most Germans, Frau Schmeck had no idea we'd supported the United States in its *Krieg Gegen Terror.* She didn't even know the name of our prime minister.

'John Howard,' Les and I answered our teacher in dull unison, in Les's case because he had no other tone. 'Best prime minister we've ever had,' he added.

'Locks up refugees and their children in mandatory detention,' I told her.

'Protects our borders,' Les insisted, fixing his eyes on our teacher.

'From terrorists disguised as refugees and children.'

Frantically trying to move on, Frau Schmeck turned towards Adrian's desk opposite. 'Adrian!' But it was too late.

'Well, I hope you don't believe in Axis of Evil,' Mahvash told Les, 'because that mean you think I am evil, and I am not evil thank you very much.'

'Me too,' added the gentle Nam-Hong from Korea.

'Iranian women are beautiful,' Mustafa interrupted, his hand on his heart. 'Really,' he turned to tell José, 'I think they the most beautiful women in the world.'

'Kein Englisch!' shouted Frau Schmeck, which was a pity because I'd have given anything to hear Les's views about the 'Axis of Evil' in front of an Iranian mother and a Korean monk.

'Adrian!' our teacher sang, almost doing a Morris dance up to his desk. 'Was ist *dein Vater* von Beruf?'

'Come again?' Adrian asked, quickly hiding his mobile phone.

'Was ist dein Vater,' Frau Schmeck asked, 'von Beruf, Adrian?'

'Me dad?' he cried. 'Gawd . . . how d'ya say professional alcoholic?'

Poor Frau Schmeck. Given such an eclectic gathering of people from all over the world, occasional turbulence was inevitable. And these were indeed turbulent times. In the last few months alone the CIA had admitted there was no 'weapons of mass destruction' threat to justify the invasion of Iraq, nearly two hundred people had been killed in Madrid by bombs planted on rush hour trains, back home there'd been riots in Redfern, in Taiwan a dead whale had exploded on the street and, just recently, millions of Americans had been rendered speechless during the Superbowl when they copped an eyeful of Janet Jackson's right nipple at half-time. This was not a good time for calm discussion in any language.

How did they do it? I wondered as I sat up the back of my carriage, watching my fellow passengers reading their papers. How did they hold conversations every day while negotiating the genders of nouns, the different cases, and the constantly changing articles, and we hadn't even started on verbs yet. I observed the solemn expressions of my fellow commuters and convinced myself that every one of them was suffering grammar fatigue, until we pulled in at Frauenhoferstrasse and three grey haired women stepped on in floral skirts with pastel coloured cardigans. That's more like it, I thought as I watched them chatting like subdued parakeets on the seat by the door. They reminded me of my favourite aunties, Nell, Merle and Doreen, off for a game of bingo in the local town hall. I was still smiling at them when all three stood up, reached under their cardigans and whipped out some kind of official ID.

'Fahrkarten, bitte,' they said, demanding to see everyone's ticket as they moved carefully through the carriage.

The *Kontrolleure*! My stomach did a somersault. They'll show you their *Ausweis*, or ID, Tom had warned me, but he never said they'd appear in floral skirts, smelling of lavender!

As two of them made their way towards me, examining tickets through their spectacles before giving an officious nod, I could see by my fellow commuters' prompt cooperation how effective the German 'honour system' was. I thanked God I had my *Monatskarte* with me. My *Monatskarte* that Tom had bought from the kiosk three weeks ago, allowing me to travel as often as I liked within the first *zwei Ringen* of Munich. My *Monatskarte* that had its own little compartment in my wallet, protected by a little plastic window. My *Monatskarte,* the hideous thought crept up my spine with icy fingers, that Tom had borrowed over the weekend so that he could catch a tram across town to pick up his Volvo with its new summer tyres from his mechanic's garage in Moosach. My *Monatskarte* that he had better have returned to its—*Oh scheisse, Tom, you utter Mutterficker*! I lost two kilos just looking at the blank little plastic window in my wallet, white and horribly vacant, until a shadow fell across my lap and I looked up to see two ghostly grey eyes that no longer reminded me of any auntie whatsoever, living or dead. They were the cold eyes of a woman who would never waste time playing bingo, not when there were pregnant freeloaders to apprehend on the underground.

'Ihre Fahrkarte, bitte,' she repeated, holding out her hand.

And as I fumbled in my wallet, going bright red under the fluorescent lights, I realised I had finally achieved something I thought impossible. I had the full attention of every passenger in my carriage.

Paying the forty euro fine hadn't hurt, but the shame stung and burned for days. As did Tom's upper right arm when I got home and punched it, very, very hard.

Don't mention the war!

'Really?' I tried not to squeal. 'To Dachau?'

I just couldn't believe it. Tom's quiet, reserved parents, whom I was finally permitted to call Friedl and Wilhelm, were actually offering to take me to a place that must have stirred such painful emotions and memories for them. I knew how I'd feel showing guests from overseas around Woomera Detention Centre, so could barely imagine the shame Germans might feel about something of the scale and horror of Dachau.

'And Tante Ilsa and Onkel Norbert said they'll come along too,' Tom called from the shower.

Really? I'd almost met Tom's aunt and uncle at Marquartstein, but due to the *Föhn,* Tante Ilsa had to be driven home with a migraine headache.

'We'll meet for coffee first,' Tom's voice echoed from the bathroom, 'and then we can all have a walk around.'

It seemed a strange setting in which to meet in-laws, but perhaps showing a guest around such places was part of some kind of national post-war healing process. Whatever it was, I thought it said a lot for my fiancé's family.

While Tom shaved, I must have changed clothes about five times. On the one hand, I wanted to look nice for my new aunt and uncle whom I'd seen in many photo frames, immaculately dressed with matching accessories. But on the other, I didn't want to walk through a memorial to a concentration camp in a floral dress swinging a handbag either.

'You going to wear that?' asked Tom, clearly disappointed to discover me head to toe in brown.

'Well, it's not exactly the Oktoberfest, is it?'

'It's not a funeral either,' he answered.

Wasn't it? I didn't think you could get a bigger, sadder grave than one of these godforsaken places, but for my fiancé's sake, I changed again.

'Tante Ilsa and Onkel Norbert don't speak much English, do they?' I asked a few minutes later, standing before him in my good jeans, damask blouse and sandals.

'Not a single word,' Tom replied, smiling as he straightened my collar and unrolled my sleeves.

On the one hour trip to Dachau I looked out my window and struggled to comprehend the statistics I'd read on the internet that morning. By the end of the war, some 32,000 deaths had been recorded at the Dachau concentration camp, but the real number possibly exceeded this by thousands. As I listened to their quiet chatter behind me in the back seat, I couldn't help but wonder how aware Tom's parents had been, even as children, of what went on within those electric, barbed wire fences just ten miles from their home. Born the same year as my father, Wilhelm would have been five years old when Adolph Hitler became Chancellor of Germany, six when Dachau concentration camp first opened its gates, and eleven when war broke out. But by the time the camp was liberated, with the population of Munich reduced by nearly a third and most of the city bombed to oblivion, Wilhelm would have been a young man of seventeen. I watched him in my side mirror, my frail, silver-haired soon-to-be father-in-law, staring sadly out his window, absent mindedly agreeing with his wife, his son, or anyone else requiring his attention, and wondered what those tired eyes had witnessed in his lifetime.

It had completely slipped my mind that Dachau, like Auschwitz, was not just the site of a concentration camp, but first and foremost a small town. As we drove through the tree-lined suburban streets, past mothers pushing prams along the footpaths, past bakeries, butcheries and the local kindergarten, Tom informed me that Dachau had a population of 40,000. So how did they feel, I asked quietly, the people of Dachau, being so strongly associated with such an infamous prison?

'I've heard it's not uncommon for pregnant women to arrange to give birth in Munich hospitals just so their children don't have Dachau on their birth certificates, eh, Mama?'

'Bitte, Tommy?'

Tom translated for his mother and I listened intently for her response, but the back seat was totally quiet.

I was waiting for us to reach the other side of the town when Tom took a surprising turn up a majestic tree-lined driveway, pulled up in a car park and stopped the car.

'Here we are,' he said.

I looked out my window at the enormous gold and white building with a row of baroque arched windows, and tried not to panic. Where were the train tracks, the barracks, the tall iron gates that said *Arbeit Macht Frei*? This place looked more like Kensington Palace than a concentration camp.

'Where are we, Tommy?' I asked calmly.

'Schloss Dachau,' he said, opening his car door.

'What Dachau?'

Tom looked at me. 'Schloss.'

'Schloss?'

'As in palace.'

'Palace?'

'Why do you keep repeating me?'

'Dachau Palace.'

'Yes, Dachau Palace, Schloss Dachau!' he cried, irritated by my confusion. 'Where we're meeting Ilsa and Norbert for coffee before we go for a walk through the town, ok?'

'I thought we were going to *Dachau*,' I hissed.

'We *are* in *Dachau*!' he hissed back.

'But I thought you meant *Dachau*,' I growled at him, 'as in *Dachau*.'

A head full of fluffy red hair protruded between us. 'Ist alles in Ordnung, Merridy?'

Yes, I assured my future mother-in-law, everything was fine. I just . . . wasn't this lovely?

I recognised the two smiling figures standing at the bottom of the grand stairs at once. Just as they'd appeared in the photos on top of Wilhelm's green grand piano, Tom's aunt and uncle were a vision in white and matching accessories.

'Merridy, liebe!' Tante Ilsa announced in her contralto voice, gently kissing both my cheeks.

Although the two sisters shared a girlish daintiness, and both squeezed my hands with the same imploring look in their eyes, Friedl's and Ilsa's choice of hairstyle couldn't have been more dissimilar. Friedl preferred a messy, curly head of copper coloured hair, whereas her younger sister Ilsa kept a neat bob, dyed strawberry blonde.

'Ich freue mich so sehr dass du da bist,' she told me, sliding her delicate arm through mine as we ascended the stairs. 'Norbert und ich haben schon so lange von dir gehört.'

Echoing every incomprehensible but kind word his wife said, the handsome, silver-haired Norbert held my other elbow until we reached the top of the stairs.

'You know why we bring you here, ja?' Friedl asked as we stood before the entrance to the palace.

I had no idea. So far it was like going to Auschwitz to see a flower show.

'Because we know you love cake!'

I did?

'Ja!' Tom's mother cried. 'Und in the Café Restaurant are most wonderful cakes you will ever see.'

The thought of eating creamy cakes when I'd prepared myself to walk through barracks where people had starved to death now seemed obscene to say the least, but I couldn't be rude to Tom's family, not when I could see how much they wanted to show me another side of Dachau, one they didn't feel ashamed of, and one that would be pleasant to share. The camp and all I needed to know about it would have to wait for another day.

Stuffed full of strawberry cake, I sat in the crowded Café Restaurant by a tall window overlooking the majestic garden in a post torte stupor. Back where I came from, the combination of children and this much sugar would have been deafening, but here, the percussion of small silver forks was actually louder than the conversation. Even the children in Germany seemed quieter than ours back home. Why was that? I wondered, searching the room for any sign of a scallywag or a rascal.

'You know we're talking about you,' Tom said, waking me from my trance.

Were they? I turned to find the two elderly sisters positively beaming at me. I looked younger than in my photos, my aunt declared. Pregnancy suited me, her sister added. I was radiant, warm, 'nett'. It was a miracle, they both agreed. Despite the language barrier, their strict Bavarian Catholic upbringing and knowledge that I'd written a book about a brothel, neither of these women ever stopped expressing their heartfelt approval of Tom's forty-two year old, five month pregnant Australian fiancée, and I loved them for it.

'And Ilsa insists I've never looked so happy,' Tom groaned, rolling his eyes.

So I whacked Tom in the chest and told him to cheer up.

In desperate need of a walk, the six of us stepped out onto the terrace and made our way towards the orchard below with its rows of blossom trees. Appearing by my side, Tante Ilsa slipped her arm through mine again and it stayed there until she realised that without a translator we could do nothing but smile at each other. Handing me over to Onkel Norbert, I was then escorted through a pergola, then passed on to Friedl, and finally back to Tom. But once we began our walk through the small winding streets of the old city, I was surprised to find Tom's father by my side, determined to pass on whatever he could of Dachau's early history. Thanks to Wilhelm's jaunty mimes and my ability to count in German, I was able to understand that Dachau could be traced back as far as 800, and that the sixteenth century *Schloss* was originally a fortress, or *eine Festung*, built around 1100, but he lost me at the *Künstlerkolonie.*

'A *Künstlerkolonie*?' I asked.

Wilhelm mimed painting.

'Up until the war,' Tom translated, coming to our rescue, 'Dachau was a thriving artists' colony.'

I had paused in front of St Jakob's parish church, wondering how the people of Dachau felt when the Nazis began building a concentration camp on the outskirts of town, when another delicate arm coiled itself through mine.

'Nobody here voted for him or his party,' Friedl whispered in her faltering English, holding me back while the others walked on. 'They did not want the Nazis, or their camp.'

'Really, Friedl?' I asked, desperate to hear more.

'The priest here,' she nodded towards the church, 'he helped the prisoners in the Konzentrationslager. He took food from farmers here, even after Nazis start locking up priests as well.'

Did they?

Friedl gripped my arm until it hurt.

'We did not know, Merridy,' she said quietly but urgently. 'We did not know what they do in there. No one knew what the Nazis do in the Konzentrationslager. Not until it is all over.'

Unfortunately Friedl wouldn't say any more, but I could feel the imprint of her fingers on my arm even after we got back to the car.

I may have sat on the couch with Tom that evening watching the soccer, but my body was back in front of St Jakob's church in Dachau. Although I was grateful to Friedl for her brief but enlightening input, it was her husband I really wished I could speak with. By the end of the war, Friedl would only have been six, but Wilhelm would have been eleven years older, and this equation led me to a question I almost dared not ask.

'Tommy?' I began timorously while they treated captain Oliver Kahn's knee injury, 'did your father have to join Hitler Youth?'

Tom began gathering our cups from the table. 'No,' he answered, standing up. 'My father always said he was such a good soccer player, they left him alone.'

Long after Tom had gone into the kitchen, I stared at the empty coffee table. Given the Nazi goal of transforming this young generation into proof of Aryan superiority and athletic prowess, it seemed odd not to have targeted sporty boys, but I dared not trespass further. Besides, like a lot of German children during those dangerous times, Wilhelm and Friedl had both been sent to stay in the country. Where exactly, with whom and for how long, I didn't feel I could ask.

'Tante Helga joined,' Tom's voice rose from the kitchen.

A second later I was facing Tom at the dishwasher.

Frau Müller from downstairs? His father's sister?

Tom nodded. 'She's quite open about it. She was with the BDM, the Bund Deutscher Mädel.' He closed the dishwasher door. 'That's the League of German Girls.'

I thought of the black and white newsreel footage of all those slim adolescent girls in their sport tunics doing rhythmic gymnastics, and tried to imagine the stooped, unhappy woman downstairs nearly sixty years earlier, twisting her youthful torso towards the sun, her arms swinging up towards the sky with the backdrop of the fresh alps behind her.

What about Onkel Norbert? I asked, following Tom back to the sofa and turning the soccer off. Had he joined too?

Wearily, Tom sat down again. Onkel Norbert was from Sudetenland, he said, the multi-ethnic area just across the Czech border famously handed over to Hitler as part of the Munich Agreement before the war broke out.

'All I can tell you about Norbert is that when his family tried to escape, he was separated from his mother and during this time he witnessed things. Things he's never been able to talk about.'

'Done by the Nazis?'

'No, not by the Nazis,' Tom said, 'by the Russians.'

Before I resolved to quench my thirst for knowledge with books and the internet, I had just one more question.

'No,' Tom answered me flatly. 'We never talked about it at home. No one did. You just didn't.'

Tom and I sat on the couch in silence, the same silence his parents had possibly shared with their parents.

An hour later, looking up from my laptop, I thought of Tante Helga downstairs, and her brother Wilhelm, both teenagers when their city was bombed in 1945. In the same year, due to Nazi laws making membership compulsory, the number of children in Hitler Youth had risen to over eight million. I wondered if they were able to discuss with anyone their feelings of betrayal, abandonment, confusion and shame when their world literally came tumbling down around them, whether they were members or not. I wondered if any of these children had sat through the horrific images on newsreels, or understood the worldwide condemnation, and if anyone took the time to deconstruct the extraordinary journey they'd been on. When I thought of my sad future father-in-law's reflection in the car mirror on our way to Dachau, or of his sister madly sweeping a garden path as if trying to remove its very existence, both of them growing old without speaking to each other, I had the distinct impression that the suffering of these children, although pale in comparison with that of so many Jewish children, had never really been properly dealt with. And then there was the next generation, Tom's and Ulrika's. On the one hand, it wasn't a subject talked about at home, but on the other, according to Tom, they learnt about nothing else at school. By the time they all graduated, Tom said, they could not talk about it easily either, so great was their burden.

'So, I hope you're not going to get obsessed with this one chapter of our past,' Tom said, leaning over my computer to kiss me goodnight.

Hoping he hadn't seen the entire Goebbels family on my screen, I promised I wouldn't. But it didn't seem fair not to allow for a certain fascination with this fateful period of German history. After all, according to one website, I was now living in the city Hitler himself called *Die Hauptstadt der Bewegung,* or the capital of the movement, home to not only the NSDAP (National Socialist German Workers' Party) but also Hitler Youth, an organisation Tom's aunt downstairs had belonged to. The most controversial club any of my aunts back home had belonged to was the Baptist Women's Scrapbooking Society. Tom may have had the Third Reich up to his chin at school, but all we had was Governor Arthur Phillip, merino sheep and the Eureka stockade. Not only had we somehow skipped the Holocaust in a class called 'Social Studies', but during my schooling our own Aboriginal history had been almost non-existent. Hopefully things had improved since the seventies, and in another fifteen years our son might even come home saying he'd had the Myall Creek massacre 'up to here'.

Mission poodle

I was beginning to notice that the Bavarian concept of 'family' was a much tighter, more intimate one than ours in Australia. Back home, my parents were lucky if they saw any of their three children twice a year, but here in Munich it seemed every few weeks we were expected to congregate in yet another car park outside a Bavarian restaurant before going in for another round of *Schweinshaxe*, *Apfelkuchen* and a *Radler*. I didn't understand the frequency of these reunions any more than I understood the spontaneous 'pop in'.

'We might just pop in on my parents,' Tom would say, suddenly flicking his indicator when we were anywhere near their neighbourhood.

'Again?' I once asked, having just said goodbye to them two days earlier in a car park. 'Are they *ill,* Tom?'

I gathered from the withering look my fiancé gave me that he considered my response somewhat heartless, and that here in Bavaria children were much more attentive to their parents. Indeed, some of Tom's friends were so busy being attentive they'd forgotten to leave home at all. Conrad and his little family lived in the same street as his parents, Veni lived next door to hers, and when Dieter finally did get married, he and his parents simply swapped rooms. This was completely at odds with our Australian tradition of leaving home as soon as possible, moving to another city, sharing a house with other young people and experimenting with as many forbidden pleasures as we could think of. Even if I did end up staying in Germany beyond the two years I'd agreed to, I just couldn't imagine any child of mine not wanting to scoot the nest the moment he smelt freedom too.

'Mum,' our strapping son would announce on his eighteenth birthday, having cleaned his room, and mine. 'I've decided to take that place offered by the admissions committee at Johns Hopkins School of Medicine in Baltimore after all.'

'Good on you, kid,' I'd say, throwing back my Weissbeer and undoing my *Dirndl*. 'Your father's just gone upstairs to check on Oma's glucose drip, so if we hurry we'll just make the red-eye to Chicago with Lufthansa.'

On the other hand, there was a lot to say for the Bavarian way. Living ten minutes away from them, Tom was able to do things for his parents I wished I could do for mine back home: fixing doorknobs, reprogramming all the digital clocks after the latest power failure, replacing light globes and, for that matter, whitegoods. While Tom's mother enjoyed her glossy ergonomic kitchen with built-in Bosch appliances, Rox was still slaving over an ancient stove with one remaining hotplate and temperamental oven door that sometimes swung open and kneecapped her. And whereas the Baumgartners enjoyed their compact laundry from Siemens, our father often had to push our vintage washing machine back across the wet laundry floor to its original place after yet another abnormally violent spin cycle. Many a time during my precious Sunday morning phone call with my parents, they'd pretend not to have heard the alarming explosion or distant crash of some other household appliance on its last legs.

'What the hell was that?' I recently asked my mother.

'What was what, Honeybee?'

'It sounded like cannon fire.'

'Oh, you mean the lawnmower? No, that's just the funny—' *BANG!* '—sound it makes when your father—' *BOOM!* '—starts it—' *POOF!* '—up.'

It wasn't until I saw my parents through Tom's eyes when I brought him home to Hobart the previous Christmas that I realised how bad things were. Watching him step cautiously through the cluttered rooms of our dear old family home, picking up the odd broken radio aerial or mug without a handle, Tom looked as if he was walking through Dresden after the war. Never mind how happy my parents were surrounded by their favourite paintings, sculptures and pottery created by local artists, and my mother's love of anything with a willow pattern design, all my pragmatic German fiancé could see were two pensioners without central heating, abandoned by their children as their house fell down around them.

'Oh, I know, dear Tommy,' my mother laughed as she hand-washed every plate and utensil before placing it carefully into our heritage dishwasher. 'But it's a dear old machine and it just needs a bit of help, that's all.'

By Boxing Day, Tom was close to cracking. I'd watched him at our old breakfast table with his head in his hands, trying to gather his thoughts while Puccini's *Tosca* blared from the radio in the kitchen competing with Margaret Throsby from my parents' bedroom, until a blown fuse suddenly rendered the whole house silent but for the quiet snoring of my father in his armchair behind us.

'They can't go on like this,' Tom said, watching several flakes of dry ceiling paint gently fall into his tea. 'They need help *now*.'

'What happened to Tosca?' my mother asked, emerging from her bathroom holding a tap.

'Wha—?' my father asked, waking with a snort. 'She jump already?'

But even after the fuse wire had been found and the house once again reverberated with smooth cultivated voices and symphony orchestras, Tom's attempts to declare a state of emergency went pretty much ignored. Plumbers and electricians would be called in good time, my mother reassured him, but first Dad had to review the Derwent Players' production of *The Caucasian Chalk Circle,* and she had to finish her upcoming talk on Russian folklore for the Hamilton Literary Society. Declaring a state of emergency would have to wait until at least some time after the following Wednesday, when they'd had their French conversation class and book discussion group.

After we'd returned to Munich, Tom and I continued a dialogue about my parents with my equally concerned brother and sister in London. Having witnessed for themselves Dad's lawnmower with its tail gun, and the sight of our seventy-eight year old mother hauling a wheelie bin down our steep garden steps, Georgina and Max decided action must be taken before the next Tasmanian winter set in. And so two months shy of turning up for our wedding day in Bavaria, my brother and sister headed for Hobart to paint our parents' kitchen, replace all the whitegoods, install a heating system, and buy them a dog.

A dog?

'Yes, Merridy, a dog,' my sister announced in her most commanding BBC voice. 'Max and I think that a four-legged, affectionate, doting companion would do both our parents the world of good.'

Not to mention help them feel less abandoned and us less guilty. I commended them on their inspired thinking, and promised George that Tom and I would throw in some money too.

'Jolly D.'

'D?'

'Decent!' George cried, as if we all went about saying Jolly D in Australia too. 'What about you, darls?' Here it came. 'Are you fat yet?'

A few weeks later my sister rang again, this time from Hobart.

'Situation here freezing but bearable. Max upstairs sleeping off bad case of window-seat-next-to-baby all the way from Beijing, but he will insist on flying Air China. Both parents currently at art gallery opening. Meanwhile ceiling in lounge room a total catastrophe, whitegoods being replaced on Tuesday, and I think we're talking poodles.'

Two days later Max rang with an update.

'Just want you to know,' he began through chattering teeth, 'that I have not taken off my beanie since arriving.'

Poor Max. Not only did he have to work in a house without central heating, he was still learning lines for his British regional one-man tour of *The Odyssey*. But inadequate heating and Homer aside, Max told me that our old kitchen was now a cheerful shade of daffodil yellow, the new oven had been delivered, along with dishwasher and washing machine, and that he'd had a long chat with a woman called Shannon from the dog pound who'd given him the number of a reputable poodle breeder on the eastern shore.

'So the plan is,' Max continued sotto voce so as not to ruin the surprise for our father asleep in his armchair, 'that tomorrow I head off to Lindisfarne to see a man about a—*Jesus!* What was that?'

I gathered something upstairs had gone bang.

'Darls, can I call you back?'

As Rox insisted we run the idea by our father before purchasing the poodle, the following morning, their time, we held a conference call between Munich and Hobart, and just as well.

'I don't want a bloody poodle!' our father roared from his seat nearest the speakerphone. 'They've got to be trimmed, brushed and shampooed every bloody month—and it all ends up costing a fortune.'

Most of us had forgotten that Aunty Gwen used to be a poodle breeder, but Dad hadn't.

'She even bought toothbrushes for them. I haven't got time to be brushing some dog's teeth every day! I've barely got time to brush my own!'

'He's a child of the Depression,' Rox explained soothingly, no doubt patting his knee. 'Doesn't like to waste a cent. Won't even let me throw out overripe bananas.'

'I'm not having a poodle!'

'There there,' Rox cooed.

A silence fell as we all remembered the constant plague of fruit flies in our kitchen.

'But you'd like a dog, wouldn't you, Roxie?' I asked meekly. 'You're a child of the Depression too.'

'Yes, but we didn't live in Punchbowl, Honeybee.'

Although we suspected our mother quite liked the idea of a canine companion, if Dad didn't want one the cause was lost. Ever since his first heart attack a decade earlier, our father's health and happiness had become our mother's number one priority. Rox was Dad's round-the-clock nurse and guardian angel, making sure he was constantly rested, relaxed, happy and hydrated. She administered his pills, escorted him on their daily walks, and insisted on his afternoon naps. Her biggest challenge, however, was keeping his blood pressure down on opening nights. Although our father loved his job as theatre critic for the *Mercury* newspaper, due to Hobart's short theatrical seasons his reviews had to be handed in to his editor by midnight. Passionate lovers of theatre though they were, this deadline put our parents under extraordinary pressure from the moment they left their home in Sandy Bay. Climbing into their blue Mazda, Rox would sit in her passenger seat, a vision in turquoise silk with matching Tibetan earrings, flip down her sun visor and use the make-up mirror to keep an eye on rear traffic.

'Ok, you're right to reverse. Mind Mrs Guildford's cats.'

But once in heavy traffic, our mother's overzealous co-piloting could sometimes hinder more than help.

'Watch out!' she'd cry as they made their way down Macquarie Street. 'This bastard behind you is trying to block you from turning left.'

'I don't need to turn left, you stupid woman!'

'WATCH OUT, WAL!'

'WHERE?'

'A BUS SNEAKING UP ON YOUR RIGHT!'

'WILL YOU STOP *DOING* THAT?'

'JUST STAY CALM!!'

Having arrived safely at the theatre and taken their house seats, Rox would then support our father by passing whatever instruments he required, like a surgeon's assistant. Pen. Program. Torch. Kool Mint. In the case of a dull monologue, a laborious scene change or an airless theatre, Rox had to monitor him vigilantly and be prepared to resort to violent poking if necessary. But when the curtain had come down and the actors were enjoying their first beverage, our parents' work was just beginning. While Rox made cups of tea to keep him alert, our father sat at his desk transcribing his scratchy notes into a cohesive and erudite review. If any of us rang during this critical final phase, our mother would pounce on the phone and speak very quietly, as if Dad was performing neurosurgery.

'Can't talk now, Honeybee. We're just home from a performance that took place down a manhole. Yes, a manhole. The corner of Bathurst and Murray. No idea. Perhaps your father's review will enlighten us all.'

But concern for her husband's health aside, Rox's edit of his final draft could be surprisingly uncompromising.

'Bullshit!' I once heard her say, reading over his shoulder. 'Why do you insult your readers? It was wankery of the highest order and you agreed with me and Marjorie Digby at interval.'

'So I really don't think we can risk it with a poodle,' Rox concluded, returning to our international phone conference. 'At least, not so soon after the *Nicholas Nickleby* experience.'

One week earlier, having made notes throughout eight and a half hours of Dickens at the Theatre Royal, and with just half an hour to get his critique written and faxed to headquarters, neither of our exhausted parents could remember where they'd parked the car.

'See, if we'd come home to a yapping poodle on top of that,' Rox concluded, 'I think it might have just—'

'Killed me!'

Nothing more needed to be said. The whole idea of getting a poodle had been to extend their lives, not kill them.

'But now we have a kitchen that evokes Wordsworth's host of golden daffodils,' our mother cried, desperately trying to change the subject, 'and dear it is beautiful!'

Two days later, I could not believe my sister's news.

'A beagle?' I repeated. 'Crossed with what, a fitness instructor?'

'Crossed with a hound!'

I suspended my enthusiasm.

'What sort of a hound, Georgina?'

'I don't know, Merridy,' my sister answered tersely. 'The woman from the dogs' home just said a hound.'

'Well, is it the kind of hound that might grow to be bigger than our parents?'

Did I really think she and Max had been so irresponsible as not to have checked how big Ella would grow?

Ella?

'Beagles are very low to the ground, Merridy. Short, stumpy little legs. Playful, affectionate, well behaved, but definitely towards the dwarfish end of the scale.'

Unbelievable. Not just that Dad had gone with them to a dogs' home, but that he was at that very moment in the garden throwing sticks in the air.

'We're giving her one week,' George said, 'and if Dad's still throwing sticks out the back, she's staying.'

'Here, Ella!' I heard my father call in a voice I hadn't heard since I was a child. '*Come on, Ella!*'

Perhaps the Bavarians had it right after all. There was a lot to be said for staying close to one's parents, looking after them into their old age and meeting them every fortnight in restaurant car parks. That way, at least you wouldn't find yourself sitting in a kitchen ten thousand miles away, crying as you listened to your father throw sticks to his new best friend. Wonderful as it was to hear their delight in their beagle hound, I couldn't help thinking they should have been making those sounds over their first grandchild in a few months' time, marvelling at his little hands and feet as he gurgled in their arms. Not a dog. But for reasons I no longer understood, just before we could all celebrate this special event together, I'd said goodbye to my parents and relocated to Bavaria, where instead of the familiar, comforting sounds of Tosca competing with Margaret Throsby and our father's lawnmower backfiring, I had to settle for Tom's non-verbal aunt and uncle downstairs, and the monotonous sweep of their brooms. Oh Merridy, I thought, as tears began to fall, what the hell are you doing here?

Uhrzeit, *or time of day*

> 'A person who has not studied German can form no idea of what a perplexing language it is. Surely there is not another language that is so slipshod and systemless, and so slippery and elusive to the grasp. Personal pronouns and adjectives are a fruitful nuisance in this language, and should have been left out.'
>
> *Mark Twain*

With my textbooks in my backpack, I strode into the *Zeitungskiosk* at our local train station at Wettersteinplatz.

'Eine Monatskarte, bitte,' I boldly told the elderly woman with a beehive.

'Ja,' she nodded, and opened her till. 'Innenraum?'

'Ja,' I told her. 'Zwei Ringe, bitte.'

With great satisfaction, I watched as a German person did as I'd asked her to, in German. I even paid her for it, and was about to leave.

'Haben Sie noch einen Wunsch?'

I looked at her. She looked at me. My heart raced.

Did I have a what?

'Einen Wunsch!'

What the hell was a *Wunsch*?

'Noch ein Wunsch?' the man next to me repeated.

Oh God, now two of them wanted me to have a *Wunsch*. Curse these *Wunsches*.

'Haben Sie noch einen *Wunsch*?' she repeated with such annoyance that I shook my head in fright. 'Auf Wiedersehen,' she said, already looking past me to the next customer.

It might have been brief, and somewhat unpleasant, but I'd just had my first conversation in Deutsch, and skipped all the way down to the platform to begin my second month of German lessons in the city.

Most of the time I sat between Natalya and José, but some days Mahvash would sit next to me, usually because José had once again got out at the wrong floor and was sitting at the same desk, but with the advanced class downstairs. It wasn't easy sitting between Mahvash and Natalya. To say that these two strong-willed, proud women didn't get on was an understatement. The only thing they seemed to agree on was that you could never wear too much eyeliner. And the competition between them in class was fierce.

'Is Akkusativ,' Mahvash would announce, leaning forward in her coloured hijab to address Natalya.

'You wrong,' the Russian would retort, leaning forward to return the serve. 'Is Dativ.'

I may have felt like Kofi Annan sitting between Putin and the Ayatollah but, quietly, my money was always on Iran. Due to Mahvash's situation at home, her Deutsch was galloping ahead at a ferocious speed. Although they'd spoken English during their long courtship across the Black Sea, once Mahvash had accepted

Dirk's proposal and relocated to Munich, he'd greeted her with a surprise announcement.

'He said from moment I arrive we speak only in German. That this was only way for me to learn!'

How sensitive of him, I thought, remembering my future brother-in-law. If only these two men could have married each other, then we could all get some sleep.

'Men,' Mahvash grumbled.

Mahvash would often look at me, shake her head, roll her eyes, and sigh, 'Men.' It was her mantra. And perhaps because I was pregnant, Mahvash decided I knew better than anyone how dreadful men could be. I could be having a cheerful conversation with someone about the summer season at the Bayerische Ballet, and Mahvash would sidle up, nudge my arm, roll her eyes, and say 'Men . . .' as if men putting on tights to dance with swans was somehow equivalent to staying out all night drinking. Not that I didn't agree with her some days.

'Well, use your brain!' Tom shouted at me from the couch. 'What do you think it means?'

Frau Schmeck had warned us about the possibility of turbulence when those of us with German partners attempted to speak German at home, and I soon found out why. While it made one partner feel extremely vulnerable, the other had to be extremely patient, and Tom and I hit air pockets just doing my *Hausaufgabe*.

'If I had one clue what the hell it meant, Tom, I wouldn't be asking you, would I?'

'Why are you being so sensitive?'

'Why are you being so horrible?'

Having given up on my homework, Tom suggested I see what I could pick up watching television.

'Hast du etwas verstanden?' he asked when the evening news was over.

Did I understand anything the robotic blond woman with enormous shoulder pads had said in the last half-hour? 'Ja,' I snapped back at him. 'Gerhard, und Schröder.'

Less than forty-eight hours after we'd begun speaking German at home, Tom and I decided to leave the *Deutsch lernen* to Frau Schmeck, and stay engaged.

'Men,' Mahvash said, shaking her head over our hot chocolates in the *Bäckerei*.

'Men,' I echoed.

'Men,' Adrian groaned, taking his cigarettes from his pocket and looking out at the oak trees.

Due to another argument with Heinzi the night before, our student from London had barely slept.

'So I left him at the party and stormed off in search of a club, only to come home at three to find a padlock on the front door! Can you believe it? Bloody *Arschloch*.'

I waited for Mahvash to say 'Men', but Adrian's story seemed to have rendered her speechless.

Once we were sitting back at our desks, most of us forgot about fights with our partners, wedding plans, homesickness. I sometimes even forgot I was pregnant, so overwhelmingly difficult was the task at hand. It was all I could do to follow our expressive teacher's every gesture and placement of lips, teeth and tongue as she introduced us to nearly a hundred new words a day. Most of the time I could keep up, especially when we were asked to work in pairs and Mahvash was sitting next to me. But if it was José, the only lesson I learnt was one in humility. The last time I got stuck with José, I ended up looking at a postcard he carried in his pocket of some Brazilian showgirls. I had no idea what the strange fellow was trying to tell me as he repeatedly pointed at them in their sequins and feathers, and then to himself. Was one of them his wife? His daughter? Was he saving up money for an operation? Or, harder to believe, was this José before the hormone therapy? I had no idea.

Never had I so wanted Mahvash to come through the door before José as the day we opened our books to the chapter called *Uhrzeit*. Had I known just how Germans tell each other the time, I might never have smiled at Tom on that jetty at Lymington last summer. Instead, I might have pushed him hard into the sea and run fast in the opposite direction.

'Halb Zehn?' young Renaldo from Argentina repeated to Frau Schmeck.

Frau Schmeck nodded emphatically and pointed to the clock. It was *Halb Zehn*, or nine thirty, time to begin our class. *Half ten?* But that was nothing. Five minutes later our teacher told us it was *fünf nach halb zehn,* and drew a large clock on the board to illustrate.

Five past half ten? I mouthed to Adrian sitting directly opposite me. But due to Heinzi flushing Adrian's new mobile phone down the toilet in another late night fight, Adrian wasn't even listening. This was not a moment to drift off. You could drift off in a German class and wake up in a fog where the only person you could still understand was José. And speak of the devil.

'Hola!' the giant greeted me, both his ears stuffed with cotton wool as he plonked his books down next to mine.

I could have cried. Curse Mahvash's dentist's appointment.

As the lesson continued we tried to stay positive, but even Mustafa, our besotted Turk, declared that from now on he would only make dates to meet German women on the hour.

'So!' Frau Schmeck said, clasping her hands in front of her, her eyes twinkling as she looked around the room.

Oh please, I silently begged her, please don't make us work in pairs. Not today. Not when I'm sitting next to Brazil.

'Hallo, José,' I mumbled a moment later.

As instructed by our teacher, we all drew clocks in our books so that we could test our partner's ability to tell the time. Except José, who drew me a small house.

'Is there a clock in the house, José?' I asked hopefully.

He shook his large head.

I looked at our teacher, who gave me an encouraging smile, as if only too aware that José was not the full euro, but what could she do? As this was the beginners class, there was nowhere else for the poor man to go, except perhaps into a larger building with wide corridors, kind nurses and bars on the windows.

'José,' I said, resigning myself to a long morning, 'why do you put cotton wool in your ears?'

The giant smiled as if often asked. He pointed to himself, then to his bicycle legs, and mimed riding a bike.

'For riding?' I asked.

'Si,' José said, happy to have solved a mystery.

I nodded too, as if we all knew the effect of exhaust fumes on our ears, and I kept smiling even when José returned to his picture of a house and added a chimney.

In the queue at the *Bäckerei*, I was happy to find myself behind Renaldo, our charming young Argentinian student working for Siemens. A perpetually happy young man and self-delegated social organiser, Renaldo was always inviting me to come to various bars and discos with him and all the younger students. So that he wouldn't think me rude, I thought I'd better explain to Renaldo why I kept saying no.

'You pregnun?' he cried, throwing his arms up in the air. 'I didn't know you pregnun! So ees my mudda!'

As young Renaldo hugged me tight, I saw all future invitations to discos evaporate like bubbles into the air.

'How ol' are you?' he asked.

I told Renaldo how old I was.

'Fordy-two?' he repeated in disbelief. 'You older dan my mudda! She thirdy-seven!'

Oh lord, even the boy's pregnun mudda was younger than me.

'I got ten brudders an seesters,' he stated with pride. 'In Argentina de women marry early and have lossa lossa babies.'

In Australia, I felt like telling Renaldo, instead of marrying early we search for partners in noisy bars until we reach thirty-nine and then take up salsa dancing and Chinese fertility herbs.

After the break I was a little mortified to find Renaldo greeting everyone who came through the door with a quiz.

'Guess how ol' Meddy ees!'

Some answers were more pleasing than others.

'An' did you know she pregnun?'

No!

'Yes!' Renaldo cried, pointing to me as if I'd turned *Brezn* into fish. 'She a pregnun!'

But it was nice to be so warmly congratulated by my classmates, except for Tooheys, who still hadn't forgiven me for my views on John Howard, and José, who counted the loose change in his pocket, shook his head and told Renaldo he didn't have enough.

'Pregnant?' Frau Schmeck cried at the door, bringing with her the smell of cigarettes from the staffroom. 'Really?'

Although we loved to hear Frau Schmeck speak English in her thick Austrian accent, as soon as the clock struck half past ten, or *Halb elf,* all English turned into a pumpkin and we were back to work.

'So die Merridy ist *Schwanger*!' Frau Schmeck announced, writing the word on the board.

The whole class copied it down into their books, all except for José, who looked horrified, possibly because the week before we'd learnt the word *Schlange*, which meant snake.

When our lesson was over and my 12.38 train arrived at Sendlinger Tor bang on time, I forgot how Germans told the time and marvelled at their punctuality instead. Not only did my train arrive every morning at 8.46 on the dot, but so did the 8.46 on the opposite platform going the other way. The chances of such synchronicity, let alone punctuality, back home were unthinkable. As were the chances of getting on a carriage free of graffiti or slashed seats. Apart from the scary plain-clothes ticket inspectors, the German public transport system, at least in Munich, was impressive in every way. As well as having up-to-date timetables, the bus and tram shelters had electronic clocks informing the public how many minutes before the next few buses or trams would arrive. If there was a delay, a voice over the PA system would make an announcement explaining why, and when the next tram or bus would arrive. Back home you could grow old waiting for a bus, not having a clue if there'd been an accident or a strike, or if the route had actually been discontinued after the Olympic Games. And this German regard for punctuality extended to social customs as well. If we were invited to someone's house for dinner at eight, Tom and I were expected to arrive at eight. If we were running ten minutes late, Tom would ring in advance to explain why. This was in stark contrast to our custom back home of arriving at least ten minutes late, lest our hosts think us rude for arriving on time.

Tom was very pleased that I was getting the hang of German *Uhrzeit* and punctuality.

'Because tomorrow,' he said as he poured an alarming amount of cream into our pasta sauce, 'we've been invited to Percy's mother's birthday lunch at the Brauereigasthof in Aying um halb Eins.'

Tante Zelda

Why the two of us had to give up a perfectly good Saturday in summer to celebrate an elderly woman's birthday in a dark wood panelled restaurant, a woman who wasn't even family and whose Christian name was a mystery, was beyond me.

'Whose mother is she again?' I asked as we drove through the Bavarian countryside to Aying.

'Percy's.'

Ah yes, Percy, who managed the building where Tom's parents lived, whose mother was Doctor Hekyll.

'Frau Doktor Gedeck,' Tom corrected me.

I found it hard to take the Germans seriously when they greeted each other with such conventional formalities. Even when we bumped into our friendly neighbour who'd lived next door for over thirty years, she and Tom greeted each other as Frau Held and Herr Baumgartner. They may have chatted over the fence, watering their gardens in their bathers, but they still greeted each other as if taking part in an Oscar Wilde play.

So did she not have friends of her own, patients even, this Doctor Gedeck?

'She's not that kind of doctor,' Tom again corrected me. 'She's an academic. And it's *Frau* Doktor Gedeck.'

Whatever she was, we were to drive forty minutes on a beautiful sunny day to sit under a mounted stag, surrounded by crucifixes and deer antlers, and help Frau Doktor Gedeck celebrate her seventieth birthday.

I soon cheered up, however, when we turned a corner in the winding road that cut through the surrounding lush green forest, and found ourselves in the picturesque 1200 year old village of Aying. And I knew by the familiar figures gathered under a tall maypole in the village centre that the beautiful white hotel behind them with shuttered windows and creeping vines must be the famous Gasthaus Brewery. Having greeted Ulrika, Horst and their children, Onkel Norbert, Tante Ilsa, Tom's parents and various others, we slowly made our way into the hotel foyer, which was decorated with elegant antique tables, enormous flower arrangements and rustic looking candle sconces on the walls. But instead of being led into a restaurant, we were shown into our own private room with a long dinner table, beautifully set for twenty, with yellow napkins, fresh flowers and silver candelabra.

While everyone decided where to sit, I did a quick tally of my surroundings: mounted deer antler: eighteen pairs (these ones still attached to their fragile skulls); antique clocks: one; framed depictions of hunting scenes: four; crucifix: none; stuffed birds: one owl with a bread crust lodged in its beak.

'Merridy?' Tom interrupted my stocktaking. 'This is Percy.'

'Hallo,' said a large bespectacled man in his fifties with his trousers hoisted up to his chest. Percy giggled nervously as he shook my whole body by the hand. 'Und hier ist meine Mutter, Inga Gedeck.'

A diminutive grey haired woman peeped out from under Percy's large protective wing.

'Alles Gute zum Geburtstag, Frau Doktor Gedeck,' I told the birthday girl, having practised all the way in the car.

But I gathered by her regal nod that Frau Doktor Gedeck was a woman of few words.

'Und how is your German coming along?' Percy enquired. 'Are you speaking it to home?'

I confessed to Percy that all I could say so far was 'the door is open', 'my bag is on the table', and 'it is three o'clock'.

Percy shook with laughter. 'Oh, that is so funny. Hast du die Merridy gehört, Mama?'

Percy's mother looked like she wanted to slap him.

'You should learn from Mama,' Percy said, putting a proud arm around the woman he still lived with. 'Mama teaches German at the Goethe Institut.'

'Really?' I asked the tiny woman. 'So you can speak English, Frau Doktor Gedeck?'

Frau Doktor Gedeck looked up at me, closed her eyes and answered in incomprehensible German.

I looked at Percy.

'My mother says her students are not allowed to speak English at the Goethe Institut. And that if you're serious about learning German, you should go there.'

I told Frau Doktor Gedeck we couldn't afford to be that serious, and that I was therefore taking classes at Inlingua. I gathered by the frosty silence that followed that Percy's mother either didn't approve of my *Sprachschule*, or perhaps hadn't understood a word I'd said.

After helping the old dowager into a chair, Percy pulled out the chair next to her.

'Sit,' he commanded me.

I desperately searched the room for Tom.

'Sit!' Percy shouted.

Curse these Germans and their direct manner, I thought as I plonked myself down next to Frau Doktor Gedeck. Why did I have to sit where some guy called Percy told me to? What the hell was I even doing here?

'Hallo, Merridy,' a voice sang in my other ear.

'Tante Zelda!' I cried, and rose to greet the beautifully preserved, poised and sprightly woman I'd met twice since arriving in Munich.

Zelda wasn't really an aunt. She had just worked in the same typing pool as Tom's mother when they left school, and Friedl and Zelda had been best friends ever since. Even before I met her at one of the Baumgartners' afternoon teas, I'd gathered from the photos on their mantelpiece that no family reunion was complete without Zelda. She was an endearing creature, clutching her handbag in a white-knuckled grip as she beamed fiercely at the congregation around her.

'Darf ich hier sitzen?' she asked, pointing to the empty seat next to me.

'Ja!' I cried, inwardly cursing Tom for abandoning me up the deep end of the pool between two German women who spoke no English between them.

As she lowered herself balletically into the chair, Tante Zelda looked around the room and smiled, quite literally, from ear to ear. In fact, if someone pushed Tante Zelda in the middle of the back while she was laughing, there's a good chance her jaws would come right off their hinges, causing the top of her head to flip back. But I loved Zelda for the way she always greeted me, squeezed my hand and welcomed me into the family, at least I guessed that's what she was doing. Tom had once confessed that everyone had trouble understanding Zelda, she spoke so fast, so I shouldn't worry if I did too.

'I'm here!' my fiancé announced, suddenly appearing on the other side of the table.

I must have looked at Tom exactly the way a baby seal looks at its mother just before it's clubbed.

'You'll be all right,' he whispered, sitting down and winking at me.

I looked at him. Did he really think so? For how long?

After she'd finally decided to just hold her handbag in her lap, Zelda turned to me and spoke with such ferocious speed and enthusiasm I wasn't sure for a minute that she wasn't singing, until she stopped, quite suddenly, as if her battery had gone flat.

'Versteh?' she asked, madly nodding at me.

'Ein bisschen,' I lied, indicating with my thumb and forefinger that I'd understood just a fraction of what she'd said.

But that was enough for Zelda. With a joyous smile, off she went again like a rocket, occasionally pausing for me to express delight, outrage, sadness or whatever response was required, until I was saved by a tap on my left arm.

'Entschuldigung Sie bitte,' Frau Doktor Gedeck said. 'Können Sie mir die Speisekarte geben?'

I blinked at her. Die shpiza—what?

'Die Speise-karte,' the old dowager repeated, pointing towards the middle of the table.

'Die Speisekarte!' Zelda cried, pointing to the vase of flowers in front of me.

'The flowers?'

'*Die Speisekarte!*' both women shouted in unison, madly gesticulating.

Now that we had the attention of the whole table, Tom finally intervened and passed Percy's mother the menu, *die Speisekarte,* from the other side of the vase.

'Dankeschön, Thomas!' Frau Doktor Gedeck sang, recovering from her ordeal.

'Menu,' I told her.

'Bitte?' she asked, offering me her good ear.

'The English word for Speisekarte,' I told the German teacher from the prestigious Goethe Institut, 'is *menu*.'

For the next few minutes, I hid in my *Speisekarte* trying to make sense of the German hieroglyphics in front of me. I knew what gnocchi was, but this one came in *Bärlauch, Sahnesauce mit Bergkäsespänen*. Before I could ask Tom what the hell *Bärlauch* was, and if *Stangenspargel* was asparagus, Zelda was once more in my ear. And as the dear woman's mirth progressed to hysterics, I felt compelled to laugh with her, even if I hadn't a clue what could be so funny.

'Da, da!' she insisted, pointing towards the door.

I looked where she wanted me to, and could hardly believe my eyes. The tallest couple I'd ever seen were taking their seats at the far end of the table. The man was so large in frame and flesh, I wondered if he'd been approached on the street by circus managers.

'Mein Gott,' I gasped.

'Ja,' Zelda agreed, holding her hand up to the sky. '*Sehr* gross, oder?'

'Ja!' I whispered. 'Sie machen eine *gut couple.*'

Zelda nodded furiously. 'Moritz und Birgid,' she said, smiling.

'Oh, you know them?' I asked.

'Meine Kinder!'

Kinder? Children? The giants were hers? 'How lovely!' I cried with joy. 'Both of them, Zelda? Not twins I hope!'

A second later I stopped laughing and stood to shake Moritz and Birgid's large hands.

'How lovely to meet you both,' I told them.

Zelda's tall children were exceptionally friendly people, and both were fluent in English, so it was with great sadness that I watched them return to their seats up the far end of the table.

'Letzte-Woche-war-die-Birgid-sehr-krank,' Tante Zelda sighed, looking fondly after them.

'Absolutely,' I agreed, with what I hadn't a clue. 'You must be very proud.'

To my surprise, after Percy had tapped his glass and made a short announcement, we all sang 'Happy Birthday' to Frau Doktor Gedeck in English, a German tradition according to Tom. But all too soon I'd returned to my quandary, trying to decide between *Ochsenlende* and *Knuspriges Spanferkel.* Unable to get Tom's attention to ask if I should order the *Schlachtplatte,* the only meal I knew how to pronounce, I once again gave in to Zelda, intent on regaling me with details in her mother tongue as if I was a native. Only by recognising one word in every twenty was I able to vaguely guess at least the possible subject matter of her conversation. Yes, I nodded, the hotel was *schön*, wasn't it? *Und meine Apfelschorle* was delicious too. No, not alcoholic. *Kein alkohol* when you're *schlange*, ha! Oh sorry, I meant *schwanger*, not *schlange*. *Shlange*'s a snake, isn't it? Yes, lots of snakes in Australia . . . How many snakes? Oh, how many months? Sorry! Five. I'm five months pregnant, Zelda. *Fünf Monate schwanger. Ja*, not very big. *Ja*, very happy. *Gut!*

No matter how often I tapped Tom's foot under the table, he was too locked in conversation with his brother-in-law about the latest BMW to help me. Could these two talk about anything else other than cars and computers?

Twenty minutes later, having ordered the *Schlachtplatte,* whatever that was, the strain of listening to my chatty companion and guessing the correct response was taking its toll. But Zelda was showing no sign of relenting whatsoever. And I gathered by her frequent nodding towards her daughter at the end of the table that her latest anecdote involved Birgid. Zelda frowned. Birgid had done something bad. Very bad. To her foot. Her leg. Zelda showed me with her hands that something was about six inches high, so I assumed that Birgid, who was already one of the tallest women I'd ever met in my life, was wearing very high heels at the time—when she'd fallen over.

'Schade!' I said, knowing the word meant 'shame', which must have been the right thing to say because Zelda couldn't have agreed more.

'Ja, furchtbar.'

But no sooner were Zelda and I both grieving over Birgid's sprained ankle, broken leg, prosthetic foot, than the dear woman began laughing her head off. And so I joined her, having no idea why. The word *apotheke* was in there, which I knew from living opposite one meant 'chemist'. But as I didn't have the skills to ask Zelda what could possibly be so funny about a chemist shop, I had to settle for asking her where it was.

'Und wo ist die Apotheke, Zelda?'

Zelda didn't think it a ridiculous question at all, and in fact seemed more than happy to give me detailed directions to a chemist shop somewhere in Giesing in which hilarious things had happened. But now that we'd got directions out of the way, Zelda found the chemist shop even funnier than before. I was still laughing with her when quite unexpectedly Zelda said the word *gestorben*, which I knew meant 'dead'. So I stopped laughing, as did Zelda, and wondered who on earth might have died, and if they'd died inside or outside the funny chemist shop in Giesing.

It couldn't have been Birgid. She sat three metres away sharing a *Brezn* with Tante Ilsa.

'Moritz und seine Freundin,' Zelda added with a sigh.

How sad, I nodded. Moritz and his girlfriend had died. No, that couldn't be right either. Moritz was at that moment helping Tom's mother with her cardigan at the head of the table. And I felt sure Moritz wouldn't have come today, no matter how fond he was of Frau Doktor Gedeck, had his girlfriend been in some fatal accident in or near a funny chemist shop in Giesing. But whoever had died, it clearly wasn't too upsetting, because Zelda was once again grinning from ear to ear.

'Die Oma, natürlich,' she added.

'Natürlich,' I agreed, knowing that *Oma* meant 'grandmother'.

Perhaps Zelda's grandmother had died in a tragic but surprisingly funny accident while picking up a prescription wearing built-up shoes. I too had recently discovered how easy it was to laugh at the misfortune of others while watching *Upps*, the only German television show I could understand. Back home it was called *Australia's Funniest Home Videos,* and although I'd always disapproved of programs that humorised horrible accidents with an accompanying inane commentary, I now sat with Tom once a week, beating the armrest of our sofa with tears rolling down my face as we both watched some poor middle-aged woman dancing on a table at a wedding reception suddenly slip off and possibly shatter her coccyx.

'. . . ist auch gestorben,' Zelda's voice interrupted my thoughts.

Oh no, don't tell me someone else had died! But this time, Zelda really did look sad. Bereft even. Perhaps the dear woman was truly Chekhovian, laughing one minute, close to tears the next. There was no doubt she was a 'feeling' creature, my favourite kind, but Christ I wished I could understand her. Negotiating whether to laugh or offer condolences in this tricky minefield was exhausting.

'Er war die Liebe meines Lebens,' Zelda said after a poignant pause.

I looked at Zelda. It was the one sentence uttered since she'd sat down next to me that I actually understood from beginning to end. *He was the love of my life.*

'Mein Mann,' she added, smiling bravely as the tears welled in her eyes.

Zelda's husband had died thirty years ago, if I understood her correctly. As I watched her desperately scrunching the napkin in her lap, I wished I knew some words that might comfort her.

'Wie traurig, Zelda,' I said, glad that I at least knew the word for sad.

Zelda patted my hand and nodded. 'Ja, stimmt.'

For a moment, we sat together quietly studying the bread basket, both of us tearily reflecting on Zelda's great loss, until curiosity got the better of me and I asked how, or *wie,* my companion's husband had died so young, or *jung.*

Zelda took a deep breath. 'Crabs.'

I looked at her. 'Crabs?' I repeated carefully.

Zelda nodded. I nodded. We both nodded at the tablecloth.

I knew the crab could give you a nasty nip, but this was extraordinary.

'Krebs!' Tom said, trying not to laugh as we pulled out of the car park. 'Krebs is German for cancer. Brustkrebs, Lungenkrebs, Leberkrebs . . . What did you think she meant?'

Despite Tom's mirth over my impression that Tante Zelda's husband had been attacked by mutant crustaceans in the North Sea, and despite the fact that I had barely understood a word the dear woman had said, Zelda's sorrow would stay with me all day. Herr Schäfer had died of a brain tumour, leaving behind two friendly, bright, rather tall children, and a devoted wife and mother who'd once worked in a typing pool with Friedl Baumgartner. And he had been the love of Zelda's life. Sometimes I felt resentful that so much of my weekends was now spent sitting in dark restaurants eating heavy meals with various kind but incomprehensible German pensioners. It was a big change from cruising around the eastern suburbs of Sydney, catching up with my friends in groovy cafés and bookshops to discuss over our lattes the latest film or play we'd seen. But I wouldn't have missed dear Zelda for anything. Sometimes I understood exactly what Dagobert Runes meant when he said, *People travel to faraway places to watch, in fascination, the kind of people they ignore at home.*

My royal dentist

I was reading Kaz Cooke's *Up The Duff*, a book both helpful and hilarious for women preparing for motherhood, when it occurred to me that apart from organising weddings, Tom and I should probably find ourselves a good obstetrician.

'Yes, that's true,' Tom said, not looking up from his computer magazine. 'We've also got to find you an optometrist, a dermatologist, an orthopaedist and a dentist.'

Sometimes I felt like Tom had bought me on eBay without a roadworthy certificate.

'Well, you say yourself you can't read street signs,' he protested, 'and that your feet always hurt, and that you've never had a proper skin cancer check-up. Plus you sleep with your mouth open, and you can't even tell me the last time you saw a dentist.'

I could actually, but I didn't think he'd approve.

Despite my fiancé's growing list of must-have inspections, I was fascinated by this stringent attitude of the Germans towards health and 'wellness' as they called it, contradictions and all. Although one could have trouble finding the toilets in their restaurants for thick cigarette smoke, the Bavarian countryside was always full of sporty friends and families trekking through the Alps with their skis and snowboards or, now that summer was approaching, their Nordic walking sticks, bicycles or paragliding gear. And although they allowed their dogs into restaurants and onto public transport, they found the wearing of shoes indoors unhygienic, were diligent hand washers, and never, ever put their feet on the seat on public transport.

It also wasn't uncommon for Tom's friends and family to recommend various 'wellness' hotels, spas, or natural therapy sanatoriums, as well as doctors. Perhaps encouraged by mandatory health insurance, Tom and his friends saw a team of specialists for every malady going. And as they'd stayed in Munich all their lives, most of Tom's specialists were old friends from school. Axel was his otolaryngologist, or ear, nose and throat doctor, Matthias was his cardiologist, Frederik was his dermatologist and on it went. I always felt Tom himself should have been a dentist, especially when he stood at the bathroom sink wearing a white T-shirt, examining his rear molars with a small dental mirror. His ten minute teeth cleaning routine even extended to gargling with sunflower oil.

'Good for the gums,' he said the first time I caught him. 'You should try it.'

I didn't like his chances.

And so, having made a series of appointments for me to see Axel, Doris, Frederik and Sebastian, who'd inspect everything from my feet to my eyesight, Tom and I made our way to visit Ekaterina, his dentist, for a check-up.

'Is she really a Bulgarian princess?' I asked on the footpath, staring in disbelief at the silver plaque on the wall in Schwabing.

'Yes,' Tom said, 'and we were at university together. That's why she's squeezed you in.'

While Tom strode inside the main entrance of the tall white building, I hastily searched through my bag for my digital camera. Wait till my friends back home got my email. 'Check out my new dentist: *Doctor Ekaterina Prinzessin Smimenska*.'

Having stepped out of the glass lift, Tom and I entered Doctor Smimenska's palatial, elegant white waiting room on the fifth floor. Although I wasn't expecting to see a woman wearing a crown and draped in the Bulgarian flag, I wasn't expecting a receptionist with a pierced nose and a green fringe either.

'Morgen, Herr Baumgartner,' Svetlana sighed, flipping her *Vogue* magazine shut, dragging her feet off her desk and putting her shoes back on.

She was so sluggish, I wondered if young Svetlana hadn't also helped herself to a little gas with her morning tea. But a few minutes later, having stapled my details into a file, our gothic receptionist managed to shuffle across the waiting area and show us into a spacious white room.

'Doktor Smimenska kommt gleich,' she croaked, before shuffling out again.

Tom politely waited until she'd gone before whispering to me: 'Bulgarian.'

Familiar with his surroundings, Tom quickly settled into the luxurious white couch by the door to flick through a glossy magazine. Not feeling quite so comfortable, I stood exactly where the Bulgarian receptionist had left me, in the middle of the room facing the enormous dentist's chair with overhanging flat screen television that looked like it had been built by NASA. Or maybe all dentists had been using such high tech chairs and screens since the late eighties, roughly the last time I'd let a stranger put his hand in my mouth.

'Have you brushed your teeth since breakfast?' Tom asked.

I gasped.

'Merridy!'

'Gotcha.'

Tom and I watched silently as the receptionist shuffled back into the room to lay various sterilised instruments on a tray as if she was setting cutlery in a diner.

'Kommen Sie hier, bitte,' she said, beckoning me to sit in the NASA chair.

And having clipped a paper towelling bib around my neck, Svetlana left me there, staring at the dark screen above my head. Maybe the princess played entertaining DVDs to take her patient's mind off all the drilling going on. I wondered if she had any in English.

'You there, Tommy?' I asked nervously.

'Yes, my love,' his deep voice answered from behind, far more interested in a spread on Japanese water features than my mounting anxiety.

A minute later I heard the unmistakable whoosh of a princess entering the room.

'Thomas! Lieber!'

'Ekaterina!'

I gathered by the almost operatic laughter, hugs and kisses going on behind me that Tom and his princess hadn't seen each other in months, during which time many hilarious things had happened.

'Hey, du schaust aber gut aus!'

'Doch!'

'Doch doch!'

I was still struggling to look around my enormous chair when suddenly her radiant face loomed before mine.

'Marion!' the princess sang, offering me her hand. 'How wonderful to meet you!'

How could Tom not have mentioned his royal dentist was a stunning, long-necked, raven-haired gazelle? And what did I do with her hand? Shake it, kiss it?

'Hello,' I said, giving her long fingers a little jiggle.

'At last someone has made a man of our Thomas!' she exclaimed in her thick accent, giving my shoulder a powerful squeeze. 'I mean a *real* man!'

Yes, I laughed. Now we could all get some sleep! Especially Tom.

While Tom and his dentist continued their conversation in German, I felt embarrassed by everything from my old jeans and scuffed boots to my neglected teeth. I didn't come from royal stock. I came from Tasmania, where my parents had slaved to put their three children through private schools instead of sending them to orthodontists, a decision they would now live to regret.

'Und du bist schwanger!' the princess sang, giving my cheek an affectionate pinch.

I nodded. That's right, completely up the duff.

'Wieviel?' she asked.

How often?

'How many months?'

'Five!'

'Fünf?' she cried, and then with a violent kick to something beneath me, made my NASA chair descend. 'You must say if you feel uncomfortable.'

I promised I felt fine.

'Because you can die, you know, if you lie on your back late in ze pregnancy.'

I laughed.

'Seriously.'

I stopped laughing.

'Ze baby can—' The princess turned to Tom. '*Quetschen?*'

'Squash,' Tom called from behind me.

'Sank you. Ze baby can *squash* ze major arteries, and zis can kill you.'

I nodded gravely. I knew that in the final trimester you shouldn't drink scotch, ride horses or take part in re-enactments of famous medieval battles, but no one told me you could die just from lying on your back.

While a princess and her pierced dental nurse took turns scraping my teeth, prodding my gums and spraying industrial shots of cold air under my tongue, I lay flat on my back trying not to think about my major arteries being quetsched.

'All ze vay von Australien,' the princess sighed wistfully down my throat. 'How—*Svetlana, foto hier!*—how remarkable . . .'

It seemed like she had her whole fist in my mouth when Prinzessin Smimenska asked when I'd last seen a dentist. There was an awkward pause, until Tom coughed twice.

'Twooh yeash?' I lied.

A silence descended on the room. I was glad I hadn't told Ekaterina the truth, that it was actually before the invasion of Kuwait. But by now I'd guessed I was in the presence of people who worshipped another god, a god of dental hygiene and oral vigilance, a people who struggled to find tolerance for my god, a god of cavities, gum disease and plaque.

'Two years . . .' she echoed, shaking her beautiful head. '*Foto, Svetlana!*'

I could tell by their low voices behind me, the princess's and Tom's, as I rinsed out my mouth that bad news was on its way.

'Vell, Marion,' my royal dentist finally said, snapping off her rubber gloves. 'Considering it is two years since you last saw a dentist, your teeth are in very good shape indeed.' Amazing. Here came the bad news. 'But it is clear to me, and Thomas tells me I am right, zat you are not cleaning properly.'

Again she kicked something hard under my NASA chair, elevating me until we were eye to eye.

'You floss?' she asked.

'Nein,' came Tom's voice from behind.

'Not a lot,' I answered, feeling less like a fiancée and more like a troublesome teenage daughter.

'Marion. Don't be put off by blood, do you hear? Gingivitis is especially common in pregnant vomen, so you must floss and floss and bleed and bleed until ze gums are strong, do you hear?'

She was magnificent. Even when speaking about dental hygiene, Ekaterina looked like she was sitting up on a decorated horse, speaking to the Bulgarian army before a great battle.

'Marion,' she repeated, leaning in so close her nose nearly touched mine. 'Ven you are pregnant, everything is swallowing. You understand?'

I nodded. Everysing was svallowing. It sounded strange, but she was a princess.

'Zis is because you have fifty procent more blood pomping around your body when you are pregnant. Did you know zis? Fifty procent. Pomping und pomping.'

I nodded. Pomping and swallowing. Fifty procent.

'Und so you have tvice as much fluid in ze body, in ze mouth, in ze nose, und in ze vagina.'

The room was silent. No doubt Tom and Svetlana were both as shocked as I was that we'd gone from teeth to vaginas.

'So let's have a look at ze fotos,' she announced, picking up a remote control and flicking it at the enormous flat screen television above our heads.

To my utter horror, the screen came to life not with the latest Pixar animation, but with a huge photo of a yellowish tooth, apparently mine.

'You see ze dark red line here at ze gum?'

Yes, for the love of God, turn it off!

'Don't vorry about Thomas!' the princess barked, as if she could hear my thoughts. 'He loves you just ze vay you are!'

No one loves me this much! I wanted to yell back at her. But she was already on to the next photo, which was even worse.

'Und zis tooth here is in a dreadful state!'

I tried to look around to see if Tom was curled up in foetal position with his hands over his face.

'Don't look at him!' the princess ordered, slapping me on the arm. 'He loves you, teeth and all! Don't you, Thomas?'

I heard a grunt, but I could also hear a Lufthansa plane taking off.

Slide session over, my dentist announced we were going to have a lesson in 'the correct brushing of ze teeth', and commanded me to follow her to the sink. As I stood before a basin in front of a large mirror, I looked at Tom on his couch pretending to be more interested in Moroccan vases, but he wasn't fooling anyone.

'Thomas, you come too.'

No!

'For cleaning ze teeth, ve don't use toothpaste. Ve use bicarbonate of soda und tea tree oil. Has Thomas told you zis?'

I shook my head. But at least now I knew who told him to gargle with cooking oil.

'And you know vat else bicarbonate of soda is good for getting rid of?' the princess asked, sprinkling the fine white powder onto my brush.

I had no idea. Lice? Tinea?

'Vind!'

Tom's plane took off for the Maldives.

As I lay in bed that night, running my tongue over my smooth, flossed, polished teeth, I prepared myself for more boot camps in the consultation rooms of Tom's old school friends. Tomorrow some guy called Sebastian would possibly sandblast the soles of my feet while Tom sat on a comfortable sofa, as if supervising the renovation of a neglected but much loved car. I looked at him, fast asleep by my side, and wondered if Tom had put all his girlfriends through a roadworthy test, or if I'd just done more miles than anyone else. Although I found this German thoroughness a little overwhelming at times, I knew his intentions were good. It wasn't as if Tom was sending me to cosmetic surgeons to have my boobs lifted and my forehead botoxed, or to hairdressers for hair extensions. Tom didn't even care if I wore make-up so much as shower with cold water from the waist down to improve my circulation. Although I drew the line at cold showers and gargling with cooking oil, I was happy to take more responsibility for my health and habits. And so having cleaned my teeth with tea tree oil and bicarbonate of soda, and moisturised every dry patch of skin on my body, I rolled over and closed my eyes, my eyes that would be tested by Doris on Wednesday, and fell into a deep sleep.

Neo Nazis and Munich eccentrics

I was sitting with my future mother-in-law and her sister in the Glockenspiel Café in Marienplatz, enjoying *Kaffee und Kuchen* after my class. Given we'd only just learnt how to tell the time in German, conversation never exactly flowed with these two affectionate women, but thanks to Friedl's little English dictionary we were sometimes able to make surprising headway. Yes, wasn't it funny that despite being German, Tom was the most *unpünktlich* or unpunctual person in the world? And couldn't he also be terribly *streng* they asked, giggling like schoolgirls.

'Streng?'

'Strict!' Friedl cried, peeping over the top of her *Wörterbuch*.

I would have said pedantic, more than strict. I could cope with the lectures I got for putting sharp knives in the dishwasher, but when Tom told me not to take such big steps when I walked he'd crossed a line.

'Pull your head in,' I repeated my response to the women. 'In Australia, we say it when someone's gone too far. Zu weit gehen.'

I gathered by the way they both nodded at me that neither sister had ever told a man to pull his head in in her life. Patting my hand sympathetically, Ilsa explained that Tom got his *Strenge* from his grandfather. *Mutter* might have been a musical, cheerful woman who laughed all the time, Friedl said, but *Vater* was as strict, authoritarian and commanding as they came.

'Und Wilhelm's Vater?' I asked, wanting to know about the paternal grandfather too.

'Furchtbar,' one sister whispered to the other, as if remembering a tyrant.

'Schrecklich,' the other agreed, shaking her head.

'Männer,' Friedl sighed, meaning *Men*.

'Männer,' Ilsa agreed.

'Pull your head in,' I repeated to the sisters, and we clinked coffee mugs. 'Prost.'

Did I want to come with them to the cemetery, Friedl asked, once we'd walked outside onto the crowded square. Every week, she and Ilsa dutifully visited their mother and father's graves at Ostfriedhof to pay their respects, sweep up the leaves and place fresh flowers between the headstones.

Perhaps some other time, I told Friedl, as I kissed her goodbye, and then watched as the two sisters carefully descended the steps of the U-Bahn, arm in arm. When they'd safely reached the bottom, they both looked up, smiled almost rapturously, and gave me the daintiest of waves. I wondered if they knew how lovable they were, and how fond I already was of both of them.

By the time I'd done a bit of shopping and reached my train station at Sendlinger Tor, I guessed by the youthful crowd gathered under the ancient brick archway in the late afternoon sun that Munich was hosting yet another big football match. But when I saw the police vans parked on the other side, and rows of heavily armoured men in black uniforms with *POLIZEI* written on their backs, I sensed they were expecting something more sinister than football revellers.

Having spotted a policewoman in front of a cinema with her thumbs tucked into the belt that held her holster, I decided to stand nearby to study the eclectic crowd gathering before both of us. Dark-eyed Goths in dark robes mingled with ferals whose matted hair and deliberately torn clothes were in stark contrast to the spiky punks who leant lazily against the wall opposite as they drank from bottles in brown paper bags. 'Schau Mama!' a small child yelled from within his *Kinderwagen*, as his mother hastily pushed him past a punk sporting a colourful mohawk. 'Er hat einen Besen auf seinem Kopf!', meaning He's got a broom on his head!

Where had they all been, I wondered. And what on earth were they here for? There must have been a thousand of them.

I'd just mustered enough courage to ask the policewoman when I heard a man's voice directly behind me speaking in a clipped English accent.

'That's the reason so many riot police are here,' he told his small group of tourists. 'Whenever the neo Nazis are given permission to march through Munich, they're so vastly outnumbered by counter demonstrators, they need protection.'

A neo Nazi demonstration? I knew this was my cue to go downstairs and get the first train home, but the curious, irresponsible writer in me wanted to stay just a few minutes longer, especially when I could eavesdrop on an English tour guide.

'Vorsicht!' the policewoman shouted as we were both nearly clocked by a rogue placard that read *NAZIS RAUS!*

The placard owner, a pale young man somewhat resembling a vampire with long lank hair, stood before me, his cigarette hanging loosely from between his purple lips.

'Haben Sie Feuer?' he asked.

I shook my head. A match? Couldn't he see I was pregnant?

One of the British tourists behind me expressed her surprise that neo Nazis were allowed to demonstrate at all, and as the rest of the group clearly felt the same way the guide had to shout them down.

'But you know the last person who put a stop to people assembling in public places in Germany?' he asked.

'Hitler!' someone called from the back.

As the policewoman turned to frown at them, the group madly shooshed each other. 'That's right,' continued the guide in a low voice. 'Since the end of the Third Reich, preserving the right to freedom of speech is something the Germans value highly. Unfortunately, this means for everyone, including the neo Nazis and the NPD, the German National Democratic Party.'

The government had restrained them in other ways, I wanted to tell them. According to Tom it was illegal in Germany to wear the Nazi uniform, to display the swastika, to deny the holocaust, to possess a copy of Hitler's *Mein Kampf*, or even to buy, sell or hire any of Leni Riefenstahl's propaganda films.

When the crowd grew restless and began chanting *Nazis Raus, Nazis Raus!* I thought the neo Nazis must have arrived, but according to our guide the noisy protesters who rose from the station below and filed past us in their black clothes, sunglasses and hoodies belonged to a group called Antifa, an anti-fascist organisation that enjoyed a reputation for being the neo Nazis' most vocal and often aggressive opponents. On hearing the word 'aggressive', I decided that this definitely was the moment to take my leave. But rather than use the underground in this uneasy atmosphere, I decided to walk all the way back to Maximilian-strasse, and go home by tram.

Sitting on the Number 19 *Strassenbahn* as it passed Munich's palatial Nationaltheater, I couldn't get over the contrast. Back in Sendlinger Tor, all hell was about to break loose but here, in Max Joseph Platz, a chamber orchestra could be heard as an elegant crowd of peacocks and penguins in tuxedos and furs had gathered on the footpath outside the famous opera house. While more passengers boarded our tram, those of us already seated watched in silence as the dark blue Rolls Royce graciously pulled up to the theatre's red carpet. And as the uniformed chauffeur opened the back door, we stared slack-jawed at what emerged from within. Clutching a tremulous little dog under one arm, a portly fellow resplendent in a purple velvet suit, matching cravat and handkerchiefs, wearing a large jet-black wig reminiscent of Ludwig II, stepped out with the majesty of a visiting royal dignitary. Watching him smile rapturously into the meteor shower of flashing bulbs, I wondered if all German opera singers arrived at the theatre's front entrance in full costume and make-up. As our tram began to rumble forward, I turned around to smile at my fellow commuters, only to remember the code of silence on Munich public transport. Back in Australia, there would have been at least one person to share a laugh with over the theatrical spectacle we'd just witnessed, but not one traveller on this packed tram wanted to dance with me. Never mind, I sighed. I'd ask Tom when I got home.

'Moshammer.'

Tom knew as soon as I mentioned the dog.

'And that's Daisy.'

I sat on the kitchen bench so I could bombard my future husband with questions as he prepared our dinner. Watching Tom put together a meal was like seeing poetry in motion. I loved the fluent way he moved from fridge to oven, spun on one foot to collect a spatula, effortlessly slid drawers open and shut, tossed pepper shakers in the air and kissed me if I got in the way.

No, Tom said. Rudolph Moshammer wasn't a famous actor. He was originally a successful local fashion designer with a menswear boutique on Maximilianstrasse. But over the years he'd become more of a local celebrity who attended balls, operas and cabarets and was invited to the opening of an envelope. And yes, the wig was meant to remind people of Ludwig II. As a young designer, Moshammer's decision to model himself on the extravagant king had proven as shrewd a business move as it had been personally irresistible. But the problem was, Tom continued as he whacked the meat into submission, that Ludwig II died when he was forty, leaving the fashionista impersonating him well into his sixties. And as he'd aged and spread, the make-up had become thicker and the bouffant bigger until 'Mosi' had become not just a caricature of Ludwig, but of himself.

'And what about Daisy?'

The Yorkshire terrier had been Moshammer's constant companion ever since his beloved mother had died ten years earlier, Tom said. Mother Else and Rudolph had been inseparable, sharing their palatial home in Grünwald just down the road, and constantly photographed together at social events. Moshammer had even written a book about their relationship, called *Mama und Ich*.

'Did it sell?'

Tom nodded. 'Almost as well as *Ich, Daisy. Bekenntnisse einer Hundedame.*'

I waited for my translation.

'I, Daisy. Confessions of a Lady Dog.'

Good grief. Even Gogol's Poprishchin hadn't gone this far. But had this larger than life celebrity really made his fortune designing fashion? I could see Lagerfeld sitting at the drawing board holding a pencil, but it was much easier to imagine Moshammer lying on a couch like Barbara Cartland, popping truffles in his mouth while dictating books about a lady dog.

On the contrary, Tom said, Moshammer's clientele had included Arnold Schwarzenegger, José Carreras, Leonard Bernstein, and various members of European royalty. 'And Siegfried and Roy.'

Tom and I had only recently caught the end of a documentary on the two famous German magicians whose long running show in Las Vegas had abruptly closed when Roy was almost fatally mauled by his favourite white tiger. Even as he'd lain bleeding almost to death in the back of an ambulance, Roy had been more worried about his six hundred pound carnivore pet. 'Don't harm the cat,' he'd gasped.

I wondered if Moshammer had in any way been responsible for the bejewelled silver cloaks with enormous stiff collars, the glittering zebra print suits or shiny white boots these two entertainers so loved to wear. It wouldn't have surprised me. After all, Moshammer's version of Ludwig II seemed just as inspired by Vegas and Liberace as by Munich and Wagner.

That night, as Tom and I watched the news, I was amazed to see Munich's streets lined with thousands of angry counter-protesters as only a few hundred neo Nazis, flanked by riot police, marched through the city with their shaved heads, heavy boots, rolled up jeans, tattoos and Lonsdale sweaters. *Lonsdale sweaters?*

'The word Lonsdale has the initials NSDA in the middle,' Tom explained, 'as in the National Sozialistische Deutsche Arbeiter Partei, Hitler's Nazi Party.'

This was why most of the marchers wore the sweaters with open jackets or shirts to cover the LO and the LE. How strange, I thought, for a British sporting label to be adopted as a kind of uniform for neo Nazis. And how strange to watch this demonstration going on in one part of the city, while just a few blocks away Rudolph Moshammer had sat in the opera box of the Nationaltheater with his dog, Daisy, enjoying an early evening performance of Mozart's *Cosi Fan Tutte*.

'I had an interesting day too,' Tom said as he collected our plates and headed for the kitchen. 'I believe you taught my mother a new expression.'

I had?

'Yes,' Tom said, turning back from the doorway. 'I told her to stop feeling so sorry for herself and the only reason she can't shake her cold is because even at seventy, she still doesn't know how to dress warmly.'

And?

'And she told me to *pull my head off*.'

Summer in Bavaria

By the time summer arrived it was hard to believe that this welcoming, vibrant, floral metropolis was the same hauntingly beautiful but austere city that had greeted me back in March.

The once leafless, empty parks in and around the city were now luscious and green and buzzing with bumblebees. The banks of the Isar were crawling with Nordic walkers, cyclists, sunbathers, picnickers and barbecues. The *Spielplätze* were full of children whose names had been written in texta on their sand toys, students sat in the grass outside the Ludwig-Maximilians-Universität in Schwabing, and tourists were everywhere. Café tables now spilled out onto the footpaths, waitresses wore the *Dirndl* and tour guides addressed groups in front of every church and statue. Standing in the sun beneath the neo-gothic Rathaus in Marienplatz, listening to all the different languages spoken around me, I could believe that around five million tourists visited Munich every summer. And judging by the constant ringing of bicycle bells, most of them still hadn't learnt not to stray onto the marked bike paths either.

'Excuse me!' an American woman howled in protest. 'This is a sidewalk, you know!'

No, I felt like telling her. Half is a *Fussweg*, the other half is a *Radweg.* The nearest 'sidewalk' was somewhere near Portland, Maine.

As if having been in hibernation during the colder months, the inhabitants of Munich now took to the hills, waterways and bicycle tracks with great enthusiasm. On weekends the *Radweg* were populated with families wearing helmets and rucksacks as they pedalled towards the zoo, the park or a *Biergarten*, often with their youngest sitting behind in the *Anhänger,* or covered trailer. Towing a toddler in such a flimsy apparatus back in Sydney would have been highly dangerous, but back home you didn't see octogenarians pedalling gracefully through the city with their baskets full of groceries either. Here in Munich the cyclist wasn't just visible, he was a protected species.

'You'll be perfectly safe,' Tom insisted whenever he got his bikes out of the garage on a Saturday afternoon. 'The Waldwirtschaft Biergarten is only a thirty minute ride, and pregnant women cycle all the time.'

I knew that. But the only helmet Tom possessed looked like something out of *Hogan's Heroes,* and when I wore it with my maternity pants tucked into my socks I looked like someone who needed constant supervision and under no circumstances was allowed near cutlery. But by the time Tom and I had reached this picturesque *Biergarten*, having cycled along the Isar River with all the other pregnant mums, octogenarians and toddlers, I was too high on endorphins and fresh air to care what I looked like. Sharing a table under the oak trees with two thousand others, Tom and I would sit with our *Fünferbrez'n, Russenmass und Halbes Hendl* (enormous pretzel, beer and half a roast chook), listen to the jazz band, and enjoy the convivial atmosphere.

Another activity Bavarians partook of by the thousands every summer was rollerblading. While Tom adjusted his blades on the footpath outside Zirkus Krone near Hackerbrücke in the city, I looked at the energetic, excited crowd gathering around us at sunset and wished I could have joined them. With its smooth, wide city streets, Munich easily lent itself to this rollerblading event held every Monday night from May until September. And thanks to the cooperation of the local police, designated streets in the city were always blocked off, allowing thousands of Bavarians to take part in this seventeen kilometre skating circuit otherwise known as Blade Night.

'Look!' Tom said, nodding to an athletic woman gliding past us on her blades, pushing a baby in its pram before her. 'That's what you can do, see? And the Kinderwagen gives you extra balance.'

I was still following the woman into the crowd, imagining myself doing the same thing this time next year, when I turned around to find Tom towering over me. It's a little exhilarating when your six foot two partner suddenly shoots up another five inches and begins gliding all over the place doing figure eights, circles and travelling backwards like Nureyev on ice.

'Let the angel past,' Tom said, suddenly pulling me into him as a man wearing a bright orange vest, helmet and whistle skated through the crowd.

The Blade Guards or 'angels' were volunteers, Tom explained, who escorted the crowd throughout the two hour event, providing help if needed. There was even an ambulance at the rear in case of an emergency.

'You don't mind me going?' Tom asked again as we kissed goodbye.

He had no idea. I watched with pride until his blue helmet joined the sea of other helmets floating towards the Olympia Stadium. On summer evenings like these, sitting on my own on a slow moving tram as it made its way through the historic streets of Munich, the orange sun reflected in windows, I felt as if I'd won a raffle.

Summer saw Tom and I settling into routines domestic as well as sporty. On Saturdays, for instance, we'd jump in the black Volvo and drive ten minutes south to do our shopping. The first time I walked up the aisles of Aldi in Taufkirchen I thought I'd been kidnapped from civilisation and forced to shop in some small village in outer Slomsk. Tom might have enjoyed their weekly bargains ranging from plasma television screens to guitars, computers to mountain bikes, but being used to the neat, organised aisles and colourful interiors of Woolworths and Coles, I found this strange German supermarket's bare walls, stacks of boxes and absence of permanent shelving grim to say the least. And then there were the unsmiling female loaders and packers who ordered us to get out of the way as they steered their manual forklift machines to replace an empty crate with another one full of potatoes, lentils or gumboots. Scarier still were the checkout chicks who swiped barcodes so fast you'd swear they'd been trained at special military camps.

'Sechsundvierzig Euro bitte,' the girl would sigh, looking bored out the window as Tom and I scrambled to gather our groceries and find our wallets.

But once I realised we could fill our trolley for less than one hundred Australian dollars, I decided Aldi wasn't so bad after all. And when I discovered their pineapple quark for sixty cents a tub and two hundred grams of truffle chocolates for one euro, I refused to shop anywhere else.

Having stocked up at Aldi, Tom and I spent many a balmy evening entwined on our blue couch in front of the open French windows enjoying the breeze as we ate our *Brotzeit*. Unlike the evening meal Tom's parents ate all year round that was more like a ploughman's lunch, we filled our breadboard with *Vollkornbrot*, every cheese we could find, smoked salmon, cherry tomatoes, dips and olives, and indulged as if it was a private party for two. Never did we enjoy this routine more than during the Euro Cup broadcast live from Portugal, mid June to July. Sometimes we'd invite Tom's friend Peter or our neighbour Gretchen over to eat with us to see Portugal lose to Greece, England slay Switzerland, or Sweden wipe out Bulgaria. I learnt to yell *Tor!*, the German word for 'goal', as we bounced on the couch with cup fever, giving each other high fives. Tom was delighted to discover I could name almost half the players on the German team, until he realised I could name everyone who played for Portugal.

'Come on, Figo, Maniche, Ricardo,' I murmured when penalty shots had been called to decide the semi-final game between England and Portugal.

'You in love with Ronaldo,' Peter asked, 'or Beckham?'

'Neither,' Tom answered flatly, sitting between us. 'She likes Figo.'

Likes didn't touch the sides. I'd become a devoted fan of Portugal's heroic captain from the moment he spat on the grass in Porto before losing to Greece. Unlike fancy-footed pretty-boy Ronaldo, Luis Figo had gravitas, nobility, and the profile of a god. And Tom knew whenever he was in shot not to touch me. But my Portuguese reverie was soon interrupted by a moment so shocking the three of us rose like a Mexican wave with our hands to our faces in disbelief. How could English Captain David Beckham's first penalty kick send the ball so far east instead of straight ahead? It was like watching a car miss the garage and park in the pool. I might have been barracking for Portugal but my heart went out to the wretched English captain as he held his face in his hands. I'd once had a disastrous opening night in an Ayckbourn play, but at least it wasn't in front of an audience of 275 million.

Another sporty event Tom introduced me to during my first summer in Munich, on top of cycling, Blade Night and watching the Euro Cup, was beach volleyball. I hadn't been on German soil more than forty-eight hours when he appeared before me in baggy shorts, a T-shirt and a boyish smile, holding an enormous canvas sports bag. Every Tuesday night for the last ten years, Tom and his band of five friends had played volleyball in his old school gym around the corner. All in their forties now, the volleyball team had seen each other through good marriages and bad, attended their children's christenings and often sought one another's professional advice. Consequently Christian was now Tom's accountant, Wolfgang his lawyer, and Veit his urologist. But the thing that Detlef, Christian, Wolfgang, Veit, Florian and my husband had most in common, according to Tom, was their extraordinary lack of talent for volleyball.

'We were so bad tonight,' he would announce, giggling as he flopped down beside me on the couch when he came home. 'I haven't laughed so much in my life.'

Although it was great to see Tom come home as if he'd been out with the Marx Brothers, never had I felt so alone as I did those first chilly weeks in Munich on volleyball nights. At no other time did I feel the full impact of what I'd done, the distance I'd placed myself from home, family and friends, forty-two years old and pregnant. But now that summer was here, Tom often invited me to come along for the ride, especially if his band of volleyball brothers were playing at Starnbergersee. With its legendary lake, or *See*, swans and aristocratic villas, I already knew Starnbergersee was one of Bavaria's most popular leisure spots. This famous lake certainly had an intriguing history and, according to my mother, even scored a mention in one of the greatest poems ever written.

'Surely you know Eliot's *The Waste Land,* Honeybee? *April is the cruellest month—*'

No, I cut her off, but I'd seen *Cats.*

'Oh,' she cried. 'You are awful.'

When I first met them at the grassy park next to Florian's place, Tom's team of jolly volleyballers were as friendly as I expected and, as each one shook my hand, took the trouble to speak to me in English. But I was disappointed to discover I was the only wife or girlfriend (WOG) in attendance. The others were at home feeding babies or putting small children to bed, Detlef explained, his eyes twinkling with the joy of having escaped for the night. Unable to sit dutifully on the grass watching six middle-aged men play volleyball for ninety minutes, I soon made my escape too. Longing to see the fourth largest lake in Germany and ponder 'sad stories of the death of kings', I made my way towards the water beyond the chestnut trees, until a minute later I was standing on a rickety jetty looking out over the sparkling, sweeping Starnbergersee.

King Ludwig II was only forty years old when he drowned here in 1886, 'in mysterious circumstances' as the guides in Munich liked to say. Known as the Swan King, the Fairytale King, or else Mad King Ludwig, the one thing everyone seemed to agree on was that the man was eccentric, not to mention that most unconventional of creatures at the time, a homosexual. But it was Ludwig's habit of building one extravagant castle, or *Schloss,* after another in which he'd often construct settings from Wagnerian operas that people most remembered him for. I'd already heard of Schloss Linderhof, two hours drive south of Munich, the beautiful baroque castle in which Ludwig would often sleep all day and stay up all night so that he could enjoy various nocturnal activities. Apparently he loved nothing more than to be rowed around his artificial Venus grotto in a shell-shaped boat while being sung to by opera singers. In winter he preferred to sit under furs in one of his many elaborately designed sleighs and go for a romantic moonlight ride through the snow. I'd seen these ornate golden chariots at the Carriage Museum when Tom and I caught the tram across town to Schloss Nymphenburg.

Tom had also taken me to King Ludwig's Schloss Neuschwanstein, the fairytale castle some 130 kilometres south of Munich that featured in the film *Chitty Chitty Bang Bang* and is said to have been the model for various Disney animations. Walking through its palatial rooms, I couldn't believe the opulence, nor how fond the man was of swans. I'd never seen so many porcelain, gold, brass or wooden cygnets in my life. Even the doorhandles had necks and beaks.

Unfortunately it was Ludwig's insatiable passion for design and extravagance, and possibly swans, while his state was plunging deeper into debt that provoked his despairing ministers to declare him mentally ill and have him deposed. Less than twenty-four hours later, and despite being a strong swimmer, the forty year old king's body was found floating in the shallow waters of Starnbergersee. Whether Ludwig II really was deranged, and whether he really did kill himself that night back in 1886, are both questions that remain unanswered. But the one thing all the historians agree on is that Ludwig's brother Otto, successor to the throne, was as mad as a box of frogs.

On top of cycling, rollerblading, wakeboarding and volleyball, just when I thought he couldn't have partaken in one more sporting activity, Tom announced he'd put his name down for the summer river surfing competition. This time, arriving at the little bridge down by the Isar River in the sweltering heat instead of sleet, the whole inland surfing phenomenon made much more sense to me. The stark parklands and frosty banks that had been empty in April were now full of picnickers who'd spread their blankets among *Vergiss mein'nicht* flowers in the soft grass. While Tom went in search of the competition organiser, Andi, I claimed our patch and enjoyed the lively banter of healthy young Germans sitting on scattered beach towels.

By late afternoon, having filmed Tom falling off his board for the umpteenth time, I was lying down on our blanket under a maple tree next to the rushing water listening to the birds singing, and the surfers cheering, when I thought I heard a trumpet. I lifted my head to listen again. This time I heard not just a trumpet, but a whole brass section—and drums.

'It's not an oompah band,' Tom would grumble whenever he heard tourists describe the traditional Bavarian bands in

Lederhosen like the one that played at the Hofbräuhaus. 'They're Trachtenkapellen and they play Blas-Musik.'

Whatever he wanted to call these bands, one seemed to be coming towards us at great speed.

'Achtung!' Andi's deep voice announced through the loud-speaker from the judge's tent as the noise grew louder. 'Ein Floß kommt!'

In the distance it looked like a bunch of castaways in Bavarian costumes were clinging to the remnants of a boat after an explosion, curiously accompanied by a band. But once they got closer, I realised that this noisy party of revellers, about thirty of them in all, were sitting on a log raft some ten metres long that stretched the entire width of the canal. As surfers quickly scrambled up the banks, the *Floß* sped towards us all like an unstoppable mini-Oktoberfest. The chap steering at the front may have looked sober enough with his knees bent and both hands on the rudder, but the party behind him, swaying to the music and holding their large beer mugs in the air, looked at least two sheets to the wind. At the back of the raft, behind a four-piece band, a brazen couple even managed a little waltz.

'Prost!' the woman yelled, raising her beer in a toast as they passed.

'Schönen Tag!' yelled the man to the spectators standing on the bridge.

And as the large raft went over the wave, plunging down and up again to the hoots of joy from its passengers, I was amazed that no one fell off.

The log rafts travelled from a town called Wolfratshausen, some thirty kilometres south of Munich, Tom explained when he finally found me under the maple tree, to just around the corner at the Floßlände. From there, the raft would be dismantled, put in a truck, then driven back to Wolfratshausen to be reassembled for tomorrow's excursion. Tom said that although log rafting had been used for hundreds of years to transport wood into Munich, as well as farmers' goods and passengers, since the advent of the railway and the steamer the rafts had been used only as a summer recreational activity.

'And do they ever have accidents?' I asked Tom as he towel dried his hair.

'No,' he answered, then cocked his head. 'Why?'

Why? Thirty people on a floating mass of logs with no rails, drinking beer, singing, some even dancing as they sped down canals, encountering swimmers, kayakers, maybe even the odd surfing competition, weren't there accidents?

'It's not all speeding down canals,' Tom said a little defensively. 'They take over five hours to get here, you know.'

Five hours? Sometimes I felt like my Bavarian partner and I weren't just from different countries, but different planets. On my planet a five hour log rafting expedition with no rails and jugs of beer would have ended on the six o'clock news with a search party, but on Tom's, it ended without incident at the Floßlände.

'I even thought,' Tom said, looking wistfully towards the bridge in the distance, 'that we might book one for our wedding party.'

I looked at my tall, wet fiancé. Was he completely mad? On our wedding day, just a couple of weeks away, did he really expect his new wife, six months pregnant, to celebrate on the back of an open log raft, speeding down the Isar with an oompah band? Hadn't we already decided to have the wedding party at Fritzi Oberhauser's restaurant? On dry land? On a floor that didn't move?

'See?' Tom said, laughing and ignoring my protests as he pulled me into his drenched wetsuit, 'who says Germans don't have a sense of humour?'

Hochzeit, *or wedding day*

It was a beautiful summer day with a warm breeze and not a cloud in the sky, a perfect day to drive out to the Bavarian countryside and get married. Being the one who could speak German, Tom had organised everything, from the flowers, to the wedding banquet menu at the restaurant, to the twenty invitations. He'd even booked a certified *Dolmetscher*, or interpreter, by the name of Verena through the *Standesamt*, or Registrar's Office, for the ceremony. A legal requirement, Tom said. 'Otherwise I might be selling you into slavery.'

But an interpreter would be much appreciated, and not just by me and my brother and sister, who'd flown over from London for our big day, but also my best friends from Melbourne, Nadine and Cameron. Unfortunately, due to a shortage of beds we were only able to accommodate one of them. The other three were staying around the corner at a clean, budget hotel Tom had found called the Etap, and any minute they would be on our doorstep bearing croissants for a champagne pre-wedding breakfast. I looked down at my brother lying on our uncomfortable fold-up bed with one black sock draped over his eyes. For most of his adult life Max had insisted he could only sleep in pitch darkness, yet by the age of forty he'd still not managed to invest in an eye mask.

'How did you sleep?' I whispered, lifting the toe end.

'Zeus does not bring all men's plans to fulfilment,' his voice croaked back.

I remembered that my brother was in the midst of a regional tour of Homer's *Odyssey*.

'Sorry we could only put you in the sunroom, Odysseus.'

'No worries, darls.'

While my brother showered and I prepared our wedding brunch, Tom busied himself downstairs in the garage preparing our wedding car, his beloved vintage metallic blue Volvo.

'Why is it called a *Schneewittchensarg*?' I'd asked.

'Because with its full glass tailgate, it looks like Snow White's coffin.'

I tried not to think about this too much, as being driven to my own wedding in a kind of hearse put a bit of a dampener on things. But Tom didn't see it that way. The Volvo P1800 ES was a collector's dream, he boasted, before bouncing downstairs in his overalls to polish his precious car and adorn it with flowers from our favourite florist. Our usual black Volvo would be driven by our friendly neighbour Gretchen, who'd generously agreed to take our Australian party with her—so long as none of them expected her to speak English.

I'd just turned our coffee machine on when I heard the familiar shriek of my sister from the street below.

'Fuckity-fuck! Get a load of their garden path! Looks like it's been vacuumed!'

I looked out the window to see the three of them, resplendent in their wedding attire, madly waving from our front gate. Having gone down two dress sizes, my sister was a vision in hot pink.

'Heard you got knocked up, darls!' she yelled up at me.

Several locals on the footpath opposite stopped in their tracks to stare. Even their dogs looked alarmed.

'So we've come to make an honest woman of you!'

I imagined Tom's joyless aunt watching in horror from behind her lacy curtains below. Herr Müller no doubt sat nearby looking equally disturbed, holding a banana to his ear and wondering why his dead brother wouldn't pick up.

'Just push! Push!' I shouted, wanting to get them inside as quickly as possible.

It was hard to believe my sister had once been engaged to a German herself. But maybe Klaus's people up in Berlin weren't as reserved and Catholic as they were down in this part of Germany.

While they all spoke on top of each other in our crammed kitchen, Max and I heard how spookily absent of human beings the Etap hotel was.

'We even checked in with a machine!' Cameron cried. 'And this morning, breakfast is all laid out, but not a human in sight.'

After an impromptu group chorus of *The Twilight Zone* theme song, Nadine told of their frustration with the woman at our local *Bäckerei*.

'The more clearly we said *Drei pretzels bitte,* the angrier she got!'

Their hysterics at Cameron's impersonation of an angry *Bäckerin* rose to a crescendo until Tom's deep voice interrupted from the doorway.

'That's because here we call them *Brezn*,' he said, 'not *pretzels*. Pretzels are American.'

Although this sober announcement silenced the room, it also prompted us to finally throw our arms around each other and declare how wonderful it was to be reunited again.

'And look at your tummy!' my sister cried in amazement.

Everyone immediately swarmed around my bulging tummy, touching it, rubbing it, smiling at it, until Georgina opened her pink pashmina shawl and cried again.

'And get a load of mine!'

Now that our apartment had come to life with the wonderful sound of loud Australians drinking champagne, eating croissants and taking photos, I almost didn't notice our shy, diminutive neighbour from upstairs hovering in the doorway.

'Gretchen,' I said, gently taking her by the hand and introducing her to my friends and my siblings.

'Gretchen!' my sister cried, springing to her feet to shake hands. 'Ich habe viel Gutes von dir gehört.'

While the others looked at each other in amazement, I tried not to wilt. I just hadn't accounted for my sister's ability to speak German, not on top of being able to squeeze into a size six pink dress with petunias on it for my wedding day. But this wasn't the time for playing victim to sisterly rivalry, I reminded myself, or for projecting my own insecurities onto others.

'Merridy!' Gretchen cried, turning to me almost accusingly. 'Deine Schwester kann Deutsch sprechen!'

'Well, there you go!' I cried, skolling the nearest glass of champagne before clapping my hands. 'Shall we?'

I sat very low in the front seat of our wedding car, much less graciously than a heavily pregnant woman ever should sit, gripping my bouquet with both hands as my whole body rattled with the vintage engine.

'What's that smell?' I shouted over the noise.

'Gasoline!' Tom shouted back. 'She hasn't been out in a very long time. Sorry!'

'That's ok,' I yelled as we swerved out in front of our other Volvo, packed with our happy wedding party, who all waved from their luxurious, comfortable, leather upholstered seats.

But the elated look on my fiancé's face as we pulled out into Grünwalderstrasse told me to shut up and enjoy the ride, however lacking in suspension.

'Goodness, you really can feel every bump in the road, can't you?' I shouted.

Beaming with *Schneewittchensarg*—joy—Tom took my hand and kissed it.

So here I was at last, I said to myself, hunched in the passenger seat of Snow White's coffin, knees apart, forty-two years old, six months preggers, in the middle of Bavaria on my wedding day. Who would have thought?

Having congregated in the car park outside the very modern looking Grünwald Rathaus, our small, well dressed party of twenty greeted each other in the warm sunshine before moving inside to the cool foyer. You'd never know from their neat, crease-free appearance that Ulrika, Horst and the kids had just driven nearly 300 kilometres from Coburg. Likewise Tante Ilsa and Onkel Norbert looked immaculate as ever, standing next to Tom's parents, accompanied by Tante Zelda. Several of Tom's old school friends had arrived, including Helmut, his motor obsessed go-kart racing partner, who always looked at me as if disappointed I didn't have handlebars and a two-cylinder V-twin engine. My sister, however, seemed to have brought out a different side of Helmut, who positively grinned at her whether she had a crankshaft or not. For some time I stood with Tom's parents and Zelda, observing the frisson between them.

'Does your sister know Helmut?' Friedl finally whispered.

No, I told my about-to-be mother-in-law. George was just a friendly person by nature.

'Das ist genug!' my sister cried, punching Helmut in the arm.

'Und sie spricht Deutsch?' Friedl asked, clearly impressed by what she'd overheard.

Leaning in, I explained to Friedl how some ten years earlier, Georgina had coincidentally been engaged to a German chap herself.

'And they did not marry?' Friedl asked.

I shook my head. 'Sadly, Klaus turned out to be a complete—'

I stopped myself just in time. It was all very well to go around calling people Nazis back home, but over here it seemed reckless to say the least, unless you were talking about Göring.

'—a complete rat.'

I waited for Friedl to translate for her curious friend.

'Eine Ratte?' Zelda exclaimed. 'O, das ist aber schade.'

Yes, wasn't it a shame. We all nodded in unison before returning our attention to Georgina and Helmut, as if observing a mating dance between a black footed albatross and a pink flamingo.

As I looked around the room at all the smiling faces gathered to celebrate our little wedding, I wished my parents could have been there too. My dear dad could at least have walked me up the stairs to the registry office, and Rox could have seen my pink 'sylph like shoes' and realised I had listened to her after all. I looked at my tall brother Max, standing at the bottom of the stairs in the midst of an intense conversation with Cameron. Two days ago Cameron had sat in a crane high over a stage in London filming a U2 concert, and now he was giving my brother lessons in how to operate his new JVC video camera. Max looked so handsome in his tuxedo, no one would have guessed what he was going through. It couldn't have been easy for him to fly over for his sister's wedding, having just broken up with Daphne, even if he did have his *Odyssey* tour to keep him busy.

'Don't worry about me, darls,' Max told me that morning. 'Every hero has to face his *Supreme Ordeal* before he can return with the elixir.'

'Darling,' my friend Nadine whispered, suddenly by my side. 'Just thought you should know, your groom's a bit teary.'

Really? What, just like Prince Frederik before he married Mary Donaldson? My smile faded as a horrible thought occurred to me—or like someone having second thoughts?

I was hastily making my way through our friendly little congregation in search of Tom when a strong finger tapped me on the shoulder.

'I hope you don't mind,' our best man said, holding an enormous basket under his arm. 'It's just a small wedding present.'

I smiled at Günther, Tom's intellectual friend with his large forehead and wild hair, whose English was better than mine.

'I just thought,' Günther continued, nodding at his hamper full of books and CDs lying among sprigs of edelweiss, 'someone like you, a writer, should be acquainted with some of Germany's greatest poets.'

I looked into our intense friend's searching eyes and saw such lofty expectations of me I considered bolting.

'Oh, what a stupid present!' he suddenly declared, wracked with remorse.

Not surprisingly, Günther's love life was in perpetual turmoil.

'Not at all!' I insisted, choosing the closest paperback from the hamper. 'What have we here?'

'Oh!' Günther cried, as if I'd just pulled Schelling himself from a hat. '*Ausgewahlte Gedichte*.' His voice cracked with emotion. 'Do you know Gottfried Benn at all?'

Couldn't say I did.

'Oh, he's truly marvellous. And—oh!' he cried again as I held up another. '*Brand's Haide* and *Die Umsiedler,* by Arno Schmidt. You've heard of Arno Schmidt?'

Not yet.

'Rilke?'

Rilke rang a bell . . .

'Wiechert?'

'You got any Goethe in there?' I asked, relieved I could name at least one German poet.

'Yes, yes!' Günther was overjoyed. 'The *Wahrheit und Vermachtnis* is here somewhere on CD, along with Oskar Werner reading Buchner, Schilkler, Weinheber and Zuckmayer.'

'Zuckmayer?' I asked.

'You know Zuckmayer?' Günther yelped.

He could have been a Belgian ventriloquist for all I knew.

'I say!' Georgina suddenly bounced up between us. 'I'm having the most fabby-dabby time with your in-laws, darl. Not a bad apple in the bunch.'

'Günther!' I said, grabbing my sister by her solarium tanned shoulders and placing her firmly in front of me. 'Have you met my sister, George?'

At last I could see Tom through the crowd, laughing with his sister as she wiped tears from his eyes. I was debating whether to go to him or leave him alone when a child tugged at my sleeve. How wonderful, I thought, to be marrying a man who could cry at his own wedding.

'Ecthuthe me,' the little voice croaked.

I looked down to find not a child but a petite woman in her sixties wearing a smart red suit and the same wig Dustin Hoffman wore in *Tootsie.*

'Hewo,' she said. 'I'm Vewena.'

'Oh, hello, Verena!' I said, trying desperately hard to remember who on earth Verena was as I shook her limp hand.

'Yeth,' she confirmed, nodding at me.

As nothing more was forthcoming except a frightening row of protruding front teeth, I repeated her name. 'Verena!'

'Vewena Fock.'

I nodded.

'Da Dohwmether,' the woman almost spat on me.

'The—Dohwmether?'

'Da Dohwmether,' she confirmed.

'Oh, the Dolmetscher!' I cried, at last remembering who Verena was. 'Our English translator for the wedding service!'

'Yeth!' Verena nodded enthusiastically. 'Tha'th me!'

How *wonderful*!

Upstairs in the *Standesamt* of the Grünwald Rathaus, Tom and I stood in front of our small gathering of twenty close friends and family and listened dutifully to Jörg, Tom's old school friend who'd grown up to become a lord mayor. With his starched white collar, clean shaven face, light voice and immaculate hair, Jörg looked as though he'd be more at home serving meals on aeroplanes. Although no doubt a fine mayor, the red waistcoat, heavy cloak and large gold chain seemed made for someone older, ruddier, less likely to ask you to return your seat to an upright position. But despite being a fairly subdued sort of chap, Jörg did occasionally allow a hint of a smile as he shared a little joke with our gathering—not that any of us Australians could understand him, except my sister.

'Ha!' George cried from her seat directly behind me. 'Oh, that's lustig.'

And standing beside Jörg throughout the whole proceedings, beaming at me reassuringly with her protruding front teeth, was our *Dolmetscher,* who still, some ten minutes into my German wedding service, had not translated a single word. Occasionally I'd look at her as if to say *Now might be a good time to tell us in English what the hell's going on.* But Verena always just smiled back at me, as if to say *Thoon, thoon . . .*

I was still lost in his immaculate hair some minutes later when Jörg woke me up with the words 'Khahil Gibran'. Having attended so many of my girlfriends' marital unions over the years, I could have recited this poem on marriage by heart. I especially liked the wise advice to love each other *but make not a bond of love, fill each other's cup but drink not from the one cup.* Given my past relationships I could have added a few tips myself. Make love with the light on, but light only the rooms you're not in. Be restrained in criticism, but forget not the option of a restraining order. Ask about each other's past, but pass not out when he shows you his One Nation tattoo. As Jörg finished his poem, I could tell by the coughing and shuffling behind me that our guests were ready to wrap things up, move on to the vows and make their way to the restaurant. But it was at this moment that our pint-sized *Dolmetscher* finally took a step forward and smiled.

'Thomath, Mewidy, fwendth and famiwy,' she began timidly. Oh no, not from the very top? 'We are gavered here today, in hohwy matwimony . . .'

I'd forgotten Max was videoing the ceremony from behind the enormous umbrella plant in the corner until Verena got up to the Gibran poem, and its large shiny leaves began to shake.

'And da oak twee, and da thypreth gwow not in each other'th thadow . . .'

Although tempted to turn around and look at my sister, I could tell by the already uneven breathing coming from behind that such a move might prove catastrophic. Our family had a dangerously low giggle threshold and, worse, Georgina was a snorter. But thankfully Verena soon completed her assignment, and passed the baton back to Jörg, who sped through the remaining vows as if he'd just remembered his evening shift on a Lufthansa flight to Düsseldorf.

'Und so von nun an seid ihr Mann und Frau!'

Amen.

The banquet room at Fritzi Oberhauser's restaurant up the road might have been attractively rustic, with wildflowers adorning our long banquet table, but it was so warm inside, even the stuffed stag hanging on the wall looked as if it was eying Tom's beer. The bride and groom sat in the middle of the table, our backs against the wall, flanked by our respective families. On my right, my brother Max enjoyed an animated chat with Karin, Tom's paediatrician friend from schooldays. And a little further down, my sister was entertaining Tom's three attentive bachelor friends we'd deliberately placed around her. On the other side of Tom sat his extended family, and then their friends. Facing me were my dear friends Nadine and Cameron, who were so busy absorbing everything around them they'd barely touched their *Schweinshaxe und Knödl,* let alone their *Maultaschen Suppe.*

'It's nothing,' Cameron explained, mopping his wet brow. 'Just one of those twenty-four hour things.'

As if Cam having spent the night vomiting wasn't bad enough, I suddenly realised why Nadine hadn't eaten her food either. How could I have forgotten that my best friend, who'd flown over especially for my wedding day, was a vegetarian?

'Darling, don't worry,' Nadine insisted, picking up a spoon. 'The potato salad's delish!'

And then I watched as she grabbed the plump hand of a passing waitress.

'Could we possibly have some more Wasser, bitte?'

In the cafés of Bronte back home, I'd seen waiters and waitresses visibly melt while my affectionate friend absent mindedly massaged their arm as she studied the specials board. But in Bavaria people were a little more formal, and as Nadine caressed her arm I watched our buxom waitress in her *Dirndl* look startled, as if no one had ever touched her or spoken to her so tenderly in all her life. Certainly not one of the customers.

'Sofort . . .' she muttered, waddling out of the room in a trance.

Our plates were still being gathered when, unable to stand the heat another minute, I knelt up on our wooden bench to push open the little window behind me.

'Could you leave it closed, please?' a deep voice commanded from the other side of the table.

I looked over at my smiling but authoritative brother-in-law sitting with his family. Was he serious?

'There is a draft blowing directly onto my wife,' Horst continued, waving his hand in front of Ulrika.

I looked at Ulrika sitting next to him, deep in conversation with her mother.

'What about the bride?' I asked cheerfully.

Horst shrugged. 'Sorry.'

What was this fear Germans had of drafts? Ever since summer had arrived, I'd found the hot, stuffy trains that took me home from my class in the city almost unbearable. But every time I opened a carriage window, within a minute some fellow passenger would stand, lean over and aggressively shut it again. Likewise, Tom would creep around our apartment, hands out, searching for the evil source of a draft until discovering the window I'd left open. We'd had many arguments about the difference between a breeze and a draft, but it was as difficult to convince Tom as it was to challenge the authority of my police commissioner brother-in-law. Having reluctantly shut the little window behind me, I sat down and looked at Nadine. In challenging situations I often looked at Nadine, and if she wasn't there I rang her.

'Darling,' my friend began, and like a hungry bird about to be offered some nutritious gem of wisdom, I leant forward. 'What a big, brave journey you've undertaken.'

Was it? She didn't think I was completely mad? Totally out of my depth, and perhaps should fly back to London with her and Cam and move into their spare room?

'What a gift for a writer,' Nadine continued. 'Just think, every little challenge that comes your way—' she nodded towards my brother-in-law '—you can just add to your author's trove to tackle on the page.'

This was why Nadine was my best friend. She had a way of turning crap into gold. But she'd also reminded me that I was more than an addition to my husband's family. With new resolve I turned around, crouched undignified on my haunches and gave the window a solid push.

'Ah,' I said, smiling at Horst as I sat down again. 'That's better!'

By the time we'd finished the enormous heart shaped strawberry, cream and vanilla chocolate wedding cake, half our guests had gone outside to stretch their legs, allowing the rest of us to spread out.

'Schläft er?' Tante Zelda asked, smiling furiously at my brother's large black shiny shoes on the bench beside me, pointing north to the ceiling.

'Jetlag,' I told Zelda, who nodded with fervour.

My hopes that Max might perform his usual party trick and give us a bit of morris dancing outside were fading by the minute. But looking beyond my horizontal brother to the end of the table, I observed my sister still happily holding court with Tom's bachelor friends.

'Prost!' Georgina cried, raising her glass.

'Damit die Gurgel nicht verrost!' Rolf replied.

'Oh, jawohl to that, Ralph!'

It was like watching Betty Grable entertain the troops in Japan.

'See, that's what you have to do,' Tom whispered in my ear. 'Have the confidence to just jump in and speak German, mistakes and all.'

'Does George make mistakes?' I cried with glee.

'Of course she does,' Tom said. 'But she doesn't care.'

While my husband caught up with other members of his family, I watched my sister charm the bachelor section, and tried to imagine her, in her stilettos, clutching her Blackberry, on a tour of Helmut's farm where he lived with his parents, their three large dogs, and a blind cat.

'*Holy Scheisse!*'

And a lethal jackal kept in a huge cage outside the stables.

An hour later my Australian party and I had retired to the long bench at the end of the room from where we quietly observed my Bavarian wedding banquet in its final stage. It hadn't exactly been the wedding day I'd imagined, but given certain circumstances beyond my control I'd left most of the decisions concerning our 'big day' to Tom, including our wedding lunch, no matter how I felt about wooden panelling, antlers and stags heads.

'No wedding speech, darling?' Nadine asked. 'Not even a funny one, for us?'

Given my own lack of Deutsch, I'd just assumed there was little point delivering a speech to a predominantly German wedding party.

'But you're the bride, love,' Cameron said, punching me in the arm. 'The predominantly Australian bride Tom asked to marry him. It's not *their* day. It's *yours*.'

Seeing myself reflected in my friends' eyes, I realised how unassertive I'd become, casting myself as an outsider even at my own wedding.

'I haven't prepared anything.'

'Darl,' croaked the voice of my brother from under the table. 'Just say the word and I'll warm them up with a bit of "Clancy of the Overflow".'

•

In the late afternoon sun, Tom and I stood in a vast green field under a blue sky, surrounded by golden buttercups, holding each other while Cameron took reel after reel of wedding photos. Having already posed for the group shots, the rest of our wedding party chatted quietly under the shade of an oak tree, the women fanning themselves with Tom's souvenir lunch menus, and the men casually holding their jackets over one arm. Weeks later we would marvel at Cameron's colourful photos taken in such an authentically rustic setting, Tom in his Armani frockcoat, and me in my dusty pink lace Sarah-Jane dress, looking for all the world as if we'd just joined the Amish community and were about to build a church. And although the highlight of my day was supper in our garden with our Australian contingent until midnight, I couldn't shake the sadness that I knew would soon engulf me when the four of them boarded their plane back to London, leaving me to begin the next big chapter of my adventure in Germany as a wife, and soon a mother, on my own.

Doctor Borg, I presume?

I admired the gentle, patient disposition of our obstetrician's attractive receptionist on the third floor of the Rotenkreuz Frauenklinik. With three phones ringing, a full waiting room, her boss still in the operating theatre downstairs and a patient standing in front of her who couldn't speak German, Frau Klingenberg was still able to smile.

'Und die letzte Regelblutung?' she asked, pen poised over her paperwork.

I looked at Tom.

'When was your last period?'

'Christmas.'

'Weihnachten.'

'Wunderbar,' she said.

Hardly.

Having left Frau Klingenberg's office, Tom and I walked a few metres across the carpeted floor to the waiting room, not really a room so much as a circle of chairs sitting around an enormous fish tank.

'Grüß Gott,' Tom greeted several other couples.

'Grüß Gott,' they murmured back.

Given how quiet Munich was, it wasn't that surprising to discover its waiting rooms were excruciatingly silent affairs, except for the polite greeting when another patient arrived.

'Grüß Gott,' a Muslim woman said from behind her burka as she sat down next to me.

'Grüß Gott,' we all greeted her in unison.

While we sat staring at the fish, I tried to calm my nerves. It wasn't just that all Tom's medical friends had raved about this world renowned oncologist, obstetrician and gynaecologist. Nor was it our discovery, having googled him the night before, that Doktor Borg had been awarded everything but the Nobel prize. It was the final words of Tom's cardiologist friend, Stefan: *Don't let Borg scare you. He's the best.*

'He will speak English, won't he, Tommy?' I asked for the third time.

'You don't think he spent the whole three years as head of oncology at that hospital in Washington speaking German, do you?'

'And do we call him Professor or Doctor?' I whispered, struggling to read the title on the door next to Frau Klingenberg's office.

'You say Herr Professor Doktor Borg,' Tom whispered back, releasing his knee from my fingernails.

Now that I'd noticed Tom was wearing his good Hugo Boss suit, I realised how much the google search had affected him too. Tom hadn't gone to this much trouble since our wedding day.

Ten minutes later, the silence was broken by a commotion in the distance. Approaching from the west, a cluster of young people in white coats was almost running to keep up with a tall green man striding ahead of them. As the air crackled with electricity, nurses' heads popped in and out of doorways like animals sensing a storm on its way. Just as Frau Klingenberg leapt up, peeped out from her doorway and ran back to her desk, a nurse came out of the ladies on our right, took one look at the advancing pack and did a U-turn. When the group got near enough, the tall surgeon in scrubs suddenly turned left into Frau Klingenberg's office.

'Genug!' he shouted over his shoulder, tossing his cap onto his secretary's desk.

As our doctor and his secretary disappeared through a side doorway into his room, his disciples dispersed like moths after a light bulb's blown, and we all sat listening to the argument taking place in his office.

'He's supposed to be on a plane to Vienna at two,' Tom translated for me. 'And if he doesn't make it, Klingenberg won't have a good day either.'

A minute later Doctor Borg appeared in his doorway, surprisingly composed and wearing a suit. As he studied the file in his hands, his bald head shone under the fluorescent light like a bowling ball.

'Why don't we offer to come back another day?' I whispered to Tom. 'When he's not in such a bad—'

'Frau Baumgartner!' the doctor announced, peering over his spectacles.

Not expecting to be first up, Tom and I leapt to our feet and fought over something until Tom realised it was my handbag.

'Will you just—go!'

While Herr Professor Doktor Borg finished making notes on my file with his golden pen, Tom and I sat quietly in our two comfy leather chairs, taking in our attractive surroundings. I guessed by the impressive collection of sculptures and paintings strategically placed around the room that Dr Borg was a serious art collector. But then again, anything with a nose coming out the side of its head looked like a Picasso to me. I tried not to pay too much attention to the pristine examining room through the open door to my right, but as I'd never been to a gynaecologist before I'd never seen a gynaecologist's chair either. It looked just like a dentist's chair, I told myself, for a patient with really, really long arms.

'Would you mind if we spoke English, Doktor Borg?' I asked timidly. 'My German's not very—'

'Frau Klingenberg!' he yelled, making us jump.

The besieged receptionist appeared at the doorway to her office.

'Zumachen!' he ordered, pointing to the door. 'Mein Gott, wie oft muss ich das sagen?'

As Frau Klingenberg pulled the door shut, Tom and I sat up straight and wiped our sweating palms on our pants.

'So ver do you come from?' the doctor asked, putting down his pen.

'Sydney.'

'Oustrahlia!' he cried, opening his arms wide enough to embrace it, Simpson Desert and all. It was amazing the effect Australia had on some Germans.

'You know Ghillong?' he asked me.

I'd once spent three hours in Geelong Hospital with an ex-boyfriend who'd fallen off his roof, so I nodded.

'My friend Harry Freeman lives in Ghillong. A brilliant oncologist. You heard of Harry Freeman?'

Tom and I smiled as our doctor recounted happy memories of fishing trips with an oncologist from Geelong, and their expeditions to the Barrier Reef. So I told him about Heron Island, a tropical paradise full of large turtles and mutton birds, where our family took holidays when we lived in Queensland. The doctor smiled at me as if clownfish swam around my head and coral grew in my hair.

'Although I remember we had to wear sandshoes when wading through the reef itself,' I added, 'in case we trod on a stonefish.'

Our doctor's smile faded, as if only an insane person would wear sandshoes into the sea, and I wished I'd left it at the mutton birds.

'So!' Borg shouted and picked up his pen again. 'How many months pregnant?'

'Six.'

'Sechs,' said Tom.

'Sechs Monate,' he wrote on my file. 'Und wie alt?'

'Forty-two.'

'Forty-two?' He peered at me over his spectacles. 'I vould have said ten years younger.'

'Really?'

'Maybe.'

Tom and I hugged our knees and laughed as we rocked in our seats. Was this going well or what?

'But at forty-two,' he put his pen down again, 'you are vat ve call *high risk pregnancy*.'

Tom and I stopped rocking. I much preferred the response of my doctor back in Sydney, Jane, who gave me a high five.

'Please,' he said, holding his arm out towards his examining room. 'I vould like to examine you.'

I concentrated hard on a tiny grey spot on the ceiling of Doktor Borg's white examining room while he examined me. It was so quiet, I could even hear Tom breathing from the adjoining room.

'Vat is ziss?'

What is this? is not a question a woman wants to hear when her legs are pointing east and west, especially from a gynaecologist.

'Oh,' I said, looking down at my right leg. 'I think it's a varicose vein.'

The doctor studied my vein.

'Any history of Thrombose?' he asked, examining my leg.

Not that I knew of.

Finally, having announced he was pleased with my cervix and the position of our somewhat large baby, the doctor left me to get dressed.

Afterwards, Tom and I sat quietly while Doktor Borg wrote a prescription.

'Stützstrumpfhosen,' he said without looking up, 'to be vorn—all—ze—time.'

'Shtootzt what?'

'Stütz-strumpf-hosen.'

'Support stockings,' Tom translated.

Was he kidding? My aunty Rhonda wore support stockings, but that was because of forty years serving behind the buffet bar at the Bankstown RSL. I still wore hipster jeans and a bikini.

Why would a youthful forty-two year old like me have to wear support stockings?

'You heard of deep wain Thrombose?' Doktor Borg asked, tearing off the prescription and handing it to Tom.

I had. But instead of telling me his concerns about the possibility of *deep wain Thrombose,* my obstetrician turned to Tom and began speaking in German. I would have understood if he'd wanted to discuss the match between Hamburg and Bayern München last Saturday, but I gathered by their frequent nodding at my stomach, legs and occasionally my head that the subject of this lengthy discourse was me.

'Could you both speak in English, please?' I finally interrupted them.

Professor Doctor Borg took his glasses off and rubbed his eyes. 'You see,' he said, leaning back in his chair, 'vat concerns me about you is ze combination of your age, ze size of your baby, und your wains.'

Had he spent his whole three years in Washington calling them *wains*?

'So, I am strongly urging you und your husband to book in for Kaiserschnitt.'

Kaiser who?

'Schnitt. Cut. Caesarean.'

Right, a caesarean. But *book in* for one? Like for a weekend at the Westin?

'Vy not?' Doktor Borg cried. 'You come in two veeks before ze baby is due, ve take you und your husband downstairs at eight o'clock in ze morning, he holds your hand, ve give you a PDA—'

A what?

'Epidural, und by ten past—you have a baby!'

At her boss's command, Frau Klingenberg sent us upstairs for an ultrasound. Most people find pregnancy ultrasounds quite moving, but since our son had already begun doing somersaults in my stomach I was less mesmerised by the faint signs of life on the screen than I was by our sonographer, Frau Doktor Henkl. I thought it took guts to wear evening jewellery and make-up with a stethoscope in the middle of the day. With her luxurious, strawberry blond hair swept up on top of her head, and beautiful green eyes blinking through her designer glasses, Frau Doktor Henkl looked more like a Bond girl than a medic.

'Unglaublich,' Tom sighed, visibly moved by the pulsating jellyfish on the screen.

'GOTT IN HIMMEL!' a woman's voice rose from somewhere down the corridor.

What the hell was that?

'MEIN GOTT!' it screamed.

I looked from Tom to Doktor Henkl. 'Are we in the birthing wing?'

'Ja,' Doktor Henkl nodded. 'The Geburtsstation is just around the corner.'

'Ooooooooooooooooooooooo . . .' another voice called out. 'Mmmmmmmmmmeeeeeeeeiiiii . . .'

While Tom and Doktor Henkl continued chatting about our baby's heart, head, legs, and possibly a penis, I sat up on my elbows and listened in abject horror. No woman could emit a frightening noise like that, I thought, unless something utterly ridiculous was being asked of her vaginal canal.

'OOOOOOOOWWWWWAAAAAAAAAAH!'

'Ja,' our glamorous doctor sighed, unable to ignore the last cry. 'Today is very busy.'

Hearing three women in the midst of labour reminded me of recent conversations with my two favourite girlfriends back in Sydney. Although they'd warned me about the pain I should expect through natural childbirth, it was the surprising details Lee and Jasmine had shared, having given birth to six babies between them, that had left the most lasting impression.

'Involuntary bowel movement?' I'd asked, shocked at Jasmine's revelation.

'You don't think you can push out a ten pound baby without emptying the bowel as well, do you?'

Leaving me to digest this information, Jasmine had then turned to Lee. 'Graham laughed. Can you believe it? A practising psychiatrist and he laughed.'

'Scott didn't laugh at me,' Lee growled, 'but he did manage to catch it on film. Since last Christmas his whole family can't look me in the eye.'

While Tom slept soundly beside me, I stared out our bedroom window at the yellow moon and struggled with my conscience.

To *schnitt*, or not to *schnitt*—that is the question:
Whether 'tis nobler to let the body suffer
The slings and arrows of vaginal childbirth,
Or to heed advice about a high risk pregnancy
And, by *Kaiserschnitt*, end them.

I might already have given birth once on primetime television and once on stage, but I wasn't sure if I was up to doing it for real. Just when I felt swayed by the many wonderful benefits of a natural birth for both mother and child, the yellow moon outside would morph into Doktor Borg's bald head, chanting 'forty-two', 'big baby' and, most ominously, 'wains'. There was no doubt I was leaning towards elective surgery, but I hoped it was for sound medical reasons and not secretly because of a few bloodcurdling screams and the remote possibility of an involuntary bowel movement.

Stützstrumpfhosen

(shtoohtzt-shtroompf-hohzen): noun—support stockings.

I'd just assumed we'd find my support stockings in the pantihose department of Kaufhof, the German equivalent of Myers, so I was somewhat alarmed when Tom pulled up outside a shop called Orthopädietechnik that sold zimmer frames, crutches and Victorian-looking girdles. For a moment I sat paralysed in my passenger seat studying the jaundiced, wigless shop window dummy in her industrial corset and matching beige *Stützstrumpfhosen.* Good God, I thought as I reluctantly got out of the car, I was going to beat my own mother to wearing geriatric underwear.

'Are you sure they don't sell them at Kaufhof?' I asked, just before we stepped inside.

Tom gave me a withering look. 'He didn't write you a prescription for lacy knickers, you know.'

Oh, I knew, I knew. If we ever had sex again, it would be a miracle.

While I moped through racks of padded floral bathers for octogenarians and medieval nighties you wouldn't bury your grandmother in, Tom exchanged a few words with the well-groomed saleslady who stood erect behind her counter.

'Und welche Gross haben wir hier?' she asked, studying my legs.

Tom and I watched as she nimbly scaled a ladder behind her, chose several small boxes, and climbed back down again.

'Kommen Sie, bitte,' she said, opening a curtain to an impossibly narrow *Umkleidekabine* in the corner.

I gingerly stepped into the tiny changing room, and nearly yelped when I realised she'd followed me in.

'Ich helfe Ihnen.'

I doubted it.

I stood like a statue in my knickers and loose smock while the woman took a tape measure from her pinafore pocket and measured my legs from top to bottom.

'Welche Schuhgrösse haben Sie?' she asked, looking up from my feet.

Back home, my shoe size was ten.

'Zehn.'

'Zehn?' she repeated incredulously, peering over my pregnant stomach. 'Zehn?'

'You're forty-two,' came Tom's authoritative voice over the top of the curtain.

'She asked for my *shoe size*,' I called back, 'not my *age*.'

'I know,' the voice insisted. 'Your shoe size is forty-two.'

How did he know?

'I ordered rollerblades for you.'

Oh, for God's sake, this was getting ridiculous. First *Hausschuhe*, then winter boots, and now rollerblades?

'Zwei und Vierzig!' the saleslady muttered, shaking her head at my large feet as she pulled out two long brown stockings. 'Mei . . .'

Oh, give me a break. I must have been the youngest customer she'd had all year. At least I still had both legs.

'Fuss, bitte,' my saleslady said, having pulled the first stocking inside out.

I gave her my right foot, which she lay in her lap, and then watched helplessly as she massaged talcum powder into it.

'Richtig,' she then said, snapping on a pair of pink rubber gloves as if preparing for battle.

Having carefully pulled the tip of the right stocking down over my toes, the woman began rolling the remaining stocking over my foot, ankle, and then gradually, with much tugging, worked her way up towards my calf. It was like pulling a sock over a rock, and I felt for her as she wrestled with it.

'Oh, sorry!' I said as I accidentally kicked her right in the solar plexus.

'Nichts passiert,' she murmured, dismissing the assault, before tucking my rebel foot between her legs again and bravely moving up to my knee.

'Are you all right in there?' asked Tom, alarmed by the heavy breathing from within.

Yes!' I called back. 'They're just terribly hard to get on.'

But as the woman gave the stocking one more powerful tug, I kicked her again.

'Ok,' she said at last, red-faced, clutching the walls with her pink gloved hands as she hauled herself up and almost fell through the curtains.

At last on my own, I looked at my reflection in the mirror. From the waist up all was well, but from the waist down, I was Aunty Rhonda.

'Come out,' Tom said. 'There's no one here.'

Just three weeks after our wedding day, I stood in front of my husband wearing a maternity smock and industrial support stockings.

'Move around in them,' he suggested, always the pragmatist.

As I shuffled stiffly around the shop, I thought of all those amputees who experience 'phantom limb', as if still able to feel their missing legs, because right now I could feel their missing legs too. They certainly weren't mine. Cased in my new *Stützstrumpfhosen*, my new legs stood rigid and proud and weren't about to bend in the middle unless someone took to them with a poleaxe.

'Am Bund hochziehen,' the lady instructed me, gesturing towards my thighs.

'Just pull them up a bit at the top,' Tom translated.

So I did, and broke four fingernails.

'Well, broken fingernails or not,' Tom said as we took off in the car, 'at a hundred and forty euros, you'd better wear them.'

Over two hundred dollars for a pair of stockings? As I sat in the front seat with my legs laid out straight in front of me, I examined the box to see what they were made of. *Orthopädische Strumpfhosen* it said on the back. *64% Polyamide, 36% Elastin.* Designed by Nazis, I muttered to myself.

'What?' Tom asked.

'Nothing,' I told him, but it certainly would explain the goose step.

Ute versus Borg

I'd never realised what a feminist minefield it was, this natural birth versus caesarean debate, until I booked in to see one of Munich's leading midwives, a *Hebamme* called Ute. As I sat in an airy room, the *Wartezimmer* of a large suburban house, I listened to the cacophony of various pregnant women grunting, huffing and puffing from within several consulting suites, preparing for their big day, and one who was possibly already having it. When the door opposite suddenly swung open, I looked up to see a large woman in shorts and a T-shirt with spiky blond hair and bare feet leading her extremely pregnant patient out into the hallway. As I watched the two of them having an enthusiastic, animated conversation about their session, it occurred to me how nice it would be to discuss my options with communicative, supportive women, instead of with a renowned doctor who spoke in German about me with my husband.

Half an hour later, having undergone a somewhat confrontingly vigorous and physical examination by my spiky haired, barefoot midwife, I was declared as fit as a fiddle and a perfect candidate for natural childbirth. With her deep voice, powerful body and colourful tattoos, I got the impression Ute wasn't used to being contradicted. I certainly didn't want to contradict her, and promised to go home and think about it.

'Who is this doctor who say you must have Kaiserschnitt?' she asked when I'd dressed again.

When I told Ute his name, she rolled her eyes.

'Suzi!' she called to a colleague in another room.

The soft padding of feet grew louder until a robust young woman in an Indian dress appeared in the doorway, panting.

'Ja was?' she asked.

I gathered by the latex baby under her arm with its dangling umbilical cord that Suzi was in the midst of some kind of demonstration.

'Borg,' Ute said, nodding towards me before she told her colleague about my doctor's advice.

While these two earthy women shook their heads, tut-tutted and conversed in low voices, I too began to feel slightly suspicious of Borg and all doctors who steered their pregnant patients away from natural childbirth.

'Listen,' Ute said, filling a calico bag with herbal ointments, Bach remedies and reading material. 'You a healthy woman, tall and strong, like your baby. Ute helps you. You don't need to be cut to have this baby, you hear? These doctors just want control of their patient to the very end. So they tell you you *high risk* and book you in at eight in the morning, and then they back on golf course by ten, see?'

I tried to recall seeing golf clubs in Borg's consulting room.

'And with the Kaiserschnitt,' Ute continued as she saw me out the door, 'there's less chance something goes wrong, and therefore less chance you sue.'

I walked to my *Strassenbahn* stop in a fog. Now what was I going to do? My head was advising me to be cautious and listen to Borg, but my loins were already dancing with Ute to the primal beat of her bongo drums.

Having agreed to let me do all the talking, in English, Tom sat quietly by my side in Borg's waiting area, flicking through a travel magazine, until I punched his arm.

'Look!' I whispered, pointing to a photo in this week's *Bunte*.

Now that I'd become aware of him, it seemed that Moshammer, the aging fashionista with the Ludwig II hairdo, was everywhere. If one of his three Rolls Royces with personalised number plates didn't purr past us on Grünwalderstrasse, I saw him and Daisy preparing coffee in the latest Nescafe commercial, or else at a party in the social pages of *Bild*, a tabloid newspaper. And then there were the television chat shows. He may not have been a raving intellectual, but Moshammer's cheeky charm, outrageous Bavarian accent and ability to laugh at himself made him a popular talk show guest. And here he was in *Bunte*, a weekly celebrity/gossip/lifestyle magazine, surrounded by a group of extremely impoverished looking men on the street, one of them in a wheelchair. Dressed in his red velvet suit, jet-black wig, darkened moustache, sideburns and eyeliner, Moshammer looked almost garish posing for the camera as he handed out Christmas presents. It looked like a scene from a sitcom, just before one vagrant unwrapped a Miele kitchen blender and another a fax machine.

'He's very involved with charities for the homeless,' Tom whispered. 'Ever since his own father died on the streets, a destitute alcoholic.'

I was already acquainted with the extraordinary story of Moshammer's rise from rags to silk ties, how he and his mother had escaped from his violent father, and that if not for the talent and determination of the young Rudolph they might have ended up vagrants as well.

'He even visits the homeless under the bridges around town during winter,' I told Tom, proud of my increasing ability to read German. 'To hand out sausages and cheese.'

Yes, Tom already knew.

'Good God,' I sighed a few minutes later. 'And did you know that he once came close to representing Germany in the Eurovision Song Contest?'

'If you're so fascinated by the man,' Tom sighed, flapping shut his magazine, 'why don't you just walk down Maximilianstrasse, pop into his shop and say hello?'

I nearly fell off my plastic bucket chair. Was the shop still there? Might he actually be *in it*?

Tom shooshed me. 'Of course,' he whispered. 'If it's not ball season in Vienna.'

A few minutes later, Professor Borg clasped his hands and leant forward over his desk. Still immersed in my *Bunte* magazine, I tried not to impose a bouffant wig on his shiny bald head, and eyeliner around his bespectacled eyes.

'I could have told you zis is vat die Hebammen say.'

Borg looked from me, to Tom, to his hands, and then took off his glasses. Here came the big guns.

'As an obstetrician viss forty years experience,' he began quietly, 'I must tell you I do not have a good feeling about a natural birss for you. Zer are a few too many stones and togezzer zey make up a mosaic, you understand? It is not just one sing. It is many sings, and I have a bad feeling in my gut.' He grabbed his gut viss boss hands. 'In hier.'

Suddenly I had a bad feeling in my gut too. And Tom had it in his. We all sat there having a bad feeling in our guts until I clapped my hands.

'So, when should we do it?' I asked.

'Tomorrow,' Borg pounced.

'Tomorrow?' I yelped. 'I was thinking more like next week!'

'You are already two veeks from your due date!' Borg protested. 'Every day ve vait ze risks increase.'

'Next Wednesday then.'

'Zis Friday.'

'Friday? Tom's taking me to the Oktoberfest this Saturday!'

'Next Vednesday's booked out. It has to be Tuesday.'

'But Tuesday's five days away!'

'You worried he'll be same star sign as your ex-boyfriend?'

I laughed at such a preposterous suggestion, then stopped. How spooky. But it wasn't really the thought of our boy being the same star sign as an ex-boyfriend that worried me so much as meddling with a person's astrological chart in the first place. The thought of our son reading Virgo horoscopes for the rest of his life when he was really a Libra just didn't seem fair.

'I tell you vat. I do you at eight o'clock next Tuesday morning. It's over in ten minutes. Piece of cake.'

Borg opened his arms for a hug. Tuesday it was.

'Und ziss vay he just makes Libra.'

Baby names and puppy dogs' tails

My parents couldn't have been happier, and although my mother swore her preference for Borg's *Kaiserschnitt* was nothing to do with Ute's tattoos, I too was relieved that we could now move on to other important issues.

'Florian's a nice name,' Rox suggested somewhat wistfully down the phone. 'Or Leopold . . .'

I'd already told my parents that Tom and I quite liked the name Henry, which they loved too, but Rox had grave misgivings that if we didn't throw a German name in somewhere, it would offend Tom's family.

'Henry Kurt?'

The only other person I could think of who lived her life by pleasing other people was Tom's mother, which made me wonder what would happen at the end of the year when these two women finally met. With their mutually over-accommodating natures, Friedl and Rox would either merge into one or cancel each other out.

'Ludwig!' my father shouted from the dining room table, where he sat sorting books for the next day's church fair.

'Our local butcher's called Olaf,' Rox continued, 'but I'm sure you could do better than that. Henry Olaf just sounds ghastly.'

'Wolfgang!' my father continued. 'Or what about this? Henry Hoffmann!'

I reminded my parents we still had time enough to come up with names, excluding famous German composers, and so changed the subject to their new beagle hound instead.

'Well, the good things about dear velvety face definitely outweigh the bad,' my mother began ominously. 'And I'm quite sure your father would say the same.'

Was one of the 'bad' things about Ella her rapid growth, by any chance?

'Didn't you get the photos I sent you?' she asked.

I certainly had. I'd rung my brother in London straight away.

'Crossed with a hound? You sure it wasn't a horse?'

But my mother assured me that although Ella had grown into a much bigger and more powerful dog than anyone had expected, she'd brought nothing but love and laughter into their lives.

'Not counting the banana lounge incident, of course . . .'

Banana lounge incident?

'Deirdre swears she was going to throw it out anyway.'

With a sinking heart, I listened as my mother tried to downplay a recent morning tea on her friend Deirdre's patio that had gone horribly wrong.

'Despite still recovering from a disastrous hip operation last year,' my mother continued, 'Deirdre couldn't have been nicer about it. And your father really was amazing, gathering every single bit of foam stuffing from her swimming pool.'

Foam stuffing?

'I wasted no time at all,' Rox said. 'The minute we got home I rang our upholsterer in Lindisfarne, you know the one who did such a beautiful job covering our two armchairs in blue velvet? He said if Ella had *just* left the frame intact, he might have been able to save it.'

Never in my life had I heard of a dog eating furniture.

'Well, she doesn't actually eat things,' my mother continued calmly, 'so much as destroy them. She's a sort of demolition dog.'

I didn't know whether to laugh or cry.

'Tell her about the lino in the laundry!' my father called out from his piles of books.

'Now that did make me cross,' my mother snapped. 'Georgina and Max had done such a beautiful job sticking it down themselves, and now the bloody hound of the Baskervilles has chewed her way through the entire thing. But Norman Harvey said they'll give us a quote on that when they come to replace the back door.'

The back door?

'Didn't you hear about the back door?'

No.

'Max had built in such a lovely little doggy door with its own flap and everything, but unfortunately Ella's grown too fat for it.'

'Not helped by all the bloody cheese you feed her!' my father shouted.

'She can't resist a bit of Mersey Valley,' Rox gushed, 'so Monkeynuts has put on a few pounds, it's true.'

Rox spoke as if the dog trotted to the fridge on her own hind legs, helped herself to some cheese and possibly a glass of wine too. But I didn't want to hear about 'Monkeynut's' diet so much as what she'd done to the back door.

'She got so frustrated, you see,' Rox continued, 'not being able to just lunge through her doggy door whenever she heard some defenceless creature outside in the middle of the night, she ended up taking matters into her own hands. Or rather teeth.'

She'd opened the door with her teeth?

'No. She ate her way around the doggy door frame until she could fit through it again.'

'Tell her about the flap!'

'And she ate the flap.'

I sat down. Was there anything else their new beagle hound had destroyed, pulled up or eaten, apart from Deirdre's banana lounge, the laundry floor and half their back door?

'Well, you remember she'd chewed her way through the cording that travels around our two front car seats?'

All I could remember now was our original plan to buy a poodle.

'Well, last week, when your father came back from paying for petrol, he found both headrests gone.'

She'd eaten their headrests?

'I never used mine anyway.'

'Tell her about the shed!' my father demanded from the next room.

Feeling the need to lie down, I took our phone to the sofa.

'Oh, Max and George had made such a nice home for her in dad's old toolshed, with carpet, blankets and everything. But Ella's shredded the whole thing, including a wicker basket!'

'Compost bin!' my father called.

My mother sighed at the growing list of complaints. 'Yes, she likes to burrow under the base of the compost bin too, scavenging for scraps until the back lawn is utterly strewn with rotting fruit and peelings. You wouldn't think she was being fed on Vermey's quality gravy beef and kangaroo meat on a daily basis!'

While my father went to investigate a suspicious noise coming from their laundry, Rox took advantage of his absence.

'I've collected all the debris in bags to take to the tip,' she whispered down the phone, 'but I've got to wait till your father's not looking. The four dollars entrance charge would break his heart. He's a child of the Depression, you know . . .'

A distant cry from my father was followed by the sound of a dog's yelp.

'What's happened?' I asked my mother.

'It's probably nothing . . .'

'*You stupid, stupid mutt!*' my father's voice rose from the laundry.

'Gerhard's a lovely name!' Rox cried, desperately trying to change the subject.

'What have you done to the ironing board?' my father's voice boomed from the back of the house. 'You gormless idiot!'

'What about Günther?' Rox gave it another try. 'As in Grass? He was a feminist, you know.'

'And the *cord*?' My father's voice rose into dangerous territory, along with his blood pressure. 'What good's an *iron,* you brainless mongrel bitch, without a bloody *cord*?'

Unhappy campers

I hated it when people did this to me, but since moving to Germany I often found myself peering over the shoulders of my fellow commuters, attempting to read their newspapers or books. If I caught sight of a few words in English, my heart skipped a beat at the possibility of discovering a fellow alien in my midst. It did the same when I recognised the author's name on a book cover, until I saw the title: *Harry Potter und der Orden des Phönix*.

Clearly fed up with my attempt to see what she was reading, the woman opposite me in the U-Bahn flashed me a warning look, crossed her legs and coughed. But it was too late. Dan Brown, *Sakrileg.* Was anyone in Munich *not* reading *The Da Vinci Code*? Returning to my German textbook that instructed me to *einen Satz machen*, I dreamt of the time when this terrifying language with its *Sätze*, or sentences, might make sense to me. The thought of actually taking part in dinner party conversation instead of examining my napkin filled me with such pleasure I even smiled, until I noticed the man sitting across the aisle frowning at me. Personally, if I'd left the house wearing *Lederhosen*, long socks and braces, I wouldn't be giving anyone dirty looks. Must remember, I told myself yet again, not to smile at strangers.

It couldn't have been easy for my Bavarian husband having a partner who kept coming through the door with weekly complaints about his countrymen. But I found it hard to believe that even when going for a walk on a dazzling summer day in this beautiful city, people seemed unable to smile back, or return my *Hallo* as we passed each other. My spontaneous greeting while power walking along the leafy banks of the Isar once stopped an elderly couple in their tracks as if I'd spat on them.

'That's because they don't *know* you,' Tom explained soothingly, 'and you don't know *them*.'

Yes, but we shared the same planet, didn't we? Having lived over forty years in a country where we at least acknowledged each other in passing, I found it almost impossible to adopt the German way of avoiding eye contact and saying nothing.

'It actually takes less effort to be friendly,' I whined.

'We are friendly,' Tom said. 'We just show it differently.'

I knew he was right. You couldn't stand on a street corner in Munich holding a map without a local asking if you needed help. I'd once been escorted to an S-Bahn platform at Rosenheimerplatz by a man and his son. But even this act of kindness was carried out with an almost regimental manner, as if smiling might turn it into something inappropriately intimate.

As our train pulled out of Kolumbusplatz station, I returned to my textbook and *Lektion* 30 titled, somewhat spookily, *Vorurteile*, or 'Prejudices'. *Wir lachen in Großbritannien zum Beispiel,* said Bob from Scotland on page 196; *ohne Probleme über alte Leute und ihre Krankheiten.* In Britain, according to Bob, they laughed at old people and their illnesses without any problem at all. I was about to laugh too when a sharp finger urgently tapped me on the shoulder. I looked up and jumped. Even Bob wouldn't have laughed at this wizened creature with her horn-rimmed glasses and spotless beige summer raincoat, no matter how many illnesses she had.

'Haben Sie mich gehört?' she barked angrily at the end of a tirade, seemingly aimed at me.

Breaking into the usual cold sweat brought on by a confrontation with a disgruntled native, in this case an octogenarian, I panicked and offered the first word that came to mind.

'Bitte?'

The woman sighed, took a deep breath, then repeated her rant that was just as incomprehensible the second time round. I looked to my fellow commuters for assistance, but they all dived back into their *Da Vinci Code*s, abandoning me to deal with Crazy Raincoat Lady on my own. Deciding she must be one of the cardigan brigade, I began searching through my bag for my train ticket.

'Nein!' the harpy cried.

'Sprechen Sie Englisch?' I asked in desperation.

The old woman visibly recoiled, as if the very idea was as distasteful as it was preposterous, and having decided I must be deaf as well as stupid she leant in for a third go.

'Da, da!' she concluded, pointing angrily towards my legs.

Did she want my seat? Couldn't she see I was enormously pregnant?

'Nein! Nein!' She even whacked my shoulder with the back of her hand. 'Schau!' she cried, pointing at my feet.

I searched the floor. Had she dropped a brooch? Directions to her anger management therapist? Had I sat on her shih tzu?

'See here,' I said, poking the knee of the woman sitting opposite. 'Could you please help? I don't speak German and have no idea what she wants.'

My neighbour frowned as if I'd yanked her out of the Louvre by the ear and with great reluctance looked up at our intruder, said something vaguely dismissive and then returned to her book. Whatever she'd said, the old woman didn't like it. But instead of telling *Da Vinci* she didn't like it, she vented her anger at me. The old biddy was still going strong when an exasperated grunt could be heard, followed by the sound of a newspaper being slapped hard on a seat. A second later we both disappeared under the shadow of my grumpy friend in *Lederhosen* from across the aisle. As he leant over my legs I almost suffocated in a fog of cigarette smoke and suede, and then watched in disbelief as he retrieved a tiny scrap of paper from the floor at my feet. Having shown it to me, he flipped open the small metal rubbish container stuck to our wall, tossed it in, and stomped back to his newspaper. I looked up at the beige raincoat. Was *this* what had been bothering her so much? Half an old bus ticket on the floor of a train? But undeterred by any disruption she may have caused, the old woman continued shuffling down the aisle, searching through our carriage for more evidence of a world gone to hell in a hand basket.

Of all the commuters I'd quietly observed over the last six months travelling on the U-Bahn every day, none had fascinated me more than Munich's elderly female population. I was intrigued by their palpable dissatisfaction and often compulsion to voice their disapproval of just about everything. It could be a girl showing her midriff, a boy with a skateboard, the forbidden ingesting of takeaway food on public transport, a noisy child or, more often, its mother. They tut-tutted, shook their heads, and were not afraid to audibly pronounce judgement. But even more extraordinary was the aggressive way in which some of these frail elderly women got on and off a train. I'd already noticed that the logical and courteous protocol of waiting for passengers to disembark from a train, bus or tram before boarding was somewhat absent in Munich, but I was amazed to find the worst offender was often over seventy with two sharp elbows and a handbag.

'WARTEN BITTE!' I once yelled at a frail stooped creature who would have head-butted my pregnant stomach if I hadn't barred her way with my rucksack. Stopped in her tracks, she looked up only to gasp at my audacity before pushing past to secure herself a seat.

On days like these, I paced the floor, waiting to hear Tom's key in the door.

'Back in Australia we have *sweet* little old ladies. But here—' I roared at Tom when he got home, '—*here* you have a breed of pensioner that has to be seen to be believed! What's *wrong* with them?'

'She's right,' Alex said later that night, looking across our dinner table directly at Tom. 'My mother would never use public transport, as you know. But if she did, that would be her.'

Out of all Tom's friends, I loved Alexander the most. With his natural curiosity and appetite for debate, dinner parties with Alex were never dull. Unlike Tom's other friends, Alex didn't slip back into German after ten minutes. And unlike Tom, Alex believed that his country was in the midst of an ongoing, untreated, national depression.

'Quatsch,' Tom groaned.

'*Nicht* quatsch!' Alex insisted.

'Doch.'

'Doch doch! You talk to any German on the street and he'll tell you how bad everything is, how much worse it's getting. Why do you think all the great psychoanalysts came from Germany? Because we Germans are the most depressed people in the world.'

'What about Finland?'

Alex took a moment to consider the happiness of the Fins.

'Apart from Finland,' he conceded. 'Ask anyone.'

'Yes, and that's why we all look so miserable every Oktoberfest, Alex.'

'I'm not talking about one day a year, Thomas. I'm talking about the other three hundred and sixty-four.'

But what about the old ladies, I asked, steering the conversation back to its original topic. Was I being unfair or were they particularly cranky in this part of the world? Why did they push past me to get to the lift or to get on the train? Why had the beige raincoat insisted I pick up a scrap of white paper on the U-Bahn?

'What you could keep in mind,' Alex said, 'is that this is the generation that survived the last war, most of them having lost husbands, sons, brothers and fathers.'

'And let's not forget they were the ones who had to clean up afterwards,' Tom added. '*Trümmerfrauen*.'

What *frauen*?

'When the war was over,' Alex explained, 'all females over sixteen were conscripted to clean up the mess, brick by brick and stone by stone. They were called *Trümmerfrauen,* or rubble women.'

While I sat quietly pondering the thought of homeless teenage girls and hungry old women pushing wheelbarrows full of rubble through the demolished streets of Munich, Alex and Tom returned to their argument about the German psyche, now with regards to their parents.

'Look at the books they grew up on!' Alex said. 'Look at Grimm's fairytales, full of dark forests and lurking evil. Look at *Max und Moritz* and *Struwwelpeter,* all fables full of warnings, punishment, threatening children with terrifying consequences.'

'*Die Märchen der Brüder Grimm* is the most popular collection of stories in the world!' Tom protested. 'And *Max und Moritz* is not disturbing. It's funny!'

Alex turned to look at me. 'Two psychopathic boys who go around maiming and killing people are finally put through a meat grinder as punishment and your husband thinks it's funny.'

I hadn't yet read *Max and Moritz*, but I had sat under a stuffed elk in Marquartstein with my jaw open as I flicked through a worn copy of *Struwwelpeter.* I'd gathered that the unhappy little boy on its cover, reminiscent of Edward Scissorhands with his bird's nest hair and fingernails two feet long, was a warning to children who didn't care about their appearance. But it was the images inside that had haunted me for days: the illustration of the little girl, Paulinchen, who'd played with matches and caught on fire; the little boy who wouldn't eat his soup wasting away until he ended up a tombstone; and most disturbing of all, the picture of little Konrad, who sucked his thumb while being pursued by a tailor with a huge pair of scissors. I sat under the elk transfixed by the sight of Konrad's little thumb caught between the shears as his blood dripped onto the floor. When I was six my parents would warn me that if I kept my mouth open a fly might fly in, or if I sat too long in the bath I'd get old ladies' fingers. But if anyone had told me that if I sucked my thumb I'd be pursued by a maniac in red breeches with a giant pair of scissors, I'd have had nightmares.

Then I remembered one of my very first dates with Tom, when he'd tried to sell me Christmas in Germany. It wasn't so much St Nikolaus who came to the front door with his 'golden book', a record of every child's behaviour, to reward the good with a lousy piece of fruit that bothered me. It was his creepy helper, Knecht Ruprecht, an ugly, hairy, red-eyed creature with horns who carried a broom made out of sticks and a large sack in which he'd put bad children. Given this was what German children had to look forward to at Christmas, Struwwelpeter could have had his own sitcom.

As I boarded my train to the city the following morning, I was almost looking forward to being scowled at for smiling, pushed past while trying to disembark, or told off for dropping a few crumbs as I ate my *Brezn*. So convinced was I that I'd reached a new understanding of German women of a certain age, I almost willed something unpleasant to happen. But the plump, elderly lady sitting opposite me with her shopping trolley brimming with rhubarb seemed oblivious to my theory, and smiled as she gazed into the blackness out her window.

'Sind Sie schwanger?' she asked me point blank as we approached Candidplatz, beaming at my enormous tummy.

'Ja,' I told her. And counting down the days, I was tempted to add.

'Das ist aber schön.' She grinned infectiously. 'Ich hab' fünf Enkelkinder.'

Five grandchildren? I repeated. 'Wie wunderbar.'

Thanks to her strong voice and clear enunciation, I was able to follow most of her detailed description of each child. But as we approached Sendlinger Tor I became increasingly anxious that we were still on the third, Lotte, who was a cheeky monkey and allergic to strawberries.

'Entschuldigung,' I finally interrupted when I saw the platform in the distance, 'leider muss ich hier aussteigen.'

'Kein Problem!' the woman sang. 'Ich wünsche Ihnen alles erdenklich Gute.'

'Dankeschön.'

'Pfiat' di Gott.'

Pfiat' di Gott means 'May God protect you'. I knew because Friedl said it all the time, as did Tante Ilsa, Tante Zelda, and even Frau Held, who lived next door. Come to think of it, I knew quite a few elderly Bavarian women kind enough to ask God to protect me whenever they said goodbye. I was still thinking about this and waving to my sweet rhubarb lady from our carriage doors when a faux alligator vinyl handbag nearly knocked me off my feet, followed by its owner, an ancient creature with a hump. Ah well, I thought as I watched her push her way through the advancing mob to secure herself a seat. There she goes again.

An audience with Mosi

What do you get a man who already has too many clothes, reads more magazines than books, has a garage full of sports equipment and a cupboard full of Marx Brothers memorabilia? Such was my dilemma as I found myself strolling down the extremely chic Maximilianstrasse, also known as 'the vanity mile', searching for a birthday present for Tom. Having passed the palatial Four Seasons Hotel on the left, then Cartier and Dior on the right, and then Louis Vuitton, I stopped at a shop between two enormous potted fir trees to admire the sumptuous window display. A silk tie might be just the thing, I thought as I looked up to read the name in gold lettering. *Gott in Himmel.* Was I really about to walk into the famous Moshammer's fashionable men's boutique nine months pregnant, wearing a stretchy mauve maternity leisure suit, Nikes and canvas backpack? Answering the question for me, a departing sheikh held the door open. Just remember, I told myself as I stepped inside, this was a man who delivered cheese and sausages to unwashed men under bridges,

As the door shut behind me the noise of the street vanished and I found myself surrounded by opulent elegance, standing under a chandelier. My head swam with the sound of Vivaldi's piccolo concerto and the fragrant smell of lilies. Against the walls, tall cabinets with glass shelves displayed beautifully arranged cravats and ties. And on every shelf or small table sat framed pictures of a smiling Mosi with his dog, Mosi with an opera singer, Mosi flanked by showgirls and, of course, Mosi sitting next to his mother. His books were on display too, including his beloved Yorkshire terrier's *Ich, Daisy. Bekenntnisse einer Hundedame.* At the rear of the shop a handsome young assistant with slicked-back hair was making obsequious conversation with a well-dressed gentleman, possibly the King of Spain. Losing confidence fast, I turned around to leave when—*holy hairpieces!*—standing beside a glass counter just a few metres away like an exhibit at Madame Tussaud's was Rudolph Moshammer.

Frozen to the spot, I watched him peruse some paperwork through the fashionable reading glasses perched halfway down his nose. He looked positively sumptuous in a black pinstriped suit with peach silk accessories and gold jewellery. But up close the enormous black wig looked surprisingly theatrical, so coarse it could have been made from a horse's tail. And above his starched white collar, I could see the line where his foundation ended, more golden peach than neutral beige. For a fleeting second I was reminded of happy days back at the Melbourne Theatre Company in the Green Room at interval, flopped in my corset and petticoats on the couch next to some restoration king as he finished his crossword.

What's the audience like tonight, Bob?

Terrible, darling. Wouldn't laugh if you lit your own fart.

Then I saw her, lying on the floor next to her master's shiny shoes. Daisy the dog stopped panting and trembling, licked her lips and stared right back at me. For one tense moment the dog and I held each other's gaze, one memoirist confronting another until, having sensed an impostor in his midst, her waxy master peered over his Versace specs.

'Grüß Gott,' I offered politely, as is the Bavarian custom.

Raising one pencilled eyebrow, Herr Moshammer's eyes travelled from my short hair to my bulging mauve stomach, matching stretchy pants and landed finally on my worn Nike runners.

'Gaston,' he called softly to his Brylcreemed fop up the back, and without uttering another word returned to his paper.

Sensing any charming exchange was off the cards, I turned towards the tie rack on my left and almost yelped. Printed onto every silk tie was a picture of Moshammer's smiling face. For a moment I played with the idea of buying one for Tom, just for a laugh, but when I read the price tag I knew it wouldn't make either of us laugh, not even slightly.

'Kann ich Ihnen helfen?'

Kann ich Ihnen helfen? usually means 'Can I help you?', but the smiling Gaston and I both knew that in this case it actually meant 'Could you instantly leave the shop, please?' I looked from Gaston's pleading forehead to his master's ridiculous bouffant wig behind him. Why not? I'd finally seen the man in person and although brief, it had been illuminating. Deciding to get Tom the complete *Blackadder* box set instead, I wished Gaston *einen schönen Tag* and, putting us all out of our misery, including Daisy, I left. Rudolph Moshammer might have shown compassion to the homeless, I muttered as I schlepped down Maximilianstrasse with my backpack, but I hoped for their sakes none of them ever visited his shop to thank him.

'Well, what did you expect?' Tom asked laughing as he hugged me in our kitchen.

Although it hadn't been pleasant being thrown out of a tie shop, I realised it wasn't Moshammer who interested me so much as the people of Munich, who clearly couldn't get enough of him. What was the big attraction of this sixty something, overweight ex-designer who wore a really bad wig and make-up and ran a tie shop in the vanity mile? Was it the memories he conjured, no matter how kitsch, of Ludwig II and the romantic era that had shaped so much of Munich's architecture, art and music? Or did they just enjoy having a colourful, camp extrovert in their midst who dared to stand out? Was it his spectacular rise from poverty to ostentatious wealth and consequent philanthropy? Or was it just that he was so kind to his mum?

'Stop thinking about Moshammer!' cried Tom from the couch, surrounded by champagne, birthday cake and wrapping paper. 'And come watch *Blackadder* instead!'

Whatever the reason for his popularity, the Moshammer brand, including wig, dog and chauffeur, was as much a part of Munich's identity as the Residenz Palace, the Hofbräuhaus and the Isar River. Love him or laugh at him, Mosi was here to stay, and no glamorous society event was complete without him.

Oktoberfest

I put the question to my Bavarian husband and his friend, Peter. Was it true that Australians had a bit of a reputation for behaving badly at the Oktoberfest? Tom squinted as if what he was about to say might hurt.

'There is a perception that some Australians come to the Oktoberfest with the sole purpose of getting blind drunk.'

'Not all Australians,' added Peter, trying to soften the blow.

'No, not all,' repeated Tom. 'Just some.'

'Surrounded by all that beer,' Peter said, with a nervous laugh, 'they probably feel like boys in a lolly shop.'

But having lived for over forty years in Australia I knew it was less to do with lolly shops and more to do with a culture that winks at excessive drinking, calls it recreation, and regards teetotallers with suspicion.

'You can't miss them,' Tom concluded. 'They're often the ones in the Hofbräu tent wearing the oversized beer-keg hats, or the Seppelhut.'

Seppelhut?

The *Seppelhut* was the large, grey, pointy felt hat with a blue and white rope tied around its wide brim. Although originally sold to tourists at the Oktoberfest as a Bavarian cliché of rural attire, these days the *Seppelhut* was more associated with 'drunken Aussies in the Hofbräu tent'.

'Aussie Aussie Aussie!' Peter cried, but one look at my face and he knew not to continue.

It wasn't until ten o'clock the next morning when Tom and I were standing in Schwanthalerstrasse in the city, waiting to see the *Einzug der Festwirte*, or 'Entrance of the Innkeepers', that I began to get an inkling of just how huge this festival was. It seemed half the city had come out this fresh autumn morning in September to see this historic parade that always opened the Oktoberfest. Having made its way from the Maxmonument statue in Maximilianstrasse, the procession had nearly finished its seven kilometre journey and, judging by the pounding of drumsticks on pigskin, would be here any second. Finally they arrived, a dozen drummers led by a small, smiling boy, followed by several flag wavers and a brass band, all marching together in their dark *Lederhosen*, long socks, red waistcoats with shiny buttons, and each hat decorated with a small red rose. Hot on their heels were several handsomely decorated horse-drawn carriages, some transporting the tent proprietors, others the waiters and waitresses in their colourful *Trachten*, enjoying a glass *Mass* of beer before their big day's work, and the rest pulled wagons stacked with enormous barrels of beer. With every brewery's recognisable banner and coat of arms, be it Hofbräu, Spaten Bräu, Löwenbräu, Hacker Pschorr, or everybody's favourite, Augustiner, a cry of thirsty appreciation went up from the crowd.

I'd forgotten what an emotional punch to the solar plexus a parade could deliver, with its rousing music, traditional costumes, horses and proud participants waving back at the crowd.

'Are you crying?' Tom asked, laughing as he threw his arms around me.

I'd just pulled myself together when a band of young boys dressed up as soldiers with blue feathers in their hats marched by, tinkling on portable glockenspiels and piccolos. But the magical bells were soon replaced by the clopping of horse's hoofs as Paulaner's wagon, decorated to the hilt with purple and white flowers, approached. I was admiring the unusually stocky, thickset workhorses, all six of them pulling this particularly heavy load, each dressed up in a kind of *Trachten* bridle, covered with ribbons and bells, when I looked down.

'Wow!' I cried, pointing at their large hoofs as they clopped by on the bitumen. I'd never seen such thick ankles or powerful, manly legs on a four legged creature in my life.

'Cold-blooded Haflinger,' Tom explained. 'Brauerei Pferde, or brewery horses.'

Was he sure? The one closest to me looked more like a panto horse with two men in it, two men from the Russian Ballet.

'They don't go fast,' Tom said, 'but they're very strong.'

I was about to point towards the smiling, moustached, bespectacled man sitting in the approaching wagon, framed with yellow and red bouquets, when Tom grabbed my arm.

'Don't point!' he hissed. 'It's Ude, our lord mayor!'

Honestly, this fear of pointing, of drafts, of wearing shoes indoors . . .

'At midday,' Tom said in my ear as we both waved back at Munich's popular mayor and his demure wife, 'Ude will open the Oktoberfest, and no one can drink any beer until he does.'

As we walked the remaining few blocks to the Oktoberfest, Tom told me that this very important beer tapping ritual took place in the Schottenhamel tent at twelve o'clock on the dot. Accommodating ten thousand people, the Schottenhamel was not only the largest of the thirty-four Oktoberfest beer tents, but also the oldest, and very popular with the younger folk. In front of an enormous crowd, and broadcast live on television, Ude would be given a special five pound hammer with which to hit the tap into a barrel, hopefully in less than five strikes. Only then could he make the announcement the whole of Munich was waiting for: *O' zapft is!* meaning 'It's tapped!' Over the years, Tom said, Ude had got it down to two hits. A record.

'Well, he'd better hurry,' I said as we crossed the road, 'because there are a lot of thirsty people down there waiting for all this beer.'

Tom stopped, nearly causing a pedestrian pile-up.

'You don't think they're all waiting for *this beer*,' he asked, gesturing towards the passing parade with all its barrels. 'Do you?'

Why not? Was it non-alcoholic?

'Do you know how many people come to the Oktoberfest every year?'

I shrugged. Given Munich's population was 1.3 million, I guessed—a few hundred thousand?

'About six million,' Tom said. 'And over the next sixteen days, they'll consume between five and six million litres of beer.'

Six million people in sixteen days? This Oktoberfest thing was huge.

Once we'd turned left off Schwanthalerstrasse, it was my turn to stop. There before us, stretching as far as I could see to the north, east and west, was the forty-two hectare fairground called Theresienwiese. Known to Bavarians as *die Wiesn,* this land had been named in honour of the festivities held here two hundred years earlier commemorating the marriage between Ludwig I and his young bride, Therese.

'And over the years, that celebration has become the Oktoberfest,' Tom said, taking my hand. 'You ready?'

I thought I was but, looking at the massive crowd inside, I asked Tom if it wouldn't be wiser to come back another year, when I wasn't nine months pregnant.

'Don't be silly.' Tom put a protective arm around me. 'Just because it's the biggest festival in the world doesn't mean pregnant women can't enjoy it too!' He gave me a kiss on the cheek. 'We just won't go on Crazyride.'

Crazyride?

Tom pointed towards the enormous machine in the distance between the rollercoaster and the ferris wheel, whose long arm swung its captive audience in wide circles through the air, upside down and at a terrifying speed.

'Or Freefall,' he said, now pointing in the opposite direction to a tall tower at the top of which sat a row of passengers who emitted bloodcurdling screams as their seats dropped in freefall, stopping just above the ground before returning them to the top for more hilarity.

I looked at Tom. 'I'm not even going on a miniature pony.'

As we walked through the entrance, I felt as if I was on the set of *Seven Brides For Seven Brothers*. Men of all ages wore *Lederhosen*, including Tom, with long socks, the older ones hats as well. They all looked as if they were about to grab an axe and cut down a tree.

I asked Tom why some had a white eagle's feather attached to their hats, and others what appeared to be a large shaving brush.

'That's a Gamsbart,' he said. 'The thick tuft of hair from the base of the chamois' neck.'

A chamois, Tom explained, was a mountain goat that lived in the Alps, and as their hair is rather expensive, the bigger the *Gamsbart* the wealthier the owner.

Making much less of a statement, the younger men chose to accessorise their *Lederhosen* with nothing more than the traditional braces over a checked shirt, and sometimes a scarf around the neck as well, but all of them, including Tom, wore the sturdy leather shoes called *Haferlschuhe*. The women's shoes ranged from dainty low pumps to short lace-up boots, both good for hours of walking or dancing on benches. And around their necks they wore either a pretty necklace or a ribbon to go with their *Dirndl*. The more mature, I noticed, favoured a longer length *Dirndl* in dark, rich colours, whereas the younger ones preferred brighter, prettier colours, and showed a bit more leg. Tom told me the former was the more authentic *Dirndl*, and dismissed the latter as 'alpine pop'. But authentic or fake, helped by the *Dirndl* corset or push-up bra, cleavage was everywhere to be seen.

'Who's the warrior lady with the lion by her side?' I asked, pointing straight over the heads of the crowd to an enormous Wagnerian statue overlooking the proceedings.

'That's the Bavaria,' Tom said. 'Ludwig I had her built about two hundred years ago, and the Doric temple behind her is the

Ruhmeshalle, or Hall of Fame, full of busts of famous Bavarians—politicians, scientists and artists.'

Tom suddenly turned to look at me. 'We can climb up inside her if you want!'

Of all places to go into labour, I told him, inside the head of a sixty foot high bronze statue during Oktoberfest on a hot, crowded day was not one of them.

'All the more reason to get it over and done with!' Tom grinned.

Ten minutes later, Tom was leading me up the statue's inner spiral staircase. It was like climbing inside mum's old electric percolator, the bronze walls stained from years of boiling coffee.

'I promise you the view is worth it,' Tom said.

'No wonder no one else is in here,' I groaned, reluctantly scaling the endless steep stairs.

'Just a bit further.'

'It's like a sauna.'

'Won't be long.'

But Tom was right. Once we reached the Bavaria's leafy crown at the top, I was relieved to find several window-size openings that not only let in some fresh air but provided a breathtaking view of the colourful, sprawling Oktoberfest below, and the city skyline beyond.

'See that revolving Maßkrug?' Tom said, pointing to a tall yellow tower to the left, on top of which a twenty foot mug of beer slowly revolved. 'That's right in front of the Paulaner tent. I wonder if we could find Miro . . .'

Although Tom's distant cousin had been living in Spain for over a decade, every year Miro brought the same delegation of friends from Valencia to enjoy the Oktoberfest. As we made our way through the tables outside the tent, avoiding waitresses with their arms full of *Maßkrug*, I thought our chances of finding Miro among the two thousand people sitting outside, let alone the eight thousand inside, were about as good as finding Wally.

'Hola, Thomas!'

Yet there he was, not Wally but Miro, waving from a table in the middle, seated with four swarthy looking men all smiling from under their handmade newspaper hats.

'Miro!'

Once we finally reached them, after much embracing, hand-shaking and cheek kissing, Miro and his amigos moved up for us and offered everything from their half-eaten banquet of traditional fare. They had *Weisswurst mit Senf* (veal sausages with mustard), *Leberkäs mit Kartoffelsalat* (meatloaf with potato salad), *Schweinshaxe und Kartoffelknödel* (pork knuckles and potato dumpling) and my favourite, *ein Halbes Hendl*, half a chicken grilled to crispy perfection with parsley and butter. And in front of everyone was the traditional *Maßkrug*, or extremely heavy beer mug made of thick dimpled glass that held one litre of beer.

'Better not,' I told Miro, patting my tummy when he offered me some of his.

Not having noticed how pregnant I was under my loose white shirt, Miro's four friends rose like a Mexican wave and with open arms embraced me all over again. Soon they were sitting on each side of me with their wallets open, showing me the photos of their wives and children back in Valencia. And the more we all agreed what a blessing *los niños* were, the more it became apparent that Carlos, Juan, Arturo and Manuel spoke no English or German, that Tom and I spoke no Spanish, and that we were all a bit dependent on Miro, who spoke all three languages fluently but was also three sheets to the wind.

'Never mind!' he shouted, raising his almost empty glass. 'Today we speak the language of Bier!'

And with that Miro's friends' mugs crashed in the middle with such ferocity, I was amazed we weren't all drenched with beer and lacerated by flying glass. So spirited was Miro's toast, it had a ripple effect through the crowd, as other tables around us put down their forks and raised their mugs too.

'Prost!' Crash.

'Prost!' Crunch.

'Prost . . .' Smash.

'Oh mei . . .'

When the singing and stomping from inside the tent behind us grew to an almighty crescendo as eight thousand people sang, 'Hey Baby', I decided I couldn't wait another minute.

'You'll be fine,' Tom agreed, now tucking into his *Kaiserschmarrn*, a mountain of sugared pancakes with raisins. 'Just stay close to the walls, keep moving, and watch out for the waitresses.'

Walking into a beer tent in full swing at the Oktoberfest was a bit like walking into a Bruegel painting come to life. Even the thick cigarette smoke added a certain Flemish Renaissance shellac to the vision before me. Dressed in their traditional costumes, the noisy revellers looked like peasants celebrating a mighty harvest, even if they were singing a pop song from the sixties, and due to the wide green and yellow ribbons hung across the entire ceiling, everyone was bathed in a golden haze.

Heeding Tom's advice, I made my way slowly along the wall to my right, underneath a row of stuffed deers' and boars' heads, enjoying being on the frontline at last. In order to keep the walkways free, especially for the fiercely busy waitresses, standing still was forbidden in Oktoberfest tents, as was trying to order beer from anywhere but your seat at a table. And so sitting at tables or standing on top of the benches, the crowd held their *Maßkrugs* high as they swayed together, singing their hearts out to the Blas Band that played with gusto from an elevated stage in the middle.

And as the revellers erupted into wild cheering at the end of the song, I kept my eyes peeled for waitresses darting in and out from the bars and kitchens to my right, some carrying trays full of chicken, pork and sausages, others multiple beers. How these women could carry up to twelve full *Maßkrugs*, six by the handle in each hand, when one on its own weighed more than three pounds, was a mystery. I was watching one woman balance one beer on top of the six in her left hand when the entire crowd suddenly rose to their feet and held their drinks high as the band led them in a rousing chorus.

Ein Prosit, Ein Prosit, der Gemütlichkeit.

Ein Prosit, Ein Prosit, der Gemütlichkeit.

Tom explained later that this short drinking refrain familiar to all Bavarians summoned everyone to drink a toast to an atmosphere of warmth and congeniality, before counting to three and taking a gulp—*Ohns! (Eins) Zwoa! (Zwei) Drei! G'suffa!*—and that the Oktoberfest tent bands played it every ten minutes or so throughout the entire day, apparently to remind everyone to drink!

On hearing the introduction to the next song, the crowd let out an enormous cheer of recognition and, linking arms, began swaying to the music as they sang a sentimental favourite, *Über den Wolken.* For the second time that day my eyes filled with tears. Witnessing eight thousand people in the Paulaner tent at my first Oktoberfest sing as one made me realise, just as the parade had that morning, that this festival wasn't only about beer. It was about celebrating a shared history, a culture and traditions that reached back far beyond the two hundred years of Oktoberfest. No wonder certain Australians who hung out in a certain tent chose to don the large Oktoberfest hats. Even if they did overindulge in the beer I understood the attempt, however clumsy, to feel Bavarian for a while. At that moment I wanted to be Bavarian too. As did the man standing next to me by the look of him. Something about his large curly moustache, spotless *Lederhosen* and pulled-up socks made me suspect he was no more Bavarian than I was.

'Australien,' I shouted, answering his first question. 'Und Sie?'

'Hannover,' he answered, smiling as he gave his moustache a twirl.

It seemed strange that a man from the north end of Germany was down here in the south, dressed as a Bavarian. A bit like an Irishman going to Scotland and wearing a kilt.

'And what do you think of your first Oktoberfest?' he asked.

I told him I was amazed to see this many people in a tent drinking this much alcohol and all under control.

He nodded. 'Yes, we are good drinkers in Germany,' he shouted. 'Of course there will be a few accidents before midnight.'

I nodded, hoping he wasn't thinking of the Australians.

'Have you been to the Hofbräu tent yet?' he asked, clearly thinking of the Australians.

I shook my head.

'You Aussies love your beer, don't you?' He nudged me with his elbow. 'You should hold your own Oktoberfest down under!'

Did he really think so? I laughed and shook my head. I wasn't so sure about that . . .

I tried to imagine the Sydney Showgrounds packed with millions of Australians drinking beer in twenty enormous tents on a hot summer day, but even before the end of the first night I saw paddy wagons, paramedics, a sea of broken glass and vomit, various dishevelled young women hobbling around holding a shoe without a heel, and one muffled voice crying from the bottom of a wheelie bin, '*I f'n love you, Sharon!*'

Taking my place once again between Arturo and Miro outside in the sun, I sat back to back with our cheerful fellow diners enjoying the food, the festive atmosphere, and the beer, or in my case *Apfelschorle*. Having often complained to Tom about a certain stiff German reserve on the streets, I now swallowed my words and enjoyed the camaraderie on display all around me. Newcomers who timidly asked if they could share a table were given a robust welcome, just as those taking their leave warmly wished each other *einen schönen Tag*. And no matter how many well wishers asked us *Wann kommt das Baby?*, nor how many times I surprised them with my precise answer, *Dienstag!* I couldn't believe it either. Tuesday. Just three more sleeps, I told Tom as we raised our glasses, and there would be three of us.

I'll be a mother in the morning . . .

To watch me calmly applying lipstick in the bathroom mirror before our Monday afternoon appointment with Professor Borg, you wouldn't have guessed I was booked in to give birth via a caesarean section the following morning in a German hospital.

But I felt strangely serene, and was looking forward to our last appointment with our professor almost as much as I was looking forward to our last night together, Tom's and mine, in our cosy home before our peaceful existence changed forever.

'You all packed to go?' asked Tom, gently knocking on the door.

I swung the door open and stood before him with lipstick on my nose.

'What do you mean, *all packed to go*?'

'With your girly stuff and your new nightie and everything.'

What was he talking about? My big day wasn't until tomorrow. Tomorrow morning I'd be all packed to go. Tonight I'd be sleeping in my own bed, wouldn't I?

'No,' Tom said, adopting a soothing tone, as if he was dealing with a dangerous animal. 'No, my love. After we've seen Borg this afternoon, we go straight upstairs to get you settled into your private room. Didn't you realise you're staying in the hospital tonight?'

No, I didn't realise. Possibly because no one had translated that bit for me! Suddenly I didn't feel serene any more.

As I sat in the front seat of Tom's black Volvo, I looked apprehensively at our front door. The next time I walked through that door, I'd have a baby with me. My baby, our baby. How surreal was that? I used to sit in empty auditoriums before opening nights and experience the same sense of disbelief as I looked at our set and told myself that in an hour's time, I'd be on that stage wearing a wig and costume, and eight hundred people would be sitting where I sat, watching us. Hopefully rocking backwards and forwards laughing, slapping each other and saying, *Isn't the tall, chinless one talented? And isn't it extraordinary she hasn't won more awards?* But as I looked at this Bavarian set in front of me now, I struggled to see myself walking through it at all, let alone holding a baby that wasn't made by some guy called Sid in the Props Department. We hadn't rehearsed. I didn't know my lines. I hadn't even had a wig fitting.

'You ready?' Tom asked.

•

By London standards, room 514 on the fifth floor of the Rotkreuz Frauenklinik was a spacious studio apartment. Two large windows looked down onto a courtyard garden, the same one we'd just seen from Borg's rooms below. And I was pleased to see I had not just my own television above my bed, but my own ensuite bathroom just inside my doorway. As Tom's already exorbitant medical insurance only covered half our famous professor's medical fees, surely it wouldn't cover this.

'Possibly not,' murmured Tom, already having made himself at home on my bed, eating one of my apples and flicking through the television stations with my remote control. 'But you get it anyway, my love.'

I was busily unpacking all my things for the next couple of days when there was a knock at the door.

'Abendessen!' sang a matronly nurse as she bustled in with a dinner tray, placed it on my bedside table, closed my windows without asking, and left.

It may only have been five o'clock but I could have eaten a horse. Sitting down next to Tom, I took the lid off my evening meal and stared in disbelief at the two pieces of rye bread, cube of butter, two slices of ham and small pile of shredded carrot on the plate.

'Brotzeit!' said Tom, reaching for a piece of bread.

I didn't mean to slap his wrist quite so violently, but I just couldn't believe someone actually thought a dry ham sandwich could sustain a heavily pregnant woman through the night, let alone through childbirth the next morning.

As the sun went down, Tom and I spent our last hour in each other's arms watching CNN, until we'd seen Donald Rumsfeld justify the invasion of Iraq for the tenth time. Yes, of course I'd be all right, I said, leaving a teary patch on Tom's shoulder as we said goodbye. It was just fear of impending motherhood, of serious operations, of non-English speaking doctors, and of Tom being late. Unlike the rest of his countrymen, Tom was always running late. But this time I believed him when he promised to be early. Twice he came back to kiss me goodbye, and then he was gone.

You really know you're alone in the world when you find yourself nine months pregnant, lying in a hospital bed in the middle of Bavaria, thousands of miles from your parents and friends, and the only comforting voice is some American weatherman warning that a tropical storm called Ivan is threatening to destroy half the Gulf of Mexico. But Tom had promised me a German birth wouldn't be that different from one back home, as all the doctors and nurses would speak English with me for a start.

'Nein!' a woman's voice shouted from the door.

It was the same robust nurse who'd brought me dry bread and ham for dinner.

'Nichts zu trinken, Frau Baumgartner!'

I'd made a herbal tea from the hot drinks stand in the corridor, more to relieve boredom than thirst, but I gathered by the vigorous way she waddled across the room to confiscate my plastic cup that I'd put people's lives at risk. I then watched quietly as my nurse reached into her pocket and untangled a long rubber hose and other paraphernalia to take my blood pressure. While she secured the cuff around my arm, I looked from her name-tag to her weatherworn face.

'Sprechen Sie Englisch, Schwester Paula?' I asked.

'Nein.'

Schwester Paula and I said nothing as we listened to the hissing air escape from my tourniquet. I wondered if she'd been to the Oktoberfest.

'Ok, so alles is normal, Frau Baumgartner,' she announced, vigorously tearing open the velcro cuff before waddling to the end of my bed to scribble something on my chart. 'Und so ich wünsche Ihnen eine gute Nacht.'

As the evening progressed, I was visited by a steady flow of nurses and doctors, most of whom, despite Tom's prediction, could not speak a word of English. But young nurses Monika and Sebastian couldn't have been happier. In fact, finding a pregnant woman in room 514 who didn't understand a word they said seemed to be the most entertaining thing that had happened to them all week.

'Nein, nein!' Monika shrieked in hysterics. '*Festhalten,* Frau Baumgartner! *Festhalten!*'

Eventually I realised Monika wasn't recommending a festival in Halten so much as asking me to clench my fist, and the three of us giggled like schoolkids until she stuck a huge syringe into my arm.

'Dankeschön, Frau Baumgartner!' they sang over their shoulders a minute later, laughing as they left with a pint of my blood. 'Gutte Nacht, Alles gute. Tchüss!'

My next visitor, a well groomed doctor who introduced herself with a warm handshake as Bettina, began telling me about 'die Risiken der Periduralanästhesie' when I interrupted her.

'No problem,' she said. 'I can speak English if you'd prefer.'

And so Bettina continued explaining the risks involved with an epidural or a spinal block anaesthetic, such as severe headache, hypotension, and possible convulsions. That was all. Nothing to worry about. Bettina was about to leave with my shaky signature of consent when she had a thought at the door.

'Has anyone told you about your breests?'

My breests?

'Yes,' Bettina said. 'As your body is not actually expecting to give birth tomorrow morning, your breests might not have milk for a week or so. Just so you know. Ok?'

Righteo.

Soon after Bettina, another nurse arrived to give me a *Klistierspritze,* whatever that was. With her peroxide hair, dark tan and cleavage, Schwester Magda looked like she might have been a Playboy bunny in the seventies, and good at it. I liked her calm, reassuring demeanour as she went about her business, as if I was the tenth pregnant Australian she'd met on the fifth floor that evening. I was still smiling amiably when suddenly, without warning, Schwester Magda pulled back my bedclothes.

'Po bitte.'

'Po?' I looked at her, utterly clueless. The only Po I knew of was one of the Tellytubbies.

'Po!' she repeated, pointing to my rear end.

As I lay on my side presenting my 'po' for her, I turned to see Magda tear the tab off a small plastic bag before attaching a long, pointy nozzle to its corner. I had an uneasy feeling that whatever Magda was about to do, it would involve that plastic nozzle, the bag and my *Po*. Sure enough, after a shocking jab right in the Tellytubby, I had the unmistakable sensation of being injected full of something that had been sitting in the fridge all day. Then I had an even more disturbing thought. I glanced behind me at Schwester Magda's name badge. It certainly looked authentic enough, but it occurred to me that any nut with a bowling uniform and badge could walk in off the street, pull back people's sheets, ask them to present their *Po* and inject God knows what up their jacksie. It could have been sweet chilli sauce or fabric softener for all I knew. It was a wonder such things didn't happen more often, especially in America. But now that she'd administered her liquid suppository, Magda leant down to face me, her nose almost touching mine.

'Frau Baumgartner,' she announced, as if my lack of German also made me a little deaf. 'In zehn Minuten, Toilette.' Magda pointed to my bathroom. 'Ok?'

'You want me to go to the toilet in ten minutes,' I repeated.

'Nort bee-fore!' she said emphatically, and moved my bedside clock so that it was just inches from my face. '*Zehn Minuten, ok?*'

Jawohl.

Was I allowed to move, I wondered as I lay for one minute exactly where Magda had left me. Details were always the first casualty of a language barrier. Very carefully, I managed to turn around without incident, and even found the remote control. Two minutes later I was watching the Kilauea volcano erupt in Hawaii on CNN News when I suddenly felt an overwhelmingly powerful urge to do the same. I struggled to control myself but the impulse to skittle to the bathroom was almost unbearable, and as I lay there squeezing my buttocks with all my might,

I wondered why they were still looking for weapons of mass destruction in Iraq. They were here. Sister Magda kept them in the fridge! I looked at the clock next to my bed. Six minutes to go? *Bastard clock!* Not even when I'd suffered food poisoning on a Greyhound bus trip from Townsville to Sydney after a dodgy T-bone steak had I experienced such a commanding impulse to release. With four interminable minutes to go, squirming around in my bed like a demented worm, I began to chant out loud.

'*Oh . . . Magda-magda-magdamagdamagda . . .*'

What was the worst that could happen if I went to *die Toilette* two minutes early, for God's sake? The baby would still have one head, wouldn't it? The planet would keep spinning, surely? Finally, with a minute to go, like some Pythonesque creature tied at the knees, I hobbled towards the bathroom, only just making it to my destination in time. Oh lord, I thought, sitting with my head in my hands, would the fun never stop?

Back in my bed and having recovered from my ordeal, I was just dozing off to sleep when there was another knock at the door.

'Enschuldigung, Frau Baumgartner,' a kind-faced nurse whispered, gliding to the side of my bed in the half-light. 'Leider haben wir ein kleines Problem.'

Sometimes German was far too easy to understand. I sat bolt upright and turned on my light. Trying hard to speak English while setting out her metal tray, syringe, plastic bottles and cotton swabs, Schwester Eva explained to me that as my *Thrombozytenzahl* was somewhat low, they needed to do another blood test to be sure. Eva couldn't explain what a *Thrombozytenzahl* was in English, but if it was low a second time, she promised to return with someone who could.

When Schwester Eva returned an hour later with a bald young doctor in a white coat and a metal stand on wheels, I tried to stay calm.

'So I am going to give you a steroid infusion,' Dr Schramm said, 'to boost your platelet level.'

Platelets helped the blood congeal, he explained as Eva deftly inserted the needle and cannula into my arm and taped it down.

They helped the blood clot, kept it thick and stopped haemorrhages during an operation. A 'normal' platelet level, he continued, was somewhere between 150,000 and 450,000, but apparently mine had dropped within hours from 140,000 to 50,000. If it dropped below 20,000, it would be too risky to operate.

I couldn't help but feel cross with Borg, who'd had me wearing old women's stockings for the last two months to prevent blood clots when it seemed I was actually more in danger of bleeding to death like a haemophiliac. But Doktor Schramm assured me that this mysterious anomaly was as unpredictable as it was uncommon, occurring in only a very small percentage of women in the very last stage of pregnancy.

'And not just old women,' Eva added reassuringly. 'It can happen any age.'

I nodded, not just old, but grateful for the information. What a night I was having. Two slices of bread for dinner, half my blood extracted, someone had planted a bomb up my arse and now I was on steroids.

Throughout the rest of the night I was so often interrupted by apologetic nurses as they woke me to take yet more blood samples, I was practically able to sleep through the whole procedure.

'Thanks, Sister Monika,' I murmured as yet another needle went into my arm. 'My horse won' fit in the lift, so we'll take the stairs, it's ok . . .'

I was running through the Kremlin carrying a javelin searching for a pipe when I was woken by more voices.

'Frau Baumgartner! Frau Baumgartner!'

'You found it?'

'Frau Baumgartner, aufwachen, bitte!'

'Watch out . . . nurse put a bomb in there . . . I'd stand back if I were you . . .'

'Frau Baumgartner! Wake up please.'

'No more Apfelkuchen, Friedl!'

Finally, realising where I was and that *I* was Frau Baumgartner, I looked up to see the old nurse, Schwester Paula, standing next to Bettina.

'She took my tea,' I told Bettina, pointing to the fat one.

'I am very sorry, Frau Baumgartner,' Bettina said, 'but your platelet level is still dropping. We think it best to operate straight away.'

I sat up and tried not to panic as I watched Schwester Paula lay a hospital gown and white support stockings on my bed.

Professor Borg had been informed of the situation and was on his way in, so as soon as I was ready, Bettina told me, they'd take me downstairs to the operating theatre.

But what about Tom? I asked. Tom was always going to be with me during the operation.

Bettina shook her head. 'As we're now giving you a Vollnarkose, this means no husbands in the operating theatre. I'm sorry.'

Following Schwester Paula out of the room, Bettina stopped at the door.

'We leave you for a minute to ring your husband and get undressed, ok?'

Luckily for me, in an unprecedented effort to be one hour early, Tom was already in the car and on his way. I was sitting on my bed in my white support stockings crying onto my operating gown when I heard him running down the corridor.

'My poor love,' Tom said, panting in the doorway.

When I finally let him go, Tom pulled something from his pocket. 'Look what I brought for you.'

I looked at the little bottle of Rescue Remedy, then back at Tom, nodding at me with naturopathic elation. *Was he serious?* Although a lot of people swore by the healing power of Bach Flower Remedies, faced with imminent caesarean section under full anaesthetic with a dodgy blood count in a foreign hospital, I needed something stronger, like vodka. But as Tom was eager to help in any way he could, I obediently opened my mouth and let him put five drops under my tongue. I even assured him ten seconds later that I really did feel much better.

Suddenly there were nurses everywhere, and before I knew it two of them were wheeling me in my bed down to the operating theatre. As we passed under a hundred fluorescent lights, I kept my eyes on Tom. Even upside down he was reassuring. And as we sped around corners, along corridors, and in and out of lifts, we smiled through our tears and even attempted the odd joke.

'Oops, we're in the morgue.'

'Stop it.'

Having reached our final destination, our nurses deposited us at the *Kreisssaal,* or delivery room, wished us luck and passed me and my trolley into the care of a large male nurse in scrubs called Gustav. Tom and I made no more jokes as we bid each other a cheerful but teary goodbye.

I was still waving at Tom's silhouette when a set of doors at my head hissed open. For a moment I thought Gustav had wheeled me backwards into the foyer of a spanking new swimming pool, so spotlessly clean were the cold grey tiled walls lit by industrial lights.

'Morgen, Frau Baumgartner,' sang a jolly woman from behind her mask as Gustav pulled up next to her. 'Haben Sie gut geschlafen?'

I half expected her to give me a token and a locker key, but instead she pressed a button that allowed us to go through an automatic gate.

'Sie kommen aus Australien?' she cried when I explained my lack of German. 'We've just come back from Perth! You ever been to Perth?'

I was so happy to hear the word Perth, I nearly burst into tears again.

'My husband and I never wanted to come back!' her voice called as Gustav wheeled me away.

'Guten Morgen, Frau Baumgartner,' a masked man said, taking charge of my trolley as he wheeled me further into the theatre. 'Wie geht's Ihnen heute?'

'Gut, danke,' I murmured as he parked me in the middle of the chilly operating theatre and left me surrounded by a dozen men and women in green pyjamas and shower caps speaking German as they merrily prepared for my operation.

'Wir müssen Sie vom Bett auf den OP-Tisch heben,' someone said, and before I knew it I was being lifted by a man and a woman onto what felt like a marble slab.

'Scheisse!' Not only was the surface cold but, alarmingly, it seemed to be moving my legs in different directions. And as my legs went further east and west, I struggled to see who exactly was getting a bird's eye view from the south.

'I hear you are an Australian,' a man at my shoulder said, as if to distract me from the nurse who'd lifted my gown up to my chest. 'Where are you from exactly?'

'Ser-Ser-Sydney!' I answered him as his rude colleague sprayed an icy substance over my lower abdomen. 'Whoa!'

'My wife and I love Australia,' he continued cheerfully.

'Really?' I asked, looking down to see if his colleague was actually doing what it felt like she was doing.

'The Barrier Reef . . .' he continued dreamily.

Was she shaving me?

'Uluru . . .'

Now where was she going?

'The Gold Coast . . .'

Was she going to just take off the top inch and leave it like that?

'The Sunshine Coast . . .'

Now she was back again.

'Kakadu . . .'

'Excuse me,' I interrupted the nice man's tour through the tropics, 'but why is she strapping my arms down?'

'In a moment we must adjust the table,' he explained, 'und tilt your body to one side to keep the pressure off the heart.'

Oh yeah, that's right, I thought, remembering what a Bulgarian princess had once told me about fatally 'quetsching' the aorta.

'Hallo, Merridy,' another upside down face greeted me.

Good God, what a beautiful voice.

'My name is Carlo, and I'm your anaesthetist.'

Carlo could have put me to sleep just by suggestion, if I hadn't been lying spread-eagled, freezing to death and having convulsions. The quiet woman by his side smiled at me with her eyes.

'And this is Schwester Engel. Engel means angel, you know.'

'Oh g-g-good.'

'Do you feel all right?'

I assured Carlo that despite my body shaking like I'd swallowed a jackhammer, and that my feet now pointed to Paris and Kharkov, I felt fine.

'This is oxygen,' he said, holding a mask over my face, 'just to help you get off to sleep.'

It could have been hydrogen for all I cared, so long as they put me out of this misery.

'Ich werde Ihnen jetzt den Katheter setzen,' a nurse called from my feet a second before she attached what felt like a bulldog clip to my urethra.

'Eooww!'

'Now, now, Merridy,' Carlo said, stroking my cheek. 'No need to cry. Just breathe deeply.'

Easy for him to say. He wasn't lying half shaved on a cold slab with his legs akimbo and a clip on the end of his penis.

'Guten Morgen, Frau Baumgartner!' bellowed a familiar deep voice, making his grand entrance from the other side of the theatre.

I tried to lift my head to see my famous professor, but I just didn't have the energy. I wanted to tell Borg that he'd lied to me, that so far my stay in hospital wasn't proving a piece of cake at all. But due to Carlo's magical cocktail, I just managed to wave my fingers and say 'no pants' before slipping into glorious oblivion.

Henry ist da!

When I opened my eyes, I was lying on my side surrounded by a pale blue curtain. On the other side of the curtain I could hear women's voices, Russian by the sound of them. Trying to remember how I'd ended up in a Russian hospital, I went to sit up when a sharp pain tore through my lower abdomen.

'Help!' I cried.

The curtain was abruptly pulled aside and, without uttering a word, a young nurse came over to check my cannula and the infusion hanging over me.

'Do you speak English?' I asked.

'Nein,' she answered, and then returned to her bench to continue with some paperwork.

That's right. I was in Germany.

'Please,' I begged her in the only language I knew. 'I'm in a lot of pain.'

Back home, my friend Jasmine had promised that after all three of her caesareans she'd been given pethidine for the pain, so I was fairly convinced my shot was just about due. But the young nurse seemed more intent on filling out forms.

'HILFE!' I called out to anyone at all, which just made the pain worse. 'HILFE BITTE!'

At last I could hear the sound of comfortable shoes running from the far end of the room behind me.

'Was ist da los?' another young nurse demanded as she ran to my side. This one even had freckles. What was this? Work Experience Week?

'Bitte,' I begged her, and at last remembered the word for pain. 'Ich habe Schmertzen!'

While the young girl checked my pulse, cannula, and chart, she also listened to her callous colleague's monotone prognosis from the bench, and nodded in agreement.

'Sie haben schon genug Schmerzbehandlung gehabt,' she snapped at me, pointing to the plastic bottle over my head.

'It's not enough,' I cried, curling up on my side.

'Sie müssen sich ruhig verhalten.'

I was in such pain, it hadn't even occurred to me to ask about my baby. I was told later that unless you've flown through a windscreen at high speed on the Autobahn, the German medical profession frowns on administering pethidine, even if you do wake up with five layers of stitches and staples following a caesarean section. But with or without suitable drugs, I seemed to have drawn the short straw and woken up in the *Aufwachraum* on the same shift as Sisters Goneril and Regan from *King Lear*.

I was just beginning to wonder if I was surviving serious post-operative pain on nothing but five drops of Rescue Remedy when finally, as if sent by God herself, Schwester Engel appeared in the doorway, followed by Tom, who walked very slowly and carefully, cradling a small white, crying bundle in his arms. Just the look on Tom's face made me forget the pain I was in. And as soon as Schwester Engel adjusted my bed and pillows, I held out my arms for our little boy, all four and a half kilos and fifty-three centimetres of him.

'Er kennt seine Mama,' our kind nurse remarked, explaining Henry's sudden peace and look of utter contentment.

If Henry felt happy lying in my arms, hearing my voice and heartbeat, I felt exactly the same way about him. Henry was here, and neither Tom nor I nor even Schwester Engel could stop smiling.

Back in my room, now full of flowers, stuffed animals and cards, I sat up in my bed with a small sandbag on my stomach, apparently to help the uterus return to normal, with Henry sound asleep by my side. Having already spoken to every member of my family around the world, I was now on the phone to my dear friend Lee in Balgowlah.

'Well, that's appalling!' she shouted. 'Didn't the Germans invent the stuff? When Dylan was born, I got pethidine *and* a glass of champagne.'

Champagne?

'We did have private insurance.'

I had to go. There was a knock at the door. At last someone had arrived with pain relief.

I could tell by the no-nonsense way she held up a suppository that Schwester Heidi and I weren't going to be sharing a good laugh any time soon, especially when she commanded me with a clap to turn over.

'Umdrehen bitte!'

Can't these people administer drugs in a pill or a needle? I thought. Do they have to do everything backwards? But within minutes all was forgiven, even the two miserable sisters in the basement, as the pain gave way to mild euphoria. Henry seemed fond of pointing, we noted while Schwester Heidi extracted more of my blood, with extraordinary grace, not unlike Raphael's *Plato*, or Michelangelo's *Creation of Adam*. Tom thought it boded well for a future as a concert pianist, I was thinking more the Bavarian ballet, and Schwester Heidi said she thought he might be a traffic policeman, a future we greeted with equal enthusiasm. I responded with enthusiasm to most things Schwester Heidi said, even if I didn't understand her. But so did Tom. When Schwester Heidi told him to go for a walk so that I could sleep, he put down his magazine, kissed me and Henry goodbye and was gone. And when she placed Henry safely in his trolley next to my bed and commanded me to go to sleep, I did likewise. In fact Henry and I both slept like babies for an hour or so until I was woken by a loud knock.

'He's here!' Professor Borg announced, swinging my door open and doing a victory lap of the room with his arms raised in the air, much to the delight of his entourage of four eager young medics holding clipboards.

After gloating about the success of the operation, complications and all, Herr Professor Doktor Borg sat down on my bed and congratulated me for trusting him after all.

'For you, my dear, a natural birth vould have been a serious mistake.'

His loyal chorus endorsed this judgement with a sombre nod.

Would it really?

The Professor took a deep breath. 'Given ze platelet level, ze position of ze baby, ze size of the baby . . . Eine Katastrophe.'

We all nodded sagely. Borg the obstetrician, one. Ute the midwife, nil.

'So!' he shouted, making us all jump. 'I vould now like to examine ze vound.'

I obediently pushed down my bedclothes, removed the sandbag and as he leaned over me, found a spot on the ceiling to study.

'NEIN!' the great man roared, making us all jump again.

I looked down, expecting to see the very worst.

'DIE STRUMPFHOSEN!' he bellowed like a great Shakespearean actor, pointing to my legs with horror.

Borg strode to my door, swung it open and shouted insults down the corridor at any staff within earshot. Frustrated that no one dared come forward, he then turned around and roared at his students. Clipboards were flung to the floor as four young medics quickly stepped forward to hoist up my hospital support stockings. Not even as an acting student in the wings at drama school had I been so violently dressed by so many nervous people. Only when the stockings were hoist high as they'd go and peace had been restored did my Professor complete his examination. After nodding with satisfaction, he stood back, smiled at me, and decreed that my support stockings were to be checked every hour. As he made his exit, he paused to look at Henry, now wide awake in his trolley.

'Henry der Platelet Killer!' the Professor shouted, shaking his fist in the air, and then swept out, followed by his obliging flock.

Left in a post-professor vacuum, Henry looked towards the door and then blinked back at me as if to say, *Who the **** was that?*

'What?' I asked later in the afternoon, convinced I couldn't have heard Tom properly.

'Would you mind,' he asked, smiling lovingly at the little bundle gurgling happily in his arms, 'if I played volleyball tonight?'

Volleyball?

Tom smiled. 'It's Tuesday.'

I knew he'd played volleyball every Tuesday night for the last ten years, but surely Christian, Wolfgang, Veit, Detlef and Florian would understand if he didn't make it just this once?

'We've just had a baby, for goodness' sake! You're holding it! You can't go off and play *volleyball*!'

Tom laughed, looked down at Henry, then back at me. Oh God. He was serious.

'Why not?' he petitioned. 'I've been here since morning, my love. What difference does it make whether I stay two more hours or leave in ten minutes?'

What good? What difference? Ten minutes?

'Then I'll stay,' Tom said, coming over and sitting on the bed. 'If you feel that way, then of course I'll stay with you and Henry. Ok?'

But he'd ruined it now. I didn't want a husband sitting on my bed, watching the German news on my television and wishing he was somewhere else playing volleyball.

'Go,' I groaned, holding out my arms for Henry. 'Go and play volleyball.'

Having handed our bundle over, Tom stood up to leave.

'But if you go play volleyball,' I said as he kissed Henry goodbye, 'and someone makes my next book into a film, you'll be immortalised as the guy who went off and played volleyball the same night his son was born. And when Russell Crowe reads out the nominations for best costume design at the awards ceremony, it's this scene they'll play, and your face they'll zoom in on, squirming in your seat in the Dorothy Chandler Pavilion.'

Tom laughed.

'That's if you're there,' I mumbled in his ear as he hugged me. 'You might be off playing bloody *volleyball*.'

But the truth of the matter was that I really didn't mind being alone at all. While Henry slept, I watched his little face, examined his hands, sniffed his soft head and spoke to him. And whenever he cried, with the help of one of the nurses I held him in my arms or lay him down next to me. I still wasn't sure if I was breastfeeding properly, but every time I asked one of the nurses' advice I was told the same thing.

'Sie müssen in das Kinderzimmer gehen, Frau Baumgartner.'

The only staff qualified to give instructions on breastfeeding all seemed to hang out in a place called the *Kinderzimmer*, which was fine if a person could walk two metres without passing out. A wheelchair, that's what I needed, or a very small moped. I was still dreaming about zooming around the corridors with Henry in the side car when I woke up to see a nurse pushing my son in his trolley towards my door.

'Where are you taking my baby?' I asked. 'Wo, bitte?'

'Ins Kinderzimmer, Frau Baumgartner,' she whispered, smiling from the doorway. 'Henry bleibt im Kinderzimmer bis morgen, ok?'

Two minutes later, worried that I'd just let a psychopath in a nurse's uniform abduct my son, I rang for help. Although Schwester Monika's English was practically non-existent her talent for charades was surprisingly good, and she was able to reassure me that keeping babies in the *Kinderzimmer* overnight was standard procedure for patients who'd had a *Kaiserschnitt*. For one or two nights, anyway.

And would they feed Henry too, I asked Monika, if he got hungry?

'Natürlich,' she said, smiling.

Well, what a nice thing for a woman who'd not slept more than two hours the night before, I thought as I snuggled down with my sandbag on my tummy. How thoughtful and kind everyone was in this hospital, really.

'Ouch!' I yelped the following morning when Schwester Heidi removed the catheter from my urethra, which hurt almost as much as when it was put in.

'Aufstehen!' she barked.

'Bitte?'

'Auf Stehen, Frau Baumgartner!' she repeated.

Stand up? Was she serious?

'Komm. Ist gut für die Wunde,' she said, pointing to my abdomen. 'Ich hilfe Ihnen, ok?'

Although Schwester Heidi was a tough and at times rude old bird, I knew she was right. I'd read in both my Australian pregnancy bibles, the one by Kaz Cooke and the other by Robin Barker, about the importance of mobility straight after a caesarean section, not just to help heal the wound, but to get circulation flowing again. But nothing could have prepared me for the pain as I put my stockinged feet on the ground and fell into the plump arms of my Bavarian nurse.

'Jesus!'

'Auf—'

'Wept!'

'Stehen—'

'Christ!'

'Frau Baumgartner!'

It must be like this when you're shot in the stomach, I thought. The impulse to fall to the floor and curl up like a dying caterpillar was ten million times stronger than the one Schwester Heidi had in mind. For a moment I stood there gripping her shoulders as I broke into a cold sweat. I'd have killed for another suppository.

'Und jetzt gehen wir zum Badezimmer, ok?'

Was the woman totally mad? My bathroom was a whole four metres away.

'Can't!' I cried, shaking my head.

'Doch!' she insisted. 'Sie müssen sich das Gesicht waschen und die Zähne putzen, Frau Baumgartner.'

All this excruciating pain just to wash my face and brush my teeth? Didn't Heidi know the Elizabethans went for years without washing their faces or brushing their teeth, and it didn't kill them. They just slapped a bit of white lead paint on their cheeks and ran a small stick over their gums. Couldn't I just be Elizabethan for a week?

'Komm!'

Several agonising minutes later Schwester Heidi and I reached the bathroom, where she temporarily left me leaning heavily on the basin, trembling at the sight of my pale, sweating reflection in the mirror. Wow. I hadn't looked this bad since I'd played the Ghost of Marley in *A Christmas Carol.* Then I remembered yesterday's photo session and felt utterly wretched. By now Tom would have emailed every friend and family member a dozen or so colourful digital snaps of our beautiful baby boy lying in the arms of a woman who looked like she'd just stuck her tongue in an electrical socket.

Having given up waiting for Schwester Heidi to return, I began my pathetic shuffle back to bed and was halfway across the room when Tom appeared at the door bearing armfuls of flowers, cards, fruit and chocolates. For a moment we stood looking at each other, my gorgeous husband, smiling from ear to ear with newfound fatherhood bliss, beaming at his stooped Australian wife with bed hair, support stockings gathered round her ankles and a half-open nightie revealing fishnet underpants barely containing three large sanitary pads.

'Hello, Tommy.'

'Hello, my love.'

Tom put his presents on the bed before coming over to collect me in his arms. So this was what it was like to be in a healthy, loving relationship, I thought, listening to the sound of his strong heartbeat over the distant stampede of various ex-boyfriends fleeing from the building.

Das Kinderzimmer

I'd been told that the caesarean might delay the arrival of my 'mature milk' for anything up to a week, and although Henry had been feeding well enough for his first two days on whatever I could give him, plus the formula they fed him in the *Kinderzimmer*, on Thursday, my third day of motherhood, I woke up to a mysterious sensation of tautness, as if something was about to explode.

Using the trapeze handle over my head, I carefully hauled myself up to investigate. As the feeling seemed to be coming from under my own nightie, I cautiously undid a button and peeked inside. Good lord! Unless I was mistaken, someone had broken into my room during the night and swapped my boobs with Pamela Anderson's. This I had to see in the mirror. It took me five minutes to shuffle my way there, but when I finally got to the bathroom, I opened my nightie and there they were in all their glory: two perfectly round, enormous, unmovable breasts. How extraordinary. From the neck up I looked like I'd been dragged backwards through dense bushland, but from the neck down I looked like a porn star. What strange motherhood magic was this? I wondered if somewhere in Los Angeles, Pamela Anderson was crying in front of her mirror, having woken up with mine.

I wasn't the only one surprised by my sudden fullness. Having been returned to my bedside from his second night in the *Kinderzimmer*, Henry did a full body dance of happiness, and then fed like a trooper until he threw up.

'You should see them, darl!' I told Lee on the phone to Australia after breakfast.

'Are they hot and heavy?' she asked.

'Yes,' I said, kissing Tom, who'd arrived with croissants.

'Like rocks?'

'Yes!'

'And do they hurt?'

'Yes! Tom! Water!'

No one had warned me about the savage thirst that could accompany breastfeeding. Not even while doing Christmas shopping in a heatwave had I experienced such an insatiable need for water.

'Well, that's fantastic, darling,' Lee continued, 'but it sounds like you might need someone to show you how to use the breast pump.'

Breast pump?

'And get the lactation nurse to make sure Henry's attaching properly. Otherwise he won't drink enough, and you could end up with mastitis.'

What was mastitis?

'Infection of the milk ducts. Not fun.'

He might have been a sleepy, cuddly thing for the first forty-eight hours of his young life, but since my milk had arrived that morning our boy had developed a greedy streak. And by dinner time, whether it was due to nipple fatigue or 'incorrect attaching', just the thought of having to feed one more time brought tears to my eyes. Having gone in search of help before leaving me for the night, Tom returned with nothing but the same advice I'd been given since arriving.

'They say you should go see the nurses in the Kinderzimmer.'

•

At two o'clock in the morning, with nipples on fire and Henry screaming in his trolley, I listened intently to kind Schwester Monika's detailed instructions of how to get to the *Kinderzimmer.*

'Sie gehen aus Ihrem Zimmer nach rechts, dann den Gang entlang bis zum Schwesternzimmer der Station Eins, gleich danach links und sofort wieder rechts, an der Geburtsstation vorbei, weiter geradeaus, dann kommt die Schwesternstation Zwei, links liegen lassen und schon kommt das Kinderzimmer auf der linken Seite. Aber folgen Sie den Schildern, Frau Baumgartner.'

I didn't understand a word she said, except *folgen Sie den Schildern*, and so, feeling confident I could 'follow the signs', and using Henry's trolley on wheels as support, I embarked on my first big journey from the safety of my room to the *Kinderzimmer.* And if anything went wrong, I assured myself as the blood rushed from my head to my feet, plunging me temporarily into darkness, *Bingo!* I was already in hospital!

To begin with, the only signs of life in the entire building were the occasional cries of other newborn babies from behind closed doors. But then I saw them, first one, then two, then another, like a disparate chorus of lost Lady Macbeths in the distance, all doing the famous sleepwalking scene, with trolleys. If Nirvana had made one more video, I was in it. I kept following the signs to the elusive *Kinderzimmer,* passing not one but two nurses' stations. This place was so far away that Henry, hypnotised by the repetitive overhead fluorescent lights, had gone back to sleep. Then just as I thought I was lost in a maze of endless corridors, another sleepwalker emerged in the distance, slowly making her way towards me.

'Hallo,' I said on approach, smiling at our similar appearance: fluffy slippers and geriatric shuffle. But instead of smiling back, the woman frowned with irritation at my trolley. Good grief, I thought, moving my trolley to the right. Even in a maternity ward at two in the morning you had to obey the German rules of traffic.

'Kinderzimmer hier?' I asked her, pointing ahead of me.

Taking her grunt as a yes, I followed the corridor round to the left until there, lit with blue neon lights like a gay bar in Oxford Street, was the entrance to the *KINDERZIMMER*.

I'd just assumed 2 am would be a nice, quiet time to visit the *Kinderzimmer*, but as I passed through the automatically opening doors it sounded like a bomb had gone off in a nursery. If my painful boobs hadn't been about to explode, I would have turned around and shuffled back to my peaceful room and CNN news updates about the war in Iraq. Instead, I kept going until I came to the main desk, behind which two nurses sat doing paperwork, their pale faces illuminated by desk lamps. In the waiting area to my left, a dozen women in dressing gowns and slippers sat almost catatonic in bucket chairs, rocking their screaming trolleys to sleep. Beyond them were three rooms, a highly active baby changing room, a small kitchen accommodating a refrigerator, and a room with darkened windows. But on my right was a doorway through which I spied a much calmer area where several mothers lay on beanbags or sofas, peacefully breastfeeding their babies. *Stillraum* it said above the door, *Stillen* meaning to breastfeed.

'Entschuldigen Sie bitte,' I said as a nurse carrying a tray of plastic nozzles sped towards me on her way from the kitchen to the *Stillraum*. 'Sprechen Sie Englisch?'

'Gedulden Sie sich bitte einen Augenblick!' she barked as she passed.

I guessed not, and so gingerly approached the two young women at the main desk instead.

'Einen Moment, bitte,' Schwester Sabine snapped, extending an angry finger that gradually curled up like a caterpillar as she continued writing her notes.

Just then my ears were blasted by the frightening sound of babies crying and waves crashing. Good grief, I thought, as a nurse came out from the dark but noisy room to my left and shut the door behind her. Was that the nursery? Was this where Henry had spent the first two nights of his life? Couldn't someone at least turn the waves down a bit? I was all for New Age sleep inducement techniques, but this was like being repeatedly dumped at Bondi.

'Was wollen Sie denn?' Schwester Sabine asked me.

Nein, she answered before I'd even finished my question. Neither she nor her *Kollegin* spoke English. So what was the problem? While I attempted to describe my predicament through sign language, Schwester Sabine regarded me with cold indifference as if the last thing she needed at two o'clock in the morning, on top of all the crying babies and their needy mothers, was a mime artist from Australia.

'Möchten Sie die Brustpumpe benutzten?' she asked, already getting up from her seat and stomping towards the *Stillraum*. I hadn't a clue whether I needed the breast pump or not, but given the peaceful ambience of the *Stillraum* I was more than happy to follow her.

As I pushed Henry in his trolley through the doorway, past the large sofas with scattered cushions, pillows, and inviting beanbags, a distant hissing sound grew louder and louder until my nurse turned off at a doorway on our right. Why was she going in there? I didn't want to go in there. I wanted to stay out here in the lovely *Stillraum*.

'Komm,' Schwester Sabine commanded over the insistent hissing. 'Bring Baby mit.'

I stood behind Henry's trolley at the doorway, frozen with horror at the spectre before me. Flanking three fluorescent lit walls of this small room sat a dozen exhausted looking women with wild hair and dark rings under their eyes. Staring up at me, each one held a clear plastic, trumpet-shaped nozzle over one breast, as if held hostage to its powerful grip. Attached under each nozzle was a small plastic bottle, some fuller with breast milk than others. And attached to this nozzle-bottle apparatus, a plastic tube snaked its way down to a vintage looking machine that hissed and pumped at each woman's slippered feet. I was seriously considering making a run for it when Schwester Sabine rose from the floor, red-faced from the effort of having plugged in a machine for me.

'Hinsetzen, bitte,' she said, pointing to the spare seat between two women on my right.

Leaving the sleeping Henry in his trolley just inside the door with the other babies, I obediently took my seat, and as Schwester Sabine attached a small plastic bottle to the nozzle that would go over my breast, I tried not to stare at the angry looking nipples of the woman sitting opposite. But I couldn't help thinking, no baby should do that to a woman, especially a relative.

'Ok?' my nurse shouted over the hissing as she handed me the nozzle. 'Zwanzig Minuten jede Brust. *Verstehen Sie*?'

I nodded. Stay with these unhappy women for forty minutes, then go back to my room and kill myself.

As I sat staring at the blank wall ahead of me, I wondered if the breast pump rooms back home were as unsociable affairs as this one. It was hard to imagine this many women sitting opposite each other at the Prince of Wales, going through the same thing, even at 2 in the morning, and not having a bit of a chinwag. For five minutes I sat holding the plastic trumpet over my right boob pondering such cultural differences, until I realised my machine wasn't hissing. Or even pumping. No matter how many times I repositioned the trumpet over my breast, I could detect no suction whatsoever, until finally I bent down to examine the black box at my feet. It may have looked like something recovered from a plane crash in the Andes, but at least I could see what the problem was. Having turned its silver knob from one up to five, I sat back in my chair and smiled at the woman sitting opposite, who looked from my pump machine to my breast with unease. Too late I realised why, and before I could say TURN THE POWER OFF! my right breast was tugged with such violent force from my ribcage, it felt as if it was stuck in an industrial Hoover.

'Jesus!'

I went to pull the thing off, but fearing it might leave me with one boob forever longer than the other, I went for the silver knob at my feet instead. Having turned it down as far as it would go, the suction nozzle promptly surrendered my poor right breast and, flooded with relief, I sat back in my chair.

'Had it on *fünf*!' I explained to my now captive audience.

One woman nodded, another almost smiled. The ice was broken.

Baby blues

On Friday morning, while Tom took Henry for a walk around the ward, I sat up in bed, topless, with my windows open and both nipples covered with *Lansinoh Brustwarzensalbe*, otherwise known as sheep's wool oil, blowing my nose.

'Oh, darl, you've got the baby blues,' Jasmine reassured me on the phone from Australia. 'Didn't anyone warn you about that? Around the third day your oestrogen and progesterone levels both plummet like a skydiver without a parachute. Add to that the sheer physical and emotional exhaustion of having a baby, plus the sleep deprivation due to breastfeeding, and it's not surprising you're a quivering, blubbering mess. But the good news is it only lasts about a week, unless of course you've got post natal depression . . . Have you got any Rescue Remedy?'

'Oh rubbish!' my mother responded briskly when she rang from Tasmania an hour later. 'That's just another old wives' tale to make women feel at the utter mercy of their bloody hormones.'

My sister and I had learnt as teenagers never to complain to our mother about 'old wives' tales' such as period pain or premenstrual tension.

'Just last night your poor father had to review some awful thing called *Menopause the Musical*. It's bad enough some women's lives are so void of meaning they have to talk endlessly about the Change, but do they have to sing about it as well? When insipid women ask me when I went through my menopause, you know what I tell them?'

Yes, Georgina and I had heard it often enough.

'It was a Wednesday. End of story.'

But Friday wasn't totally blue by any means. Before Tom left for the afternoon, he came with me to the *Kinderzimmer* where we were warmly greeted by a team of friendly nurses. Schwester Inga may not have spoken a word of English but when it came to the universal language of patience and kindness she was fluent, and having seated me on one of the comfy sofas in the *Stillraum*, the devoted lactation nurse showed me how to position myself and Henry, and how to help him attach properly.

'You do believe me, don't you?' I whispered to Tom, after she'd gone to help someone else. 'After midnight, they send the mean nurses out until the sun comes up and then they have to scuttle back down to the basement.'

But whether Tom believed me or not, sitting next to him as I fed Henry in the *Stillraum* was one of the happiest hours I'd spent since Schwester Engel had handed a small bundle to me in the *Aufwachraum* four days earlier.

Much later that night, however, long after Tom had kissed us both goodnight, I sat on my bed crying, this time convinced I had mastitis. In desperation, I finally opened the pamphlet that had come with Tom's little bottle on my bedside table: *Rescue Remedy contains Star of Bethlehem for shock, Rock Rose for terror and panic, Cherry Plum for lack of self-control, Impatiens for agitation and Clematis to counteract faintness and bemusement.* It had everything except *Nog's hoof* for dealing with stressed staff in the *Kinderzimmer.*

And so preparing myself for another unpleasant confrontation with Schwester Sabine, I flicked through my English/German dictionary and memorised the words for *nipples, pain,* and *need help urgently.*

I was standing in the queue at the dimly lit nurses' desk when I turned to see a woman in her dressing gown behind me, smiling down at Henry.

'Süss,' she said. 'Ein Bub, oder?'

Bub, pronounced 'boob', was the Bavarian word for 'boy'. I nodded with pride. Henry was indeed a cute *Bub.* Beautiful even. Wanting to return the compliment, I peeped into her trolley and nearly yelped. I'd read that the soft unformed baby's skull could temporarily appear 'moulded' after its passage through the narrow birth canal, but when they said 'cone-shaped' I never believed they literally meant a head shaped like a cone.

'Bub?' I asked her, realising what totally different birthing experiences we'd had.

'Nein,' she said. 'Mädl.'

And we both smiled at her happy, cone-headed baby girl until an angry voice interrupted.

'Ja, bitte?'

Sensing I wasn't going to take *nein* for an answer this time, Schwester Sabine barely tolerated my frenzied mime routine until she abruptly stood up and stomped over to the kitchen.

'Komm!'

Standing me directly under the fluorescent lights by the fridge, the peevish nurse demanded I show her my *Brustwarzen*. I often appreciated how illustrative German words could be, but calling a nipple a 'breast wart' just seemed crass.

'You must feed to they are very bad!' Schwester Sabine shouted at me. 'Understand?' She then rudely pointed to my breasts. 'Das ist ganz normal.'

Normal? Was she insane? I cupped one in my right hand and shook it at her. 'Das ist nicht eine normale Brustwarze!' I felt like John Cleese doing the Parrot Sketch. 'Something ist *wrong* mit dieser Brustwarze!'

With a grunt, Schwester Sabine spun around, yanked open the top door of the fridge and slapped two packets of frozen peas on the bench. I watched helplessly as she pulled open a drawer full of tea towels and wrapped one around each bag of peas before shoving them against my chest.

'Auf den Busen halten. Verstehen Sie?'

'Put them on my breasts?' I asked in disbelief.

'When they not freezed any more,' she continued, 'breng back!'

For a moment I stayed in the kitchen where Schwester Sabine had left me, holding two frozen packets of peas to my chest. This was the moment when the lights were supposed to come up and all the extras posing as mothers laughed as they tossed their latex babies up in the air, while the show's suntanned presenter walked onto the set in hysterics to give me a bear hug, followed by Schwester Sabine, who'd let down her hair to reveal it was actually Kate Winslet. This was the moment all the women from the breast pump room were supposed to come out, holding their plastic nozzles attached to grotesque rubber breasts, followed by some sheepish guy from the art department holding a vacuum cleaner. But instead, I woke up to the sound of crashing waves and babies crying under the harsh fluorescent light of the *Kinderzimmer* kitchen.

I was making my way back to my room later that morning, having returned two packets of soggy, slushy peas to the *Kinderzimmer* freezer, when I noticed my door was open. Although I'd been hoping for just one heavenly hour of uninterrupted sleep, I was hopeful that Tom had arrived already.

'Grüß' Dich, Merridy.'

Sitting around my bed were five grey haired people smiling at me. I greeted my mother and father-in-law, Tom's aunt and uncle and, of course, Tante Zelda warmly and opened Henry's presents on my bed while they admired the new addition to their family, still sleeping peacefully in his trolley. Thanks to my classes with Frau Schmeck, my German stretched just far enough to answer most of their questions, although I had to condense the last four days, including childbirth, into three words.

'Ich bin müde.'

My kind in-laws couldn't have been more sympathetic. Yes, childbirth was tiring, they all agreed before the inevitable pauses approached like potholes in the road, until there was no escaping the gaping chasm of a language barrier.

After one unbearably long silence, Tante Zelda boldly began a new conversation in fluent Bavarian, by the sound of it, smiling from ear to ear as she pointed madly to my ceiling. Whatever had happened, I gathered it was terribly exciting. Perhaps her mother was with the Luftwaffe and had once paraglided over the building. Or as a sleepwalker she'd once woken up on the roof. The possibilities were endless. Throwing me a lifeline, Tom's father kindly explained what Zelda was talking about, but unfortunately it was in German.

'Und unten im Garten laufen Patienten,' he concluded, pointing out my window.

'Wirklich?' I asked.

Really? was a question I often asked my father-in-law.

'Ja,' he nodded, and then gestured to the courtyard below. 'Im Kreis in Schlafanzughosen.'

I looked longingly at the door. These were kind, thoughtful people with good intentions but without Tom here to translate for us, their visit was excruciating.

'So,' I asked them, biting the *Kugel*. 'Wie geht's?'

As usual, Wilhelm mumbled something as he pointed to his heart and shook his head, Tante Ilsa and Onkel Norbert shrugged their shoulders, Friedl closed her eyes and gave a nod, leaving only Zelda feeling so-so. Before I'd become acquainted with this somewhat German stoicism, I used to think everyone over sixty in Munich was unwell.

'Nein danke, Friedl!'

With a nervous look at her husband, Friedl left my windows open and returned obediently to her seat.

I hadn't meant to yell at the dear woman, but I just couldn't indulge this German fear of drafts and summer breezes one more time.

'Zu warm, Merridy?' Zelda asked, frantically attempting to resurrect the conversation.

'Ja, Zelda,' I answered. 'Ich bin heiss.'

Zelda blinked at me.

'Sie auch?' I asked her.

Zelda looked at the floor and shook her head until it almost came off. My in-laws stared at their shoes, a doorknob, or a spot on the wall. Had I said something wrong?

By the time Tom finally arrived, he found me fading on the bed while his family tenderly passed Henry from one to another, murmuring sweet nothings to him. If German could sometimes sound a little harsh, the Bavarian accent with its softer consonants and melodic lilt more than made up for it. Henry was *ein Mäusl (moyzel,* or little mouse), *ein Schatzl (Shatzel,* or little treasure) and *ein kleines Wurstl (Voorshtel,* or little sausage*)*. Each of his tiny fingers and toes was a miracle to behold. And the more they rejoiced the more I thought of my own parents, who'd be here in another five weeks. I couldn't wait to hear my mother compare Henry to a 'pearly silkworm' or some such creature, or to hear my father sing the same songs he used to sing to us as children, old ditties from his childhood, including *Hallelujah, I'm a bum, Hallelujah, bum again . . .*

'He's a child of the Depression,' Rox would remind us poignantly.

Left in peace at last, I told Tom about my night with the peas, how surprised I was to find his family waiting for me, how I'd snapped at his poor mum when she'd tried to shut my windows, and finally of the strangely awkward moment with Tante Zelda.

'You never say *Ich bin heiss*,' Tom explained, chuckling as he helped himself to one of the apples from my fruit bowl. 'You say, *Mir ist heiss*.'

But wasn't it better to say *I am hot* rather than *Me is hot*?

Tom shook his head. 'One means *I am hot,* and the other means, *I want sex*.'

Oh no.

'*Ich bin heiss* means *I'm hot!*, as in ready for—'

'Yes, yes!' I cut him off, horrified that I'd asked Tante Zelda if she felt like sex, and in company too.

'Which reminds me,' Tom continued, munching on his apple as he flicked on my television, 'the other day when you were talking to my aunt downstairs about the weather?'

Oh God. Had I accidentally asked Helga if she'd ever ridden on a horse naked?

Again Tom shook his head. 'But the word for humid is *schwül*.'

That's what I'd said. I said how *schwül* it was.

'Yes, but you forgot the umlaut. You said *schwul* with an *oo,* instead of *schwül* with a *ew*.'

Which means?

'Gay.'

Could one little umlaut over a *u* so drastically change the meaning of a word? While Tom munched on my apple watching CNN news, I studied the wall beyond, trying to remember how his frail aunt had responded when I told her how much I hated homosexual weather. And that Sydney, where I came from, could be horribly homosexual in summer. And then I wondered if this was before or after I'd asked Tante Helga if she felt like sex as much as I did. Boy, I'd groaned as I'd fanned my face at her front door, I wanted sex so much I was going to have to go upstairs and lie down.

And then there were three

I was so prepared for post natal depression I'd almost made up a spare bed and cleared out a shelf for its underwear. I'd been told, given my history with PMT, that I might be a prime candidate, so I expected its unwelcome arrival like an old hungover boyfriend any minute. Occasionally I thought I could hear it snoring on the couch with its dirty boots on our coffee table, darkening my thoughts with its gloomy presence. But I soon discovered that my blues were the lightweight kind, easily chased away by a phone call home, a power nap, a banana, or a good long look at our baby boy sleeping peacefully in his cot. The fact was, hormones and exhaustion aside, I still could not believe my extraordinary good luck. It was only a year ago, single and forty-one, that I'd mustered the courage to accept—with remarkable good cheer it has to be said—a future that didn't include a partner, let alone a baby. It had been a good future too, crammed to the hilt with friends, family, nutritious books, films and evenings at the theatre, part time study, writing, acting and yoga. But this was even better.

Those first weeks of motherhood had other pleasant surprises in store for me as well. Although my caesarean wound still had me shuffling around our apartment as if I was expecting a telegram from the Queen, my skin was glowing and my hair was worthy of a shampoo ad. No one mentions what final trimester pregnancy hormones can do for a woman's hair. But the biggest surprise my body had in store for me was when, hours before I left hospital, Professor Borg asked me to step onto the scales.

'Let me get this straight,' said Lee, on the phone from Sydney. 'Before you got pregnant, you weighed sixty-four kilos.'

'Correct.'

'And five days after giving birth, you weigh sixty-three.'

'Correct.'

'Over your entire pregnancy, from gestation to birth, you've lost a kilo.'

'Correct.'

The line went dead.

A few minutes later, Lee rang back just to remind me of the things she'd done over the last ten years to lose the weight she'd accumulated over three pregnancies, including climbing Mount Fansipan in Vietnam, swimming across Lake Macquarie, and nearly dying on the Kokoda Track, just so she could fit into her old jeans again. I told Lee I was really sorry and, before I hung up, wished her all the very best for her Tasmanian white water rafting expedition.

If motherhood turned me into a nurturer during those first weeks of autumn when the leaves in our garden changed from green to orange, fatherhood turned Tom into a hunter and gatherer. While still managing his family's properties, and suddenly inspired by a magazine article on ceramic tiles created from digital images, Tom began setting up his own showroom in the groovy Glockenbachviertel just three stations away. There the locals would gather outside his shop window to view the multitude of creative things one could do with a digital photo. You could have seashells on a tiled bathroom floor, Che Guevara lampshades, or the musical score of Beethoven's Fifth Symphony on kitchen wallpaper. You could even have your naked girlfriend or boyfriend blown up on your ceiling—so long as they didn't mind.

I loved visiting Tom in his shop almost as much as I loved catching the train to Schwabing on the other side of town. Accommodating Munich's most prestigious university, Schwabing may have had a more exciting pace and youthful energy, but the Glockenbachviertel was home to the city's gay and lesbian community and, with its artists' workshops and young designers' boutiques, had a gentler, more creative vibe. With their groovy bars and cosy cafés, both of these boroughs provided me with the perfect antidote to living in Harlaching, home to the obedient, quiet and elderly. Just the thought of them could cut through the monotonous swish of the Müllers' broom on our front path, and remind me not to lose hope.

'Little thing!' Georgina squealed in our doorway, a vision in lime green with matching pashmina scarf and stilettos. Whenever she could get time off work, my sister would fly over from London for a family visit.

'You're nothing but skin and bone!' she'd cry, nearly knocking Tom backwards as he came up the stairs behind with her overnight bag. 'Where is he, then?'

I loved Georgina's visits. In this quiet Bavarian setting I found her loud, British exuberance positively refreshing. Refusing Tom's offer to change into *Hausschuhe* as soon as she arrived (Georgina just wasn't a house shoe sort of person), my sister would spend the next forty-eight hours, stilettos clacking over our wooden floorboards, entertaining us with stories from London. Nursing a transfixed Henry in her arms, she'd fill us in on friends whose childbirths had nearly killed them, whose babies were screamers, or whose marriages were now on the rocks. But on the career front, Georgina had much more positive news. Not only had she recently been presented with a gong for her television program by none other than Cherie Blair on behalf of the Work Foundation, George had been approached by the secretary to a renowned Egyptian businessman.

'But I can't be media spokesperson for Mohamed Al-Fayed, Merridy,' George announced earnestly as she helped herself to more camembert. 'I mean, *gorgeously* charming as he is, he's utterly convinced that Prince Philip and Prince Charles plotted to kill Diana, Princess of Wales, in a French tunnel. Man's nuttier than a dukkah!'

Georgina was the only person Tom and I had ever seen nurse a baby while operating both a BlackBerry and a television remote control at the same time.

'You don't mind, do you, darls?' she'd ask, already flicking through the stations in search of BBC World. 'Only I really should keep an eye on—fuckity-fuck! What the hell's Barnaby doing in Kathmandu?'

An intrepid reporter could be standing in a trench in Iraq or in a trench coat outside Westminster and my BBC financial correspondent sister would know him.

'Peach of a man. Prat of a girlfriend.'

While staying with us, Georgina was always keen to get out into the Bavarian countryside for some fresh mountain air before heading back into the smog and stress of inner-city London life. Nothing pleased her more than a trip to the Alps, to Marquartstein, or a scenic walk around Chiemsee, but no matter how often we reminded George to bring sensible walking shoes, she only seemed to possess heels so pointy you could have thrown them at a dartboard.

'You mustn't worry about me,' she'd insist, sinking into the wet grass in her stiletto boots as we walked around the lake at Stanbergersee. 'They're Italian suede, totally waterproof.'

But the third time George forgot to bring sensible shoes, Tom lost patience with her and declared our planned trip up to Blomberg in the Alps no longer possible.

'Don't be silly!' Georgina cried. 'I negotiate steep stairwells in these things every day, Tommy darl! I'll be fine! Course we're going to Bomburger.'

Blomberg, Tom told her, was a mountain with a ski lift and a *Rodelbahn* that wound all the way from its peak to the bottom, where he had intended to wait with Henry while we two sisters went on the ride of our lives.

'We can still do that!' George cried with excitement. 'In these shoes I can easily hop on a ski lift and go on the Rodelthingy!'

'You don't *go* on it,' Tom snapped, fed up with my sister's bubbly enthusiasm. 'You slide down it, very fast!'

'Oh, brilliant!'

It wasn't until Georgina stood before the dour ticket seller at Blomberg two hours later that she finally got the message. As the woman's cold grey eyes travelled from my sister's pink Cartier sapphire pendant down to her strappy high heels, we could almost feel the temperature drop.

'Nicht mit diesen Schuhen,' the woman announced flatly, pointing to my sister's feet.

'Really?'

The ticket seller closed her eyes and shook her head.

'Oh, buggeration!' George cursed, trotting past fifty Germans dressed in sensible pants and hiking boots. 'Woman has no idea what she's talking about.'

Tom may not have been able to show my sister all the natural Bavarian landmarks he'd have liked, but due to her real popularity with our bachelor friends, we threw some great dinner parties for her. Again, Georgina's choice of clothing could sometimes overshoot the runway, but never so much as the first time. Luckily I smelt her perfume before she'd entered the room.

'No, darls!' I whispered, heading her off in the corridor and escorting her straight back to our bedroom.

Helmet and Siegfried had just arrived, I told her, and were having a beer with Tom in the kitchen, all of them wearing jeans and pullovers. My sister and I both looked down at her floor length black evening dress, string of South Sea pearls and diamante drop earrings.

'Fuckity-fuck, darls,' Georgina said. 'That was close.'

Before my sister flew back to London, we always made sure to ring our parents in Hobart. Although we'd see them before the end of the year when they flew over to meet their grandson, it was great to have a two-way speakerphone conference call and hear how they were going with their new dog.

'Well, funny you should ask,' Rox began, sounding a little breathless when we caught them late one afternoon. 'We've just come in from taking Ella for a walk.'

'Oh terrific! And how was that?' Georgina asked, jollier than all three Railway Children put together.

'Well, old Monkeynuts does like to charge off into traffic,' Rox began with an unconvincing laugh, 'or else into other people's gardens. And when we take her down to Nutgrove beach she will insist on tearing up and down the dunes and over the rocks, which can be a bit tricky for me and your father, not being as nimble on our feet as we used to be.'

Didn't they have her on a leash?

Rox emitted a high-pitched giggle, never a good sign. 'Well, she chews through one a week, I'm afraid.'

My sister and I looked at each other. Chews through?

'But we've had a bit of a breakthrough there.'

Georgina and I listened intently as our mother described the several metres of chain our father had discovered in the old wood shed out the back of our family house.

'. . . and I find that if I wrap the other end around my body, and then a few times around my right arm, I'm able to keep quite a firm grip of her.'

This just wasn't the comforting image the three of us had had in mind when discussing a loyal canine companion for our aging parents in their dotage. They were supposed to be taking leisurely walks with a poodle, not winding each other up in yards of old chain before being pulled up sand dunes, over nettles and through thorny bracken by a large beagle hound.

'So if you two don't mind,' our mother concluded, 'I might just go and join your father. After we've taken Ella for her daily walk, we often like to lie down.'

Never mind, I told my sister. Soon our parents would be putting Ella into the dog kennel for four weeks while they flew over to see us all and have a well deserved holiday. The plan was to spend the first ten days of November with us in Munich before flying to London to stay with my brother and sister, then return home via Malta. No trip overseas was complete without a trip to Malta. Not just because of its beautiful harbours and ancient cities built by the Knights of Saint John, or because of its famous swirly coloured glass and cobalt blue water, but because Malta was where my mother's family had emigrated to in the sixties. Sadly, the only remaining relative in Malta these days was cousin Bobo, an ex-Olympian high jumper who now worked as a physiotherapist in Valetta. And although my parents always enjoyed catching up with cousin Bobo, the real drawcard of this small island nation was an eccentric elderly family friend and relic of the British empire called Hortense. My brother Max and I were the only ones who still hadn't experienced Hortense's famous hospitality, perhaps because no one could mention the woman without doing an impersonation of Queen Victoria played by Margaret Rutherford. In fact no conversation about Malta could pass without my mother, father and sister imploring me to get on a plane and go there.

'Just to meet dear old Hortie. Oh, Merridy, you must! She'll be dead one day, and then how will you feel?'

I was never heartless enough to tell them.

Ancient ruins in Munich

I stood at every window of our warm apartment with a five week old Henry in my arms, marvelling at the metamorphosis going on outside. It was like waking up in a glass snow globe that some giant from above had shaken. Even the petrol pumps at the *Tankstelle* opposite looked beautiful when seen through a constant veil of soft white flakes descending from the sky, some of them as big as a twenty cent piece. A thick blanket of snow covered everything in sight, transforming our frostbitten garden out the back into a vision of white.

Never having lived in a place where it snowed, I wasn't familiar with the quiet that came with it either. Cars glided slowly down our street as if they had no engines. And as our elderly neighbours walked their small dog along the crusty footpath cleared by a snowplough, I could hear every footstep and every word they uttered, as if the snow had turned our street into an intimate film set with hidden microphones. As I looked out on this picturesque winter's morning in November 2004, I couldn't have been happier. Not only was this going to be my first ever authentic white Christmas, and first festive season as a wife and mother, but in a few hours' time the cherry on top would be arriving at Munich airport.

I stood at the arrivals gate next to Tom, shivering with cold and excitement, holding their first grandchild. I'd presented my parents with other achievements I knew would delight—a mermaid made out of shells, my first attempt at scones, a papier mâché volcano—but this was definitely a first. Henry didn't have any burnt raisins or seaweed glued to his head, neither Mum nor Dad would ask me how I'd made him, and hopefully Dad wouldn't toss him into the attic when I wasn't looking. The thought of witnessing my parents meet their first grandchild made this a rather emotional as well as felicitous occasion.

'Is that them?' Tom asked, squinting at two elderly Nordics coming through the doors wearing backpacks and matching ski suits.

'Don't be ridiculous.'

The last time I'd seen the 'ancient ruins' was in March at Hobart airport when they'd waved me off to begin my new life in Munich. Since then, my seventy-eight year old parents hadn't exactly been idle. On top of their writing courses, German lessons, French conversation classes, dog walking and book club meetings, my father was still the theatre critic for the *Mercury* newspaper, and my mother was a very active member of the Hamilton Literary Society, or 'the Hammos', as one author had affectionately called them. Constantly on the lookout for guest speakers, Rox had recently scored gold.

'Robert Dessaix!' she cried with elation down the phone. 'To talk about his favourite Russian writers. And the exquisite fellow's even allowing me to pick him up in our ghastly car!'

After one hundred smartly dressed Austrian businessmen, several backpackers, two pilots and three flight attendants had walked through the sliding doors, I began to wonder if my parents had been detained in customs again. Surely, after what had happened at Heathrow the previous year, Rox hadn't brought another Tasmanian devil hand puppet. Or maybe we'd missed them altogether and they were already on a bus into town.

'You and Tommy mustn't come and pick us up, Honeybee,' Rox had croaked down the phone from Tasmania, having spent an entire week cleaning the house in preparation for their return.

'You two have enough to worry about with a new baby. Your father and I will just hop on a bus or something.'

My mother's preference for finding her own way rather than being picked up from a German airport on a bitterly cold winter morning after she and my father had been in the air for twenty-five hours drove me crazy. But such was her nature. Had Rox been on the *Titanic* she'd have given up her place on the lifeboat, and Leonardo di Caprio would still be alive today: 'No, Leonardo dear, you sit there. We'll just hop on a bus or something.'

The longer they took, the more anxious I became about sleeping arrangements over the next ten days. As Tom and I could only offer one narrow couch in our living room, the best solution all round seemed to be that my parents stay with Tom's parents in the comfortable 'guest room' of their cosy city apartment, just five minutes away in the car. Although we'd be with them every day, the thought of these four very different personalities sharing living quarters without even a common language made me nervous. Just days earlier I'd watched my in-laws eat their early *Brotzeit* dinner in silence, and thought of my own boisterous parents back home, my father pouring the wine as he shouted over the *7.30 Report:* 'Kerry's interviewing the bloody chimp again!'

Ever since Tampa, my father would only refer to John Howard as a simian primate, which was restrained compared to what my mother called Philip Ruddock.

'Then put the Verdi back on, Wal! I'll kill myself if I have to listen to that grimacing, monobrowed dimwit again!'

It wasn't all 'television rage', however. If Bob Brown made an appearance on *Lateline*, you could hear my mother's cries of jubilation three houses away. But something in the reserved nature of my Bavarian in-laws made me doubt that Wilhelm and Friedl ever yelled at Gerhardt Schröder, let alone ate dinner with Mozart's *Queen of the Night* trilling fortissimo from the kitchen. Trying to imagine my parents sharing living quarters with Tom's was like trying to imagine them at a Vipassana 'ten days of silence' meditation retreat in the Blue Mountains.

I wondered how easily they'd all be able to communicate with each other. It didn't help that both Tom's parents were whisperers and both of mine were slightly deaf. And although both our mothers had a smattering of the other's language under her belt, just how much German my mother could speak or understand was still a mystery even to her. Thanks to her conversation classes, Rox's grasp of French was impressive, and after a glass of wine most of her Italian came back, but two courses of German For Beginners was yet to be put to the test. The first time our parents had completed the course was ten years earlier.

'Who would have thought both my daughters would come home engaged to Germans?' she'd asked Rodney, 'the dear homosexual' still teaching German up at the college.

Who indeed? Neither Georgina nor I had ever shown the slightest interest in Germany. We hadn't even met our fiancés on German soil. George met hers in Knightsbridge and I met mine on that jetty in Lymington.

'Rodney was terribly sad to hear that Georgina's fiancé had turned out to be a Nazi, as were we all, but I assured him that Tommy is *much* nicer than Klaus, and that George is now seeing a lovely Frenchman. Or is that over and she's back with the Arab? Anyway, our class had to laugh about both of you wanting to marry Germans, because it *is* funny when you think about it, isn't it?'

Hilarious. Wait till they started conjugating *trennbare Verben.* That'd wipe the smiles off their faces.

The doors opened again, and after several airport cleaners emerged, my heart skipped a beat as I got a glimpse of two familiar figures pulling trolleys in the distance. I'd recognise the womble-like gait of my father and the dainty geisha shuffle of my mother anywhere, but what on earth were they wearing? The outlines were distinctly A-shaped, like two daleks on the wrong set. And then it came back to me: Ingrid Eisenhofer's coats. Ten years earlier Ingrid, my sister's best friend in London who had introduced me to Tom, had very kindly lent our visiting parents two winter coats for their remaining tour through Europe.

Unbeknown to Rox and Dad, the coats had been custom made from vast amounts of soft black leather for Ingrid's tall, stylish, aristocratic Bavarian parents who lived in Munich. But when the coats had finally been delivered, Herr and Frau Eisenhofer were not pleased with the way they looked. Having lived through the war, Ingrid's parents felt that these stylish knee-length black leather coats, drawn in smartly at the waist with a black leather belt, were too reminiscent of Himmler and Hess, and so, having no desire to draw such attention to themselves, they'd left the expensive garments in the wardrobe of their daughter's Chelsea apartment, hoping never to see them again. Luckily, our parents weren't quite as statuesque as Ingrid's, and on them the oversized coats looked anything but sinister, especially when worn with their luminous Nike walking shoes.

It was a wonderful reunion when Mum and Dad finally reached us. Although here to meet her grandson, Rox was most of all anxious to see me. For the last five weeks she hadn't been able to shake the image of her youngest daughter, starving and ignored in a German hospital, learning how to breastfeed from a Kaz Cooke book. But my father made no bones about the main attraction for him as he let his luggage fall from his hands and held out his arms to hold the precious bundle he'd travelled ten thousand miles to see.

'Hello there, little fella!'

As they both marvelled at the twitching, gurgling baby in my father's arms, I savoured the moment I'd waited so long to see, and Tom captured it forever, circling us like a moon, taking photo after photo.

Strange bedfellows

I watched my poor mother and father struggling to sit upright around Friedl's coffee table. Too late, it occurred to me that taking my elderly, exhausted, disoriented, jetlagged parents straight from Munich airport to a place where they had to make polite conversation in German was perhaps not the best idea. And when I watched my mother smiling with her eyes closed and my father's head occasionally flopping forward, I just knew the decision to stay awake until dinnertime had to be renegotiated.

'Oh, how exquisite, Freda,' my mother said, mustering all her strength to squint at the silk butterfly brooch Friedl was proudly showing her. 'Just like the ones they sell at Salamanca market, isn't it, Wal?'

'It *is* from Salamanca market, Rox,' I told her. 'Friedl's thanking you for the present you sent her.'

'Is she, Merridy? How nice of her. How nice of you, Fiddle. I love butterflies.'

No wonder they were plummeting fast. On the way to my in-laws' apartment, Tom and I were appalled to hear about their long flight from Hobart to Sydney to Singapore to Vienna, and finally to Munich. Not only had my parents sat right up the back of a stuffy plane for over twenty-four hours trapped against the window by an immovable snoring Scot, but due to there being no more room in the overhead compartment, they had to nurse their enormous leather coats on their laps.

'Dear Roxie,' I said, patting my mother's knee while the others were looking at photos of alps. 'Are you all right?'

'Nothing that a long shower and a glass of scotch wouldn't fix, Honey-buzz.'

She looked miserably at Tom's parents' drinks cabinet—stuffed full of Friedl's antique china dolls.

'I don't suppose any of their heads come off and you can pour yourself a Glenfiddich.'

Having guessed we were discussing thirst, Friedl suddenly jumped to her feet, disappeared into the kitchen, and returned with a tray of apple cider.

'What's this then, Friedl?' my father asked, gulping down his tall glass of bubbly amber liquid. 'It's glorious.'

'Apfelschorle,' Friedl answered, clinking her glass with my mother's.

'How lovely, Fritta,' my mother said with her eyes closed, 'but I don't think Wal should be drinking it. He's a diabetic. You're a diabetic, Wal,' she said, swinging her body to face him. 'Drinking a fuzzy drink after a long dehydrating flight could kill you.'

I knew by her tone of voice, tenuous grasp of names, and now using the words 'kill you' in a sentence that my mother had passed a threshold, and we had to get her horizontal as soon as possible. But just as I helped both my parents to their feet, a frightening noise like Scottish bagpipes came from behind the living room door.

'Christ!' my mother gasped, grabbing my arm. 'What the hell's that?'

The noise from beyond grew increasingly loud until my normally shy father-in-law re-entered the room playing a piano accordion.

'Well, isn't that something!' my father said, collapsing back onto the couch as Wilhelm gave an impromptu performance of Bavarian folk tunes.

'What fun,' my mother echoed, close to despair.

I watched my parents with their eyes half open, hypnotised by the accordion's wheezing bellows and Wilhelm's fingers struggling to reach the right buttons, until my mother sank her fingernails deep into my arm.

'Georgina,' she said, now delirious with fatigue, 'how do we get off this plane?'

The following morning we were relieved to find my parents in a much better state, having had a good night's sleep in the comfortable guest bedroom. While our fathers stood at the French windows having an animated conversation in German and English about the Luftwaffe, the RAF and ME110s, our mothers sat together on the floral couch, each clutching her little dictionary for security.

'You dear woman,' Rox said, patting Friedl's hand. 'You must sit down now and stop fussing over us.'

'No. *You* are a dear woman,' Friedl replied, patting my mother's hand. 'I am—' She quickly flicked through her little *Wörterbuch* for the word she was looking for. '—silly.'

'You are *not* silly, Friedl,' my mother snapped, casting a cross feminist eye in Wilhelm's direction. 'I won't have you saying that. I think you're very clever indeed.'

'*You* are very clever. I cannot be lib-rar-ian like you.'

'But you speak English, having not learnt it since you were a child. That shows a keen mind.'

'You are artistisch.'

'Well, so are you!' Rox cried, and then quickly searched the room for evidence. 'Look at that gorgeous clock!'

For a moment both women contemplated the cuckoo clock on the wall above the piano.

'And I love how this bold yellow wallpaper gives the room an omnipresent golden haze of spring.'

Friedl looked nervously at her walls, but Rox hadn't finished.

'As if clumsy bumblebees might come flying out of the piano at any moment.'

Friedl looked uneasily at her grand piano, then back at my mother, and gave her a warm smile.

After morning tea, having wrapped ourselves in overcoats, hats and scarves, we all set off for a leisurely stroll through the old city. As my parents and I slowly descended in the smallest, slowest elevator in the world, I couldn't help but smile at them in their black leather coats, luminous sports shoes and two faux fur hats I'd never seen before.

'What you staring at?' my mother growled, looking up at me.

'You look like Uncle Vanya and Raisa Gorbachov off to an aerobics class.'

'Nasty.'

'Punch her, Raisa,' my father ordered.

My mother tried, but there just wasn't room.

While Tom led the way down Nymphenburgerstrasse towards the city pushing Henry in his pram, I watched our mothers follow him, their arms entwined, each telling the other how lovely she was, apologising for everything, possibly even the war, and singing the praises of each other's offspring. The two fathers at the rear were happier pointing at this ancient wall, that statue and this church.

'Well, isn't that fascinating?' I kept hearing my father exclaim, and 'Fancy that!'

Now and then I went to him and took his arm, as I could tell by his heavy breathing that the winter walk was taking its toll, but Dad always insisted he was fine.

'Can't understand a word the dear fellow says,' he whispered, 'but enjoying every minute.'

We'd just entered Munich's historic museum and gallery quarter, and as the six of us stood in front of the vast square of Königsplatz I waited for the right moment to discreetly tell my father that this was where the Nazis used to hold their mass rallies. Having grown up in a house that had vibrated on Sunday nights with Lancaster planes as Dad sat five feet from the television watching *The World at War,* or *A Warning From History,* I knew this was the kind of information he'd relish. Even when we were children, our father had taken us to see *Mary Poppins* and *Chitty Chitty Bang Bang* closely followed by *The Battle of Britain,* making me the only child at school who knew that nannies might fly with umbrellas, but if you shot a pilot from a Spitfire his goggles filled up with blood. However, as Wilhelm was telling my father something about the Glyptothek, as if he'd be more interested in the royal family collection of classical sculptures, I decided to go tell my mother about the rallies instead.

'Oh, and that's the Antikensammlung, is it?' she asked Friedl, pointing to the original site of Nazi headquarters. 'I just adore anything Greek or Roman.'

I had to respect my in-laws' more benign, less Nazi-obsessed tour of their beloved city. Their reluctance to mention the war, coupled with the notable absence of any signage marking the infamous Führer's presence in this city, reminded me that this was a country still coming to terms with its past in its own way, and not with the same insatiable appetite as the History Channel.

'Look, Wal,' my mother cried, just before we left Königsplatz behind us. 'Friedl says that gorgeous building on our left with the Doric columns is the Music Academy.'

I watched helplessly as my parents admired Hitler's Führerbau, where the infamous Munich Agreement was signed in 1938 before all hell broke loose, as if they could hear nothing but *The Trout Quintet* floating from its windows.

At last we reached my favourite square in Munich, Odeonsplatz. To our left was the elegant Renaissance Hofgarten, to our right the towering yellow baroque church known as Theatinerkirche, but it was the colossal stone edifice in front of us that impressed my parents the most. Again, it was a well known Nazi landmark.

'Wow!' they gasped, taking in the grand open stage of Munich's Feldherrnhalle framed by three massive arches. While Tom continued pushing a restless Henry in his pram across the square, I escorted our parents up the steps, passing between the two enormous lion statues, one on each side. When we'd reached the top, we turned around to admire the view of Ludwigstrasse, one of the four grand royal avenues of Munich, stretching all the way to the Siegestor in the distance. Seeing my in-laws turn away to examine the bronze statue behind them, I sidled up to my father.

'Later on,' I whispered at his shoulder, 'I'll show you photos of *guess who* standing right where we are now, speaking to thousands of *you know whats* below.'

I did a vague moustache gesture and a tiny Nazi salute.

'*Hitler?*' my father cried.

'Shh.'

'Eyes over here now folks!' a loud American voice suddenly yelled from below.

We watched as a plump woman wrapped up in a pink woollen coat, matching scarf, beanie and gloves ascended the stairs before standing in front of us to address her small camera-laden group shivering in the square below.

'Can ya'll hear me up the back there?' They could have heard her in Minsk. 'Originally built in 1844 during Ludwig the First's reign, the Feldherrnhalle was originally a memorial to the fallen generals of the Bavarian Army. But in 1923, this building and square you're standing in was the scene of the first protest led by Adolf Hitler and his fledgling Nazi party.'

My father was all ears. Naked women on horseback wouldn't have distracted him now.

'The Munich Putsch, as they called it, ended with sixteen protesters being shot in the street just here on our right. Unfortunately, the young Adolf sustained only a minor shoulder injury.'

'Bummer,' called an Australian voice from the back.

As a ripple of laughter went through the small crowd, I glanced nervously over my shoulder to see how my Bavarian in-laws were coping with this commentary. Flanking a statue of a half-naked warrior holding a flag, Wilhelm and Friedl listened to the pink beanie with their usual unreadable expressions. Not offended, nor interested, just a picture of stillness and perhaps resignation, as if used to hearing their ancient city defined by its worst chapter.

'About ten years later, when Hitler had become Chancellor of Germany,' the guide continued, 'thousands of his soldiers stood right where you're standing now to witness the new recruits pledge their loyalty to their Führer.'

I looked at Tom in the distance and imagined him pushing our pram through endless rows of black helmets, shiny boots and red armbands depicting swastikas.

'Now,' the beanie continued, 'if y'all follow me round to the side here in Residenzstrasse, I'm gonna show you where Hitler made a shrine to honour the "martyrs" of the Putsch . . .'

We were still standing in the vacuum left by the tour guide when Wilhelm slowly shuffled over and pointed to the enormous yellow church on our left.

'Theatinerkirche,' he said quietly.

Resuming our hosts' tour, my parents and I looked at the towering façade and agreed it was a stunning example of baroque architecture.

'Bombed.'

It was the first word I'd ever heard my frail father-in-law utter in English.

'Alles,' Wilhelm added, gesturing feebly to the historic buildings around us, now restored. 'Bombed, zerstört. Kirchen, Geschäfte, Krankenhäuser, Schulen, Häuser, Wohnungen, Fabriken. Alles-destroyed.'

For once even my mother didn't know what to say.

'Please don't do that, sir!' the guide's loud voice interrupted from the shrine in the distance as she berated one of her group. 'It's illegal to do that salute in Germany, and don't think I'm joking.'

As we made our way to Marienplatz, our fathers continued bonding over churches. Munich was full of them, and with every excursion into one Dad expressed his sorrow at its destruction by the Allied forces, followed by his delight in its astonishing restoration, both responses pleasing Wilhelm no end. Although my mother also loved nothing more than a rococo façade or a gothic steeple, she was easily distracted by the *Trachten* shops Friedl kept showing her with the Bavarian national costumes on display.

'Oh, please let me buy you one, Merridy,' she implored at a shop window, pointing to yet another dummy with stiff blond plaits, dressed as an alpine goat-herdress. 'I just can't think of anything more becoming on you than this.'

I looked at my mother and wondered how to tell her without offending my mother-in-law that if she came anywhere near me with an embroidered frock, matching bustier, apron and a puffy-sleeved-blouse, she'd lose an arm. Instead, I calmly reminded her that I'd already worn a *Dirndl* on stage at the Theatre Royal in *The Sound of Music* back in 1976, and if she really wanted to see me in one she could always look back through her photo albums.

'That's true,' Rox said, turning to Friedl. 'She looked ever so sweet playing the second youngest von Krapp child.'

'Von *Trapp,'* I corrected her. 'Brigitta von Trapp.'

We had just stepped into St Peterskirche, the oldest church in Munich, and were admiring the Baroque interior when Henry made it clear he was inconsolably hungry.

'Wirklich, Friedl?' I whispered before carrying my screaming bundle into one of the ancient confessional boxes, amazed at my

Catholic mother-in-law's suggestion. 'You tell me if someone comes, won't you?'

And so leaving both women standing watch outside while their husbands perused the murals, I breastfed Henry inside one of the oldest churches in Europe.

Finally we'd reached our destination, and just before descending into the Ratskeller restaurant for lunch, we stood in Marienplatz with thousands of other tourists from around the world to witness the Glockenspiel strike midday. I enjoyed watching my parents' faces as they looked up at the little stage set in the tower, on which life-sized knights jousted on horseback, followed by the dance of the barrel makers, and all accompanied by forty-three charmingly out-of-tune bells. When the fragile golden bird had chirped three times, the delighted crowd clapped and began to disperse. My mother had just declared the whole experience 'heavenly' when my father lost his footing and fell backwards almost into Henry's pram. 'Whoopsidaisy!'

Taking him firmly by the arm, Tom said it was time to sit down for lunch.

It was after lunch, when we were leaving the restaurant stuffed with meat, dumplings and potato salad, that we knew something was seriously wrong. At first Dad couldn't get out of his chair without help, and although he swore he could walk to the door without assistance, his weight on Tom's arm told another story.

'Oopsah!' he said, almost crashing into a coat rack, and then 'Whoa!' as he nearly impaled himself on the deer antlers by the door. 'Those bloody things are everywhere, aren't they?'

It was only when my mother and I had tucked him into bed back at Tom's parents' home that she told me about the vomiting.

'Yes, we didn't want to worry you, Honeybee.' It was a sentence I'd heard all too often. 'But he did get a bit travel sick on the way over.'

Did she mean that on top of sitting up the back of a packed aeroplane for twenty-four hours nursing their enormous leather coats in their laps, my father had to use one of those paper bags?

'Three.'

This reluctance to 'worry' us with bad news until days, weeks, months had passed drove my brother and sister and me crazy. If either of our parents had serious health scares, we never heard about it until after the operation.

'Yes, we had just a bit of a car accident last week,' Rox had once told me over the phone when I was still a student at NIDA.

A bit of a car accident? While I'd been sitting on a dirty carpet in Darlinghurst, sharing a flagon of cheap riesling and discussing Chekhov with my new best friends until the wee hours, my parents had been trapped in their car upside down in someone's destroyed living room in Sandy Bay, falling in and out of consciousness while the fire brigade tried to cut them out.

'But we're both doing much better now, although your father still feels a *tiny* bit funny in the head . . .'

While my father slept peacefully in the guest room, I sat on the Baumgartners' floral couch feeding Henry under a shawl, listening to the women in the kitchen beyond.

'My dear good woman, can I help you wash up?'

'Wash?'

I watched as Friedl came out of the kitchen holding my mother by the hand and showed her the bathroom next door.

'Here,' she said, graciously opening it for her. 'You wash.'

'Oh. Yes. Thank you, Freda,' Rox said, almost bowing as she retreated into a room she didn't need.

Like an ornithologist observing the unusual dance of an exotic bird, I watched my mother hovering in the doorway before tentatively following her hostess back into the kitchen for a second try.

'Dear Freda, what I meant was, can I help you wash up the dishes?'

'You want washing up?'

'Yes! You let me—wash up—for you.'

Again, Friedl led my mother out of the kitchen, this time to the laundry. 'You give me clothes und I wash for you, ok?'

'Oh!' my mother exclaimed at the laundry door. 'All right. Thank you, Freda.'

'Ja?'

'Thank you so much. You're very kind . . .'

I knew it wasn't easy for them being out of their comfort zone without their radios, music, book clubs, wine and Kerry O'Brien, but as Dad's health returned to normal, I believed we were all enjoying our little family holiday—that is, until my mother pulled me into the guest bedroom towards the end of their ten day visit.

'I thought you liked Chopin!' I said when she'd told me she couldn't take another of Wilhelm's impromptu late night piano recitals.

'I do, but he's got no timing! Plays the Number Nine like it's the One Minute Waltz!'

And then there were the cold dinners in the middle of a European winter.

'If that dear woman emerges from her spotless kitchen one more time carrying a tray of white bread, salami and cheese I'm going to scream. And not even a glass of wine to wash it down. I tell you, this lack of vegetables is playing havoc with my digestive system.'

What about all the lunches at restaurants?

'Oh, their generosity is boundless, but it's all pork and potatoes in those places, isn't it?'

I nodded. Nothing made my heart sink faster than opening a menu written in gothic font and seeing *Schweinshaxe* and *Knödl*.

'And every time I ask for a cup of tea, dear Friedl gives us some tepid herbal concoction that I swear has sugar in it.'

I just couldn't tell my mother that I'd seen Friedl pouring sugar into the teapot at Marquartstein.

'And the cakes!' Here came the cakes. 'This afternoon it was a strawberry and white chocolate cheesecake! How that dainty lady keeps her trim figure and doesn't kill her diabetic husband I will never know. The only reason *your* diabetic father's still alive is because I stab his hand with a fork every time she offers him a piece.'

I patted my anxious mother's knee.

'Welcome to my world, Rox.'

I was just going back to check on Henry when she asked me one more question.

'And why does that intelligent woman insist she's stupid?' My mother looked at me imploringly.

Maybe Friedl felt the need to apologise in the presence of a woman the same age who'd raised children while enjoying a career, I told her, and who'd recently gone back to university to get her MA. It hadn't been easy for women of their generation anywhere, but Friedl had grown up in a time and place where women were still encouraged to live by the three Ks: Kinder, Küche and Kirche, meaning children, kitchen and church, and a woman who chose to work was called a *Rabenmutter* or 'raven mother', meaning a bird that neglects its young.

'Well, they'd better not call you a Rabenmutter when you go back to work.'

I had no intention of staying that long, I told her. Despite a female candidate called Angela Merkel perched to become Chancellor in the upcoming elections, even in the twenty-first century this wasn't a country that encouraged women to pursue careers. Due to a lack of incentives for them to join the workforce, incentives including promotion, equal pay and available childcare, many mothers deliberately chose not to.

'But once Henry's at school you'd be free,' my mother reasoned.

I shook my head. 'Unless you sign them up for after-school activities, primary schoolkids come home at midday.'

'What on earth for?' she asked, her eyes almost popping out of their sockets.

'Lunch, followed by homework, with guess who?'

Rox was speechless.

'Anyway,' I said at the door, 'I'm not going to discuss feminism with someone who wants to buy me a full dress with puffy sleeves and a matching apron.'

But the truth is, I didn't want to tell Rox how miserable I sometimes felt, that despite a career on stage and television and recently as a published author, no one ever asked me about my life before Tom. Except Friedl, who occasionally enquired how many more words of my book I had to write, only to shake her head and say, 'Poor Merridy.' I didn't want to tell my mother that Horst, my brother-in-law, had welcomed me by directing Tom to speak to me only in German, or that my bilingual obstetrician often spoke about my pregnancy with Tom in a language he knew I couldn't understand, instead of directly with me, the patient. Or that the only subject the women in Tom's family ever discussed with me was babies and the joys of impending motherhood. Or that everyone except me seemed to have forgotten that I'd promised to stay in Munich for only a couple of years, and that I regularly lay in bed at night wondering how much longer I could last here without screaming. Maybe I was more like my mum than I cared to admit. Maybe I'd only tell her about these things days, months, years from now, when they were well behind me.

On their last day, Tom decided to treat my parents to a surprise. Only an hour and a half south of Munich by car, Salzburg was one of their favourite cities. Flanking their grandson in the back seat, they sounded like excited children as they listed all the places they wanted to revisit: the famous horse fountain, the ancient fortress, the baroque cathedral and, of course, Mozart's birthplace. Even the fact that it would all be under snow didn't curb their enthusiasm. And not knowing when exactly I'd get to see them again, I cherished every moment. Except perhaps the one when we arrived, and all nearly froze to death on the Mozartsteg bridge while my mother struggled to take a photo of us with her cumbersome new Kodak camera.

'Hang on, Honeybees, I'm still having a bit of trouble—focusing—in the—rain.'

By the time she finally got the lens cap off, none of us felt much like smiling any more.

Having stuffed ourselves on Wiener Schnitzel at the famous Stiegl Keller restaurant, we waited again while Rox tried to take a photo of the enormous white Salzburger Nockerl dessert that stood like Mount Everest in the middle of the table.

'How nice of you, dear Tommy,' she said when Tom finally commanded her to sit down and let him take photos with his digital camera. 'But I insist we give you the money to develop them.'

'It's a *digital* camera, Rox,' I hissed at her.

My mother looked at me curiously, but wisely knew not to proceed any further.

When the time came to leave, it happened again. My father couldn't get out of his chair, at least not without assistance. Agreeing to forgo the cathedral, we made Dad drink a large glass of water and helped him back to the car. While both my parents and Henry slept in the back seat all the way home to Munich, I sent my sister in London a text message: 'Dizzy, wobbly father arriving tomorrow morning urgently needs to see a doctor.'

Ten minutes later George texted me back. 'Appointment with Doctor MacManus. Utter bastard but will see at 2.'

'Dad's fine, darls,' Georgina said the following afternoon.

It had been a particularly difficult and teary goodbye that morning at the airport, so I was glad she'd rung with such comforting news.

'Labyrinthitis. Middle ear infection that gives you vertigo. So long as he takes his pills and doesn't go for a spin in the London Eye, he should be fine.'

For the next several days, Georgina continued sending updates. Although he still suffered from the occasional dizzy spell, Dad seemed to be in fine form, she said. Every morning he and Rox left her house in Shepherds Bush, dressed in their Nike walking shoes and the Eisenhofers' long leather coats, clutching a battered copy of her London A-Z. And every evening they returned, exhausted but happy, having revisited their favourite galleries, museums and theatres, including the Tate Modern, the Wallace Collection, Covent Garden and the National Theatre. At the end of the week, my sister said, they'd fly to Malta and stay with dear old Hortie, and then, finally, back to the comfort of their own home and their enormous dog, Ella.

'So go back to your life in Munich, darls,' my sister said. 'Our parents are just fine.'

A Mutterzentrum *in Schwabing*

Back in Sydney, I used to love to begin my day sitting in my favourite café with a double-shot latte and a David Sedaris book. The only thing that could ruin this perfect morning ritual was the dreaded Mothers' Group.

'I don't care if you said sorry, Giovanni. Go back to the rubbish bin and get your sister's glow-in-the-dark pony!'

Go to Starbucks, I'd beg them telepathically. *It's got couches!* Sometimes they heard me, but other times I wasn't so lucky.

'Leave the straws alone, Paris, and come sit over here next to Mr Wombat.'

'Fingers out of the sugar bowl, Odette.'

'I'll just put these tables together and ask for some menus, shall I?'

Peeping over my book, I'd watch helplessly as half a dozen battle worn creatures who hadn't visited a hairdresser in months spread themselves over three tables, staking their territory with their large shapeless bags full of bottles, nappies and teething biscuits.

'No, Dimity, you've had three Wiggles Ricey-Bites already!'

Over the din of their crying babies and the milk frother as it made the first round of babyccinos, I'd read the same paragraph three times before finally surrendering my book for the floor show. Watching the mums, I could never understand what rogue hormone it was that enabled them to enjoy a conversation while dribbling toddlers emptied the contents of their handbags at their feet.

'Poo! Who's done a fluffy?'

And as I watched their offspring exchange sticky credit cards, suck on each other's car keys and attempt to insert lipsticks into one another's ears, I made a promise to myself. Whatever the future may hold, never, ever would I join this tragic organisation called a *Mothers' Group*.

'Hi, is that Lara?' I asked the American voice on the other end of the phone in Munich. 'I read about your English speaking mothers' group on the internet and was just wondering when and where you meet.'

As I hurriedly made my way across town on this snowy November morning, catching the U1 and then the U3, I wondered what it was exactly about Schwabing that made me want to run all the way there. Was it the grand Renaissance and Romanesque architecture of Ludwigstrasse that stretched from the city to the north, or the majestic Ludwig-Maximilians-Universität that loomed over me as I surfaced from the Universität U-Bahn? Or perhaps it was Schwabing's bookshops, cosy cafés and bars that lined Schellingstrasse, many of them full of students who'd parked their bicycles outside. And then there was its history. During the Weimar era, Schwabing had been the bohemian and intellectual heart of Munich, home to writers, artists and great thinkers, including Thomas Mann, Brecht, Kandinsky and even Lenin. But all that changed in the years leading up to the Second World War when Germany's most expressive artists fled from the oppressive new regime, especially from Schwabing when it was hijacked by the Nazis.

Poor Tom. Ever since I'd taken myself back to Dachau while he'd minded our son for the day, the small pile of novels beside my bed had been replaced by heavy tomes on Nazis, the Holocaust and anything at all by Antony Beevor, until it had become a leaning tower of Hitler. My never-ending source was The Munich Readery, an English secondhand bookshop on Augustenstrasse with comfy large leather lounge chairs, run by a friendly, incredibly well read American couple, John and Lisa.

I felt like a sleuth as I took to the streets to find addresses mentioned in various books and was amazed to discover Tom's parents lived just a few buildings down from Hitler's first digs.

I could have conducted tours along Schwabing's Schellingstrasse. Number 33, for instance, had once been the photographic studio of Hitler's personal photographer, Heinrich Hoffmann, until he moved his business across the road to number 50, also Nazi Party headquarters. I'd often pause on the footpath outside this building, now a gift shop, not just because it was here that Herr Hoffmann introduced Hitler to his seventeen year old assistant, Eva Braun, but in a city that had gone to such trouble to remove all landmarks, signs and symbols of the Third Reich, this one remaining eagle carved in stone above the entrance captivated me.

Moving further along Schellingstrasse to number 54 was the Schelling Salon, where Hitler apparently ran up such a tab, despite being a teetotaller, he was forbidden entry. And just one block further at number 62, right on the corner of Schraudolphstrasse, was Hitler's favourite restaurant.

Braving the icy wind, I paused outside the Osteria Italiana, once the Osteria Bavaria where the dictator used to eat his lunch either with Eva Braun or with his Nazi colleagues, and marvelled at its unchanged façade. Apparently the interior hadn't altered much either. You could still sit at the table near the door where Unity Mitford regularly sat, waiting for a chance to meet her hero. I had long been fascinated by the Mitford sisters, not just because of the funny family dynamics portrayed in Nancy Mitford's entertaining novels, but because the five of these siblings could not have been more diverse in their political beliefs, ranging from communism to fascism. And of the five sisters, none was so fanatical as Unity, the youngest and plainest of them all.

Already a keen fascist, Unity was only nineteen when she followed her older sister Diana, renowned for her beauty and for marrying Oswald Mosley, founder of the British Union of Fascists, to hear Hitler speak at the 1933 Nuremberg Rally. So taken was the youngest Mitford with her hero's impassioned performance there she moved to Munich the following year, attended German classes and hung around Hitler's favourite haunts in the hope of meeting him.

Her efforts were finally rewarded when, unable to continue ignoring the tall, pale young woman staring at him from across the room in the Osteria Bavaria, Hitler invited Unity to join him. Delighted to discover not only that the young Mitford's grandfather was a close friend of Richard Wagner but that her middle name was Valkyrie, Hitler rewarded Unity's devotion by making her a permanent member of his entourage. But so desperate was she to prove her allegiance to her Führer and his beliefs, when England declared war on Germany in 1939 Unity found a quiet bench in the Englischer Garten, the enormous park in the middle of the city, and shot herself in the head, possibly upsetting no one less than Eva Braun.

She is known as the Valkyrie, a jealous Eva once wrote in her diary, *and looks the part, including her legs.* But Viking legs or not, Unity's suicide attempt was surprisingly unsuccessful, and with an inoperable bullet lodged in her brain she went on to survive another nine years in her mother's care until 1948, when she died of meningitis. Such were my reflections as I paused with Henry outside the Osteria Italiana on the corner of Schellingstrasse, just before turning right up Schraudolphstrasse to find my mothers' group.

I never realised how much I craved the company of English speaking women until I saw those dozen or so prams parked on the footpath just several buildings further up the street. What typically thoughtful, constructive and practical creatures we women were, I thought as I parked Henry's pram among the others, to facilitate these social get-togethers once a week for a chat and a playdate, and support each other through this challenging chapter of our lives. What a brilliant concept the Mothers' Group was.

Impatient to meet my new best friends, I tried to sneak a peep through the glass façade, but it was covered with too many signs taped from within: *Kinder Flohmarkt! Kinderwagen kaufen/verkaufen, Tanz Kurs für Kinder.* But there, right above the door handle, was the only sign I needed to understand: *Freitag 10–12, Englische Gruppe.* Giddy with excitement, I pushed open the heavy glass door and was immediately engulfed by the noise and warmth of a packed, heated room and the aroma of over-percolated coffee and at least one soiled nappy.

It was a narrow space no bigger than a classroom divided in the middle by a large, worn red sofa. At this end of the room was the kitchen area where many women and a few men stood and sat around a table eating homemade cakes and biscuits from tins. But occupying the other end were at least twenty people sitting on old sofas or beanbags, drinking from mugs and catching up as they watched their toddlers explore the vast array of toys scattered across the floor. Through the glass windows at the back, I could see a small, empty courtyard outside, enclosed by a tall brick wall.

I stood still for a moment just listening to the familiar and wonderful sounds of English. I hadn't heard people this loud and animated in months, and it took my ears a moment to adjust. Instead of the poised, upright people outside, everyone here leant on walls, flopped on sofas or spread out on beanbags as if they'd all taken muscle relaxants. Tom got nervous if I just pointed at things, but here I saw hands moving through the air like threshing machines. After the decorum on the streets of Harlaching, the stillness on Munich's public transport system and Tom's well behaved family, walking into Lara's *Mutterzentrum* on a Friday morning was like discovering a hidden speakeasy.

'Merridy?' a laughing woman with fabulous hair called as she almost fell through the crowd before me.

I shook Lara's hand like Stanley discovering Livingstone on the shores of Lake Tanganyika.

'So you found us all right, then?' she asked.

'Yes,' I cried. 'I just walked along Schellingstrasse and turned right at Schraudolphstrasse like you told me to and here you are!'

'And here we are!' she sang, erupting into contagious laughter. 'And where is—?' Lara asked, gingerly peeping over my shoulder.

I peeped behind me too, until my stomach did a violent backflip and I tore outside to find Henry still sound asleep in his pram. I'd once left my brand new wooden clarinet that my parents had bought me for my thirteenth birthday in the Didgeridoo Café in Hobart, but this was about a billion times worse.

Back inside, holding Henry in my arms, I quickly kicked off my shoes as everyone else had done, and let Lara lead me through the crowd to the couch. Having hastily introduced me to an Indian woman sitting in the middle of it, Lara shouted her apologies before running off to answer a ringing telephone. For a moment Roshan and I said nothing but watched her tiny daughter chew on the ears of a wooden mouse.

'Have you lived in Munich long, Roshan?' I finally asked over the noise.

'One year.'

Something about Roshan's granite expression told me she wasn't in the best of moods.

'I've told my husband,' she continued in a clipped British accent, 'either we go back to London before Christmas, or I take Shilo and go without him.'

I nodded, wondering why Lara had left Henry and me with the one miserable person in the entire room.

'Your husband's German, too?' I asked.

'God, no!' she exploded. 'Do I look like a bloody masochist?'

What was it about my face that said *Place next to difficult people,* or *Copes well with nutters*?

'Oh dear,' I said, 'I think your little girl might have swallowed something.'

And while Roshan turned to help Shilo regurgitate a mouse's ear, I deftly made my escape with Henry to the back end of the room.

Having settled ourselves on some scattered cushions in the soft toys corner, Henry and I watched the older babies and toddlers crawling over their mothers, scaling shelves, getting bogged in beanbags and occasionally clocking each other in the head with blocks. In some previous life, I vaguely recalled this being my idea of a nightmare, but sitting in the midst of this chaos now, I couldn't have been happier. Here were women and men who'd met Germans, who'd relocated for them, who'd become mothers or fathers in a foreign country. Here were expats forging a new life in Germany, just like me.

'They all speak English anyway,' an American voice declared from the sofa behind me. 'And if they don't, I just point at what I want and shout.'

'Oh, I know!' her British friend replied, sounding remarkably like my sister. 'Whenever I go to the gym or to Vidal Sassoon's or to one of Valentin's BMW functions, they can't wait to practise their English, so you just think—why bother?'

Having quickly glanced at these two voguishly shabby women who had time to go to gyms and Vidal Sassoon, I guessed that neither of them regularly found herself sitting under a stuffed stag's head at a rustic wooden table with no one to talk to but Tante Zelda. And the thought began to dawn on me, just because I'd found my tribe, it didn't mean we'd all speak the same language.

'So how long did you say you'd been here?' a loud Australian voice shouted across the room.

'Six years,' a tall African American woman standing near me hollered back. '*You*?'

'Two!' the Australian yelled. 'How d'ya like it so far?'

'I'm loving it, actually! Took a while, though. What about you?'

'I hate it!'

'Really?'

'Can't wait to get out!'

'Hold it right there!' my neighbour shouted. 'I'm coming over.'

Me too! I wanted to shout. *I'm coming over too!*

'Mamaaaa!'

All conversations halted as an ear-piercing scream rose from within a box of tambourines, maracas and castanets to my right. By the time Lara had run from the other end of the room, pulled her distressed daughter out and untangled her hair from a triangle, I found myself standing in a small group of women who all seemed to know each other. Having been introduced to Lara's four friends over a percussion box, I began my interrogation. How long had they been here, why had they come and how did they all meet?

'I don't think any of us planned to end up living in Germany, did we?' Rowena asked her friends, leading us over to the kitchen table.

'Italy maybe,' sighed Heidi from Arizona.

'South of France,' said Lara.

'Spain,' Dagmar added wistfully, in her Scottish accent.

'Let's face it,' said Jane from Oxfordshire, 'who wakes up in the morning and thinks—"I want to live in Bavaria"?'

But it was very encouraging for me, I told them as we sat down at a table covered in crumbs and used coffee mugs, to meet other women who'd met a German chap, given up everything to relocate, and that it had all worked out. Hadn't it?

The women all smiled at each other.

'Actually, it didn't work out for any of us,' confessed Dagmar from Scotland whose mother was German hence the name. 'Rainer dumped me the minute I arrived. Took one look at my bags and freaked.'

'Martin and I lasted all of three weeks,' said Heidi.

'And let's not even discuss my soccer player,' added Lara.

I seemed to be the only one at the table still with her original German fiancé.

'My God!' Jane cried when I told them I'd arrived less than a year ago, four months pregnant to the first Bavarian I'd ever met and without a word of German under my belt. 'You were thrown into the deep end, weren't you?'

But why hadn't they all jumped on the first plane home? I wanted to know. If Tom had broken my heart, there was no way I'd stay in Germany on my own.

'I just didn't want to go back with my tail between my legs,' Rowena confessed.

'I'd packed up my life,' added Jane. 'Literally had nothing to go back to.'

'I was all set to go,' Dagmar said, 'when I got offered this amazing apartment.'

The others agreed. I had to see Dagmar's rooftop apartment with views of the Englischer Garten. It even had a lift, a rarity in these beautiful old buildings in Schwabing.

'You know why I didn't want to go home?' Heidi asked in her breathy voice, wide eyed. 'I'd just begun to dream in German.'

The others nodded knowingly, and for some reason I did too.

And how had they supported themselves all this time, I wanted to know. For the last ten years, Rowena from Brisbane had worked as an interior designer for a German architecture firm, Lara and Jane taught English at Ludwig-Maximilians-Universität, Dagmar edited a magazine for Germans wanting to learn English, and Heidi worked as a senior nurse in an old people's home. And then it was my turn.

'Are you going to try to get work here as an actress?' Lara asked.

I nearly spat out my coffee. Me? Here? Never mind how long it would take me to be fluent in German, had they ever seen the photos from the latest Kammerspiele production outside the Schauspielhaus on Maximilianstrasse? A pregnant bride in a blood spattered wedding dress ate an apple in front of half a light aeroplane protruding from the stage. An old man slept naked on the floor under a dead horse suspended from the ceiling. Theatre in Germany, it seemed to me, went for the jugular. Across the Austrian border my inspiringly talented friend Melita Jurisic had just learnt the role of Medea in German for Barry Kosky's production at the Schauspielhaus Wien. But if there was one actress I could imagine sitting starkers under a spotlight in a bath full of eels, it was Melita. The last time I stepped on stage I was dressed in a grey wig, slippers and apron, holding a tray of kippers.

'Habt ihr den Erste Hilfe Kasten gesehen?' a woman interrupted us.

As I listened to my new friends discuss the whereabouts of the first aid kit with Astrid in fluent German, Heidi quietly explained to me that a few of the German mothers always came along on Fridays too, in the hope that their kids might pick up a bit of English.

'Which is fine,' she whispered, 'but I wish they wouldn't let them run around naked, you know?'

We both looked across the room where two naked toddlers bounced up and down on the beanbags.

'We've only just washed all the covers again after last week.'

What about childcare? I asked my new friends. I'd probably be needing some in a couple of years, given my rapidly fading hopes of leaving earlier. Did they have any advice?

'You mean you haven't already applied for a place at a Kinderkrippe?' Dagmar asked.

What was a *Kinderkrippe*?

The women went quiet. Even the small cardboard box slowly shuffling its way around our table paused, then farted.

A *Kinderkrippe* was a morning crèche, a day care centre or a nursery. But to get a place in one was almost impossible, Jane said, unless you registered during pregnancy.

During pregnancy? When I was pregnant I didn't even know if the foetus had arms and legs, let alone if I'd be needing a *Kinderkrippe.*

That was a pity, Lara sighed, because the waiting list at her local had just reached four hundred, Jane's was five hundred and Rowena's was over six. Worse still was the small intake each year.

Twenty? According to these figures, Henry would get a place in a *Kinderkrippe* just after he got his driving licence.

'You could always look for a good Tagesmutter,' Lara said.

A *Tagesmutter,* Rowena explained to me, was a woman qualified to look after up to five toddlers or babies on a daily basis in her own home. 'It's exactly the same as family day care.'

I tried to imagine looking after five small toddlers at our place, but just while I was changing a nappy, one poured milk into our oil heater, another stuck his fork into a powerpoint while the smallest rolled off our balcony. If I could go without childcare until Henry was three, Heidi cried, I wouldn't have to worry about a *Kinderkrippe* or a *Tagesmutter,* because by then Henry would be old enough to go to *Kindergarten.* Surprisingly, there were almost enough places at these church-supported and voluntary community *Kindergartens* in Germany to cater for every child from the age of three to six.

''Cause you know when they're six they have to go to Grundschule.'

Yes, I'd already heard about primary schools in Germany, I growled. They began at 7.30 am and sent children home by midday, making it impossible for a whole generation of mothers to join the workforce full time.

High school hours varied too, Rowena sighed, depending on the subjects your child chose, and the school he or she got into. I was surprised to learn that in Germany children chose from three different kinds of high school. According to their marks they could either go to *Hauptschule*, *Realschule* or, if they wanted to complete their *Abitur* (HSC) and go on to university, a *Gymnasium*.

'Over here,' Jane said, 'a Gymnasium is not a sports hall.'

The five of us had to temporarily suspend our conversation when a small celebration erupting by the fridge made it impossible to hear. What had happened? I asked my friends as we watched people hugging the German mother. Had Astrid finally found the first aid box?

'Letzte Woche hab ich mit Lukas einen Probetag im Waldkindergarten mitgemacht,' Astrid answered Heidi, nodding towards her naked son still bouncing on the beanbags. 'Und heute hat er einen Platz bekommen!'

While the others jumped up to congratulate her, Heidi explained to me that Astrid's son Lukas had just been offered a place in a *Waldkindergarten*.

I knew that *Wald* meant 'forest', but nothing could have prepared me for what came next.

'In the middle of the woods?' I whispered to the four of them. 'Parents drop their three year olds off at a forest for the day? No building? No heater? No toys? *No toilet*?'

'Some Waldkindergärten ask the kids to bring their own potty, don't they?' Lara asked Heidi, as if she was talking about a pencil case.

Heidi wasn't sure. 'I thought they taught the kids to make a hole in the ground.'

A hole in the ground?

'It's not like they're just dropped off by the side of the road,' Rowena said, laughing at my shocked expression. 'And there are two qualified teachers with them all day.'

'And let's not forget,' Dagmar added, 'this is where the word *Kindergarten* comes from.'

From a hole in the ground?

'From some very clever German chap two hundred years ago who noticed how young children thrive in nature, in every way.'

That's right, Jane continued. The Danish had rediscovered the *Waldkindergarten* back in the sixties, and now they were popping up again all over Germany, with waiting lists as long as your arm.

'And these children turn up every day,' I asked, still struggling with the concept, 'even in the pouring rain?'

My friends nodded.

Even in the snow?

They nodded again. 'They can always huddle in the Wagen.'

I turned to Heidi. Did she say *Wagen*?

'Like a trailer,' Lara explained, 'or a caravan.'

I felt like reaching for my Ventolin inhaler just thinking about it. Having been a bronchial asthmatic kid who spent one afternoon a week blowing into a Spirometer, I didn't like my chances of surviving winter in a *Waldkindergarten*, with or without a *Wagen*.

'If it's *really* cold, they do cancel,' Heidi said, 'but I think it has to be minus ten.'

I shouldn't have been that surprised by the concept of the authentic German *Kindergarten*. I'd seen them from tram windows often enough, two neat lines of small children dressed from head to toe in sensible, waterproof, windproof clothing, being led by their teachers through rain, slush and snow to play in their local *Spielplatz*. Back home, the only children in the woods for any extended period of time in subzero temperatures were the ones being looked for by helicopters and search parties with sniffer dogs.

According to studies, Astrid continued when she'd joined us at the table, children who attended *Waldkindergärten* developed a stronger relationship with nature, with each other, their bodies and senses; they tended to be much more verbal than their indoor peers, they slept better, had stronger immune systems, improved fitness levels, physical stamina and—'wie sagt man Blutkreislauf?'

'Blood circulation,' Lara translated.

Here we go again, I thought. Tom was still trying to convince me to have cold showers from the waist down every morning to improve my circulation, as well as gargle with sunflower oil for my gums, so it was probably only a matter of time before he suggested we drop Henry off at a forest every morning.

I didn't know if it was all this talk about *Waldkindergärten* or if it was the flashbacks I was having from my own childhood in Queensland, spending entire days with the kids from our street in the surrounding bushland, catching tadpoles down at the creek, collecting mulberries on the side of the road, or spending our afternoons climbing in the mango trees, but I had a sudden urge to get out of this hot, stuffy room and go for a walk in the fresh Bavarian air.

'You wanna come with us to Türkenstrasse?' asked Lara, already stacking the kitchen chairs on top of the table. 'It's a bit of a walk but there's a great café with a Spielecke.'

But after twenty minutes of bracing winds and light rain on the streets of Schwabing, I was ready for a stuffy, warm room again. And for the next two hours we sat at our table in a café called Zeitgeist, just near the *Spielecke* scattered with ravaged, worn, torn, chewed, stained toys. And as we breastfed our babies and let our toddlers empty our handbags at our feet, passing around our car keys, credit cards and lipsticks, my new best friends and I continued our conversations about motherhood, in-laws, childcare, formula milk, Aldi, homesickness, and *Waldkindergärten*. And while I enjoyed their company like a starving plant enjoys the rain after a long dry season, in the far corner of the café a woman sat with her double-shot latte, trying to read her David Sedaris book and wishing we'd gone to Starbucks instead.

Newsflash from London

Having been cooped up in our centrally heated apartment for days on end as it continued to snow, I'd declared a state of emergency and insisted on a winter's morning walk through town. The Sunday traffic was almost non-existent and as we pushed Henry's pram through the old city, Tom and I enjoyed having Munich to ourselves to do a bit of window shopping. The little *Christkindlmarkt* stalls stood lifeless in the malls, boarded up until the following morning when they'd open their wooden shutters to reveal shelves of painted candles, handmade wooden toys and some of the most exquisite Christmas decorations I'd ever seen. Other stalls with mugs hanging from the eaves would seduce passers-by with the smell of *Glühwein* and the promise of a hot drink that might put one in the mood for ice-skating at the temporary rink nearby at Karlsplatz. Having left Odeonsplatz and making our way down Prinzregentenstrasse towards the Englischer Garten, we noticed a small crowd standing on the Eisbach bridge, transfixed by something in the rushing water below.

'Oh no,' I said as the crowd cheered. 'It's minus five. You've got to be kidding.'

'I bet it's Manfred,' Tom said, laughing as we approached.

Only a few months earlier I'd stopped to join the locals and tourists on this bridge overlooking the Eisbach, meaning 'icy creek', to watch the intrepid surfers below. Stretching some eight metres across, the Eisbach wave was much more powerful than the one Tom surfed on in Thalkirchen, and despite being only a metre high in places was notoriously dangerous. Instead of being made by a ramp in the riverbed, the Eisbach wave was made by rocks and slabs of concrete on which many shoulders, knees, ribs and arms had been broken over the years, hence the sign, *Surfen und Baden verboten!* But no matter how many signs the city council put up, or how many surfboards they confiscated, the intrepid river surfers kept coming back until the authorities decided to turn a blind eye—an amazing achievement considering how diligently they policed the streets. Tom sometimes watched a television show that followed a group of *Polizei* around Munich as they waved down the odd cyclist gently pedalling through the city and fined him for riding through a walking zone. I never knew what was more worrying, that there were people who watched such a program, or that I'd married one of them.

Impatient to see, I worked my way through the crowd of coats, scarves and beanies until I had a dress circle view of the show going on below. And sure enough, there on the snowy banks of the Eisbach with a surfboard under his arm stood Manfred in a wetsuit and crash helmet, waiting for his turn. I'd only just managed to get my head around people sending their small children to kindergartens in the forest throughout winter, but river surfing in November?

'Hallo, Manfred!' Tom called to his friend from behind me.

'Hey!' our friend cried, waving back at us. 'Wie geht's?'

Wie geht's, I mumbled to myself as I made my way through the crowd and down the icy path to the banks below. *Wie geht's* he asks, like everything's normal and he isn't about to jump to his own death in the freezing water.

'Where are you going?' Tom shouted after me.

'To take photos!' I shouted back. 'If I'm going to write home about this, I need proof.'

I was still taking photos of Manfred surfing the wave when my mobile phone rang.

'It's not good, darls,' my sister said from London.

Turning away from the noise of the wave and the crowd, I walked up the snowy bank through the trees until I could hear Georgina clearly.

'He was up all night throwing up. Can't walk in a straight line to save himself, his speech is slurred and getting worse, and if I didn't know our father better, I'd say he was blind drunk. We called an ambulance this morning and went with him to Charing Cross Hospital. They've got him on a saline drip awaiting a complete evaluation. Rox and Max are by his side, say he's doing fine, but I think we can safely say Malta's off.'

I'd forgotten our parents were due to fly out to Malta the following day. For a moment my sister and I said nothing, but listened to each other sniff.

'If this is a middle ear infection, Merridy—' we waited for an Ealing Broadway train to finish thundering past her wall '—I'll eat my arse.'

Although bad news, George's update at least gave me the green light to take the action I so badly wanted to, and within an hour Tom had booked Henry and me on a flight to London the very next morning. Tom would follow a few days later, after he'd put in an appearance with his family at Marquartstein. George was so thrilled when I rang with the good news, we nearly forgot we still had one small problem.

'Jesus, darl. Where the hell am I going to put you all?'

Max didn't have enough room to swing a cat in his bedsit around the corner, and Georgina's sofa bed was already taken by our mother. My sister lived in one of those tall, narrow, four-storey Edwardian houses with each room accessible only via the central staircase, prompting my mother to call it 'the lighthouse'. It wasn't uncommon for my parents to wake up in George's living room every morning as the 5.36 to Epping shook them out of bed, only to stand in the doorway and have a senior moment.

'Where's the kitchen, up or down?'

'Not sure, but the bathroom's two up, isn't it?'

'Darls!' my sister cried down the phone the following morning as we sped along the Autobahn to the airport for our eight o'clock flight. 'You're not going to believe this! Do you remember mad Jocelyn? Prince Valiant haircut Jocelyn? Barking BBC foreign affairs correspondent Jocelyn who lives in the basement flat next door to me? Yes you do! One bung eye, bit of a tick, always depressed? Well, I thought she was in Baghdad, so rang her on her mobile and bugger me if she isn't in the Ukraine covering the latest elections! I asked her if the three of you might be able to camp at her place for the next couple of weeks while she's gone, family emergency and all that. And do you know what the dear old bung-eyed thing said? She said yes! Said it's a bit of a mess, wasn't expecting visitors from Germany and all that, but just shove her things to the side and make yourselves at home!'

'What do you mean you can't get in?' my sister asked a few hours later, throwing her heavy handbag onto the driver's seat in the middle of Heathrow car park.

The stress of finding us all accommodation, preparing a story on the growth of Tescos in Ireland and looking after a seriously ill father was clearly catching up with her.

'Can't you just hold him in your lap?'

'No!' I cried, more angry with myself for having forgotten to bring our baby capsule to London.

'What about we just put a belt on him?' Max suggested cheerfully from the other side of the car.

George and I scowled at our younger brother until he stopped smiling.

'Look at him!' I snapped, raising Henry's little body in my arms. 'He can't even sit up yet!'

I gathered by his bowed head and shaking shoulders that Max found the image of Henry flopping about in a loose safety belt terribly amusing.

'But, darls,' continued my sister through gritted teeth, 'can't you just hold him in your lap and have the belt around *both* of you?'

'No, *darls,* it's illegal. He's supposed to lie in a Maxi-Cosi!'

'A maxi-*what*?'

'A Maxi-Cosi! The legal safety restraint for babies the world over. And you haven't got one!'

'Well, of course I haven't bloody got one!' my sister shouted back at me. 'What would I put in it? A pineapple?'

My sister and I glared at each other across the roof of her Nissan Blue Fairy, ignoring the uncontrolled snorts from our brother, now bent over double in hysterics.

Just before midday, having forced the stiff door to Jocelyn's basement flat open, Georgina and I followed our intrepid brother, who crept down the dark corridor like Harrison Ford in *Raiders of the Lost Ark*.

'Did you know,' George whispered from behind, 'in all these years I've never been down here?'

We stopped at the doorway to what looked like a dark cave on our left.

'I'm going in,' I said, handing my brother his babbling nephew.

Once I'd pulled Jocelyn's heavy curtains aside, we all gasped. In the middle of her bedroom, a mountain of sheets, towels and clothing was piled on top of an unmade bed. Next to the bed a crate with an exotic looking scarf draped over it supported a hefty reading list including *Pity the Nation, The Israel-Hezbollah War, The Clash of Fundamentalisms* and, somewhat disappointingly, *The Da Vinci Code.* Laid out on the floor was a well read newspaper pinned down by a bowl of pistachio shells and a small pile of dried orange peel. Despite orange juice stains, I recognised the new president of the Republic of Ukraine straight away, one picture taken before his handsome face was ravaged by dioxin poisoning, and the other afterwards. This theme of toxic damage continued as my eyes travelled over the messy desk in front of me where, among all the bills, newspaper clippings and scattered BBC access passes for Prince Valiant, sat a mug of something that may once have been tea, or soup, but was now growing.

'Fuckity-fuck,' Georgina's voice echoed from another room.

Following the sound, Max and I made our way down the narrow passage until we found ourselves in a living room furnished with nothing but two miniature beige couches, a coffee table and a television. On top of the coffee table were two half-empty pizza boxes, and on top of the television sat a wastepaper basket full of rubbish.

'Perhaps she was just about to do some vacuuming when she got the call from the Ukraine,' my brother suggested.

'Or perhaps she was about to do some vacuuming when she remembered she didn't own a vacuum cleaner.'

'Shall I put the little fella down here?' Max asked.

'No!' I snapped. 'Don't put him down anywhere!'

We looked around for our sister.

'Where are you, darls?'

'I think I'm in the bathroom,' said a small voice right behind us.

Gingerly peeking over our sister's shoulders, Max and I looked at Jocelyn's bonsai bathroom. Damp towels hung from every hook, door, and rail, or else lay crumpled on the wet floor, possibly left there since she'd covered the fall of the Berlin Wall.

'Nagasaki,' Max sighed.

Every square inch of surface space around the tiny bathtub was crammed with empty shampoo bottles, squeezed toothpaste tubes, open face creams, moisturisers, dried out mascaras, broken lipsticks and my favourite, used tissues. I'd just spotted it in the corner when my sister, like a special commando seeing an unexploded land mine, leapt forward and flushed it.

'Good decision.'

'Just in case.'

'Absolutely.'

Suffice to say the kitchen next door to the bathroom was no happy ending. The three of us crept in with our noses twitching until we discovered, under the bench to our left, a dishwasher full of dirty dishes. The bench opposite was covered with various half-eaten meals. The oven and the fridge beyond were in need of industrial cleaners, and there was a nasty surprise waiting for us in the microwave.

'What can I tell you, darls?' my sister sighed, having discovered a washing machine full of fetid towels. 'The old girl's covered a lot of war zones these past few years.'

But our brother had a better explanation for Jocelyn's bombsite: 'You don't think she's been broken into, do you?'

For a moment the three of us cheered up at the possibility. It was so much less disturbing to imagine criminals had done this to Jocelyn's flat rather than Jocelyn herself. But this theory only made sense if the offenders had stayed long enough to order pizzas, read *The Guardian,* have a shower and help themselves to a wide variety of skincare products.

Needless to say, it was a fraught drive to the hospital, not only because Henry screamed the entire way, but also because my sister, now running late for work, drove like a maniac. Even when she wasn't running late, George drove like a maniac. Having survived twenty years living in central London with a demanding job and a busy social life, George had lost all tolerance for obstacles and respect for rules. 'Oh bugger this!' she'd say at a red light before suddenly swinging into a left exit. 'Oh bollocks to that!' she'd yell at the sight of a delivery van parked in an alley, before putting her foot to the floor and throwing her car into reverse. I'd held on to the ceiling as we'd mounted median strips, driven up on footpaths, across paddocks, and gone the wrong way up one-way streets. But most distressing was George's ability to do all these things while talking on her mobile phone: 'Suze! You're back from Corfu! Did you hear about Felicity's wedding? Disaster. Who knew Nigel was allergic to horses?'

Having parked right on Fulham Palace Road, I followed my sister and brother into Charing Cross Hospital's vast beech and glass entrance, past its chemist, café, telephone/internet area and florist shop, until I stopped in my tracks to show Henry one of the largest tropical fish tanks I'd ever seen.

'Saw a dead one in there yesterday, didn't we, Max?' my sister called over her shoulder as she clacked ahead in her stiletto heels.

Leaving the fish behind, I joined my siblings around the corner where we waited with a large group of nurses in front of three ancient looking lifts. I had to stop myself from staring, but you just didn't get this many Kenyan, Indian, West Indian or possibly Mongolian nurses waiting for a lift back in Munich. And you didn't have to wait this long for the lift either.

'Yeah,' my brother groaned, reading my mind. 'You wouldn't want to be dying for medical attention down here, would you?'

No television location scout would have chosen the men's ward on the first floor of Charing Cross Hospital for a sexy new series about young doctors. No shiny surfaces and white light bouncing from wall to chiselled cheekbone here, I thought as we marched through the dull yellowish corridors with their bumpy walls, high ceilings and fluorescent lights. Nor would any wardrobe department have dressed their extras in the array of moth-eaten, faded tartan dressing gowns that shuffled past, some of them attached to mobile saline stands.

'Oh lord!' I cried, stopping in the doorway of a communal bathroom.

In the middle of the room, lit by a lonely light bulb hanging from the ceiling, stood a bathtub with Victorian looking pipes and taps. All that was missing was the guy from the Michael Leunig cartoons. Gently touching my arm, my brother informed me that this was where he'd helped our father shower twice in the last two days. I looked at him, and Max smiled.

'Yeah, darls. Me and the old man have become intimately reacquainted this holiday.'

I spotted them as soon as we entered the ward, a picture of unity in the far corner by the windows. Slightly stooped with scoliosis, our mother stood at the side of our father's bed with her arm around him. She looked like a small bird with a protective wing around a catatonic chicken in striped pyjamas.

I prepared myself for heartbreak. George had already warned me that as this mystery illness had swiftly progressed, so had our father's personality retreated. They'd asked the doctors all the usual questions except the less medical one: *Where has he gone?* I was grateful for the warning. For the first time in my life, my father didn't acknowledge me, my brother or my sister as we touched his arm and kissed his forehead. Instead, he slowly held out his arms for Henry, as if someone had finally brought him the only thing he really wanted. For some minutes we stood around the bed, all together for the first time in over twenty years, as my father sang a quiet ditty to his grandson about a 'tiny king'. I glanced up at my exhausted mother still standing by his side, my eyes full of tears.

'Don't be sad, Honeybee,' she whispered. 'He hasn't smiled like this for days.'

Doing shifts at Charing Cross

Every morning at eight-thirty, long after Georgina had left for work at the BBC, my seventy-eight year old mother began her journey on foot from Shepherds Bush to Charing Cross Hospital. Despite the smog and noise of heavy London traffic, Rox insisted the half-hour exercise did her good. All morning she'd sit by her husband's side, chatting about anything, trying to stir him from his apathy. When visitors had to leave the hospital in the middle of the day, she'd go to the pizzeria across the road, have some lunch, chat to the waitresses and write Christmas cards to all her friends back home, before returning to her post until well after dark. Although it couldn't have been easy sitting for so many hours in a bedside chair that didn't support her curved spine, Rox never complained. Nor did she express any sorrow that her normally affectionate, chatty husband now barely spoke to her.

'Where are you, Bug?' she'd sometimes ask, stroking his cheek as he stared at the wall.

Preferring to go by train, I'd set off in the late morning, Henry in the baby sling, a backpack full of nappies, and cross the road to Shepherds Bush station. After so many months of quiet, well behaved Germans and their tidy U-Bahn, I found the grime, noise and chaos of London's underground tube exhilarating—so much so that I even forgot about the wonderful *Mutterzentrum* I'd recently discovered back in Schwabing that would be waiting for me when we returned. Feeling ridiculously happy for someone whose father was seriously ill, I'd sit among the late morning commuters with their turbans, saris, hoods, suits, piercings, mohawks, tattoos and beanies and read the front pages of their newspapers. According to the *Daily Mirror* and the *Sun*, the two leading stories of the day concerned the 'MRSA', whoever they were, and a young British celebrity whose new breasts were now each bigger than her own head.

Arriving at the hospital, I'd find my parents in the same repose, my father looking despondent and my mother by his side, holding his hand. Having settled Henry on Dad's lap, I'd say hello to Hamish, the Irish bookie two beds away, and to Charlie, from the western Caribbean, in the bed opposite, always reading his bible. Georgina arrived as soon as she could get away from 'the Beeb' and, being a freelance actor and teacher, Max visited whenever his unpredictable schedule permitted. Some afternoons, having travelled from Bristle on Tule, or Wattle on Iffy, Max would arrive at the hospital looking like he needed a bed himself.

And then there was Tom. Just a few days after I'd kissed him goodbye, like a breath of fresh Bavarian air Tom arrived with the Maxi-Cosi. Although he coped admirably with Jocelyn's little bombsite downstairs, and even looked at home sitting on the tube between a half-eaten Big Mac and a woman wearing a yellow helmet and rubbish bags on her feet, it was Charing Cross Hospital with its unbelievably slow lifts, yellow walls and the smell of hospital food that Tom found the most challenging. But if Henry was the only one who could make our father smile, Tom was the only one who could make him sit up straight.

'Quick!' Dad would whisper at the sight of his son-in-law coming round the corner. 'It's the hydration Gestapo. Pour us a bloody drink, will you?'

Perhaps he was thinking of the previous European summer in which nearly ten thousand elderly people had perished in a heatwave across France, but Tom made it his mission to pour as much water down our father's throat as possible.

'Drink up, Wal,' he'd say, filling Dad's cup again. 'The important thing is to keep hydrated, ok?'

'Thanks, Tom. Very kind of you.'

He even marked the water level on the bottles to check how much Dad was drinking.

'Don't worry about your bladder, Wal. The walk to the toilet will do you good.'

'Thanks, Tom. Cheers.'

But as soon as we caught sight of Dr Chetlapalli and his entourage coming round the corner for their daily examination, Tom would swiftly scoop Henry up in his arms and head downstairs for the fish tank, while my mother would rise into a half-curtsy.

'And what are we doing for Mr Eastman?' Dr Chetlapalli would ask his students standing around the bed.

'Isn't he heavenly?' my mother would whisper.

I hadn't seen Rox like this since her crush on Don Dunstan. Back in the seventies, at the sound of the silver haired politician's mellifluous voice from our old black and white television set, there'd be a crash of pots and cutlery from the kitchen followed by the patter of running feet until we looked up to see our breathless mother standing in the doorway clutching a meat hammer, commanding total silence so she could catch every syllable that came out of the South Australian premier's mouth. Likewise, if some butter-fingered nurse at the end of the ward dropped a bedpan or a visitor sneezed while Dr Chetlapalli was talking, Rox would hiss at them like an angry python. Once, when my sister's mobile phone interrupted his examination with Tom Jones' 'It's Not Unusual', Rox threatened to toss it out the window.

It was Dr Chetlapalli's fifth visit in as many days. Tom had again taken Henry downstairs to see the fish, and my mother was having palpitations by the window.

'And what are we doing for Mr Eastman?' the doctor asked his entourage as usual.

'We're having doubts about the labyrinthitis diagnosis,' piped the brave young woman next to me. 'The patient is having trouble with language,' she continued, 'which could indicate aphasia.'

We all looked at her.

'Plus a loss of balance and coordination,' said the spotty young man standing next to my mother, 'indicating ataxia.'

We all looked at him.

'A penny for your thoughts, Dr Varkesh?' Dr Chetlapalli asked the tall man standing next to my father.

We all stared at Dr Varkesh, waiting to hear what aphasia and ataxia meant.

'I think we should now consider the possibility that Mr Eastman's had a stroke.'

Just at this critical moment in our father's diagnosis a mighty hullabaloo broke out in the corridor. A second later, two very stressed looking nurses entered pushing a trolley on which an angry geriatric sat up swinging his bony arms at imaginary windmills, spewing abuse at all and sundry. At least it sounded like abuse. The language was indecipherable.

'Oh Christ no,' my mother groaned as they parked Gollum in the bed next to Dad's, stuck a cannula in his arm, hooked him up to an intravenous drip and left.

'Tileorasi!' he yelled after them.

'Quiet!' Dr Chetlapalli roared.

The creature instantly pulled his sheets up to his nose, and while his wild eyes explored the walls and the ceiling we took a moment to study him. Nothing conveys mental instability quite like patchy hair stubble and missing teeth, but the resemblance was uncanny, and later we all agreed: if he hadn't died in Paris just a few days earlier, we would have sworn Dad's new neighbour, minus his trademark *keffiyeh*, was Yasser Arafat.

Long after Dr Chetlapalli and his students left, and Yasser had gone into a catatonic state, we sat contemplating all the things the deep-voiced Indian doctor had told us, until Rox whacked our groggy father in the arm.

'There you go, Bug,' she said. 'We'll know for sure after your MRI scan tomorrow, but it sounds like you've had a stroke. And Dr Chetlapalli says that's why you're all depressed.'

With a weary sigh, our father slowly turned to look at her.

'So shut up,' Rox concluded.

Even Yasser woke up from his vegetative state to join us for a laugh, until he pointed to the chair at the end of his bed and yelled at it.

'BGAINO EXO!'

Max and Dad often bought each other books from the humour section, especially if they had the word 'worst' in the title. Whether it was wedding speeches or Victorian inventions, they loved to read out loud to each other until they were both crying with laughter. And never did our father need a good laugh more than after his MRI scan. Having to lie absolutely still deep inside an enormous magnetic resonance imaging scanner had not been the most enjoyable way for a seventy-eight year old claustrophobic recovering from a stroke to pass half an hour. But at least we now knew that the part of Dad's cerebellum most affected by his stroke controlled balance and appetite, and not memory or movement. Or laughter by the look of it. Although it was wonderful to see our father wiping away tears as Max read from Tony Robinson's *The Worst Jobs in History,* when he got up to

Henry VIII's 'Groomer of the Stool' we made Max put it away, in case it actually killed him.

But Dad wasn't the only one in need of a laugh. Having been kept awake all week by mad Yasser's sporadic explosions of rage, the entire ward was close to mutiny. Even Charlie in his bed opposite looked like he wanted to clock someone with his bible.

'Fucking Cypriotic nutcase,' growled Hamish the bookie, peering over his racing guide.

Not only did we now know Yasser came from Cyprus, but he seemed to believe himself commander of an invisible Greek army sent to invade Turkey sometimes, unfortunately, at four in the morning.

It was early evening, and before we all headed off to Genie's Bar in Holland Park to celebrate Georgina's birthday, Rox thought it would cheer our father up if he could see us all in our finery.

'Just fetch a couple of Yasser's chairs, will you, Max?' she asked my brother. 'He won't mind, he thinks they're Turks.'

Although we finally arranged ourselves in a glittering line around him, our father only had eyes for the 'tiny king' babbling in his lap.

'Pass us the water, will you, Rox?' my sister said, breaking our silence.

After scrutinising various objects on our dad's bedside table, Rox passed Georgina her mobile phone.

'I said *water*!'

'Oh! I thought you said *portable*.'

Portable?

'Well, don't you call them portables?'

'No!' we all shouted at her.

'But they're portable phones, aren't they?'

We were still laughing when an officious nurse pushed her way into our circle and reeled at the sight of Henry on my father's lap.

'Who's baby is this?'

Ours, I told her, terrified she'd seen Tom and me changing his nappy on the bed.

'How old is he?' she demanded.

About nine weeks.

'*Nine weeks?* Don't you people watch the news?'

We stared at her blankly.

'Haven't you heard of MRSA?'

MRSA. The initials on the front page of the newspapers I'd seen on the tube. The initials for some anti-terrorist taskforce that sat in plain clothes on Boeing aircrafts waiting to hurl themselves at anyone caught trying to light his shoe, so I'd thought.

'MRSA is a virulent and deadly super bug currently found in large hospitals,' she snapped at me, 'including this one. It's been on the news for weeks.'

I glared at my sister, a BBC journalist who sometimes appeared on the evening news.

'Don't look at me!' George protested. 'I'm in finance! Unless you can float super bugs on the stock exchange they mean bugger all to me!'

'Babies have to be at least six months old before entering a hospital ward like this,' she continued. 'There's no way at nine weeks he's got the immunity to fight a super bug. Take him out of here at once.'

Before she could say *Staphylococcus aureus* bacteria, Tom and I were stuffing our things into my backpack.

'Do you know where Genie's Bar is?' Georgina asked as we hurriedly kissed my bewildered father goodbye.

'No, but I'll call you!' I said, scooping Henry up in my arms before he developed lesions. 'I'll call you on the portable!'

A birthday celebration at Genie's cosy wine bar in Holland Park was exactly what we all needed. Even Rox thoroughly enjoyed herself, entertaining BBC journalists and the occasional banker. Given we had a small baby with us, Tom and I couldn't stay very long, but Max and I were glad to see our sister receiving gifts, compliments, and all the attention she deserved. Not only had Georgina fed and accommodated us all throughout this crisis, but being the only one in our family both willing and able to deal with the enormous amount of paperwork to be done, she'd often stayed up to negotiate with bureaucrats on the other side of the planet.

'It's Georgina again, Tiffany, calling from London at two in the morning. I'm very well, and you? How wonderful to hear, and did you get the neurological report I faxed stating my father's stroke was not a pre-existing condition and therefore the MRI scan *is* in fact covered by his travel insurance? Terrific. Otherwise he has to pay over one thousand pounds, Tiffany, and that's not really a good result considering how much your company's taken out of his bank account over the last forty years, is it?'

And once Georgina had conquered their medical insurance company, she took on their airline.

'It's Georgina again, Craig, calling from London at four in the morning. Oh, I have to go to work in an hour but apart from that I'm excellent. Yourself? Well, happy birthday to you. Now, about upgrading these return tickets from economy to business. Yes, so you said last time, Craig, but I've got a letter here signed by two neurologists and a GP who beg to differ.'

It was our father's twentieth day in Charing Cross Hospital when Dr Chetlapalli announced he had good news and bad. The bad news was that our father wasn't allowed to fly anywhere for at least another six weeks. But the good news was that he was well enough to be released, and spend Christmas at home. After three weeks of tests, nutters and staring at the wall, nothing could have made Dad happier. From his daughter's lighthouse in Shepherds Bush, he could continue his recuperation in the best way possible, Dr Chetlapalli said, surrounded by his family.

From the minute we sat our father down on Georgina's sofa bed, the pink returned to his cheeks, his appetite came back and, best of all, he discovered his favourite television station.

'And you didn't even know you had the History Channel!' Dad cried, as if he'd unblocked Georgina's sink.

Soon my sister's house shook with the sound of Mustangs, Spitfires and air raid sirens. No meal or conversation could take place without the accompanying soundtrack of panzer tanks or newsreel footage of bombs exploding, until George called an emergency meeting in the kitchen. While Germany invaded Poland for the third time in as many days, it was agreed that in the interests of our father's ongoing recovery, and everyone else's sanity, there should be less indoor television and more outdoor family walks. Cutting Neville Chamberlain off mid speech, Georgina presented Dad with some new rules, and his Nikes.

'Oh, isn't it heavenly,' Rox sighed a minute later, floating down the stairs to the front door, 'when you turn that bloody war off . . .'

Christmas Day was a day none of us would forget. Surrounded by flowers from her favourite florist in Chelsea, coloured Christmas lamps and candles, we sat at my sister's round dinner table and enjoyed a sumptuous turkey from Lidgates with wine from Australia. Although my father's gaze would occasionally settle for long spells on a spoon, a crumb or a leaf, he was becoming easier to distract from such reveries, and occasionally even led the conversation like he used to.

And as everyone prepared for our afternoon stroll up to Holland Park Gardens, knowing what awaited me back in Bavaria, I soaked up the cacophony of my wonderfully loud family. While my mother accidentally pulled out Georgina's entire cutlery drawer in the kitchen below, and my brother sang Scottish ditties to a mesmerised Henry, my sister ran upstairs in search of something to hold our father's fleecies up. Henry's pram might have proven the ideal walking frame, providing Dad with excellent support as well as a view of his grandson, but it also meant his hands weren't free to deal with any sudden wardrobe malfunctions.

'Just because you've lost ten kilos in five weeks,' Georgina muttered, tying her gold Gucci belt around Dad's waist on her return, 'doesn't mean we have to have another Blythe Road incident.'

The Blythe Road incident is one our family agreed to keep in the vault. Suffice to say, it happened at approximately 2 pm on Christmas Eve, we were returning from Holland Park Gardens, no one was ready for it, and we were in Blythe Road.

•

But the next morning we sat around the television set in numb silence. While we'd all slept peacefully in our beds and sofa beds, somewhere just off the west coast of Sumatra the plates of the earth's crust had shifted, displacing hundreds of cubic kilometres of water and sending powerful tsunamis towards coastlines bordering the Indian Ocean. A BBC seismologist described how some fishermen far out at sea possibly felt nothing more sinister than a small wave pass under their boats, but that this wave was so many miles long and was travelling at such ferocious speed along the ocean bed that by landfall it would have been a powerful, destructive and unstoppable force of nature. One tourist described looking out her beach resort window to see the sea being sucked out almost to the horizon, leaving curious bathers and even fish flipping on the wet sand, as if someone had pulled the plug out of a bath. Instead of running to higher ground, families had even collected on the shore below, she said, wondering where the water had gone.

Glued to my sister's television, we went from breakfast to morning tea, from lunch to dinner, as bulletins came in from various coastal towns and villages in Indonesia, Malaysia, Thailand, Myanmar, Sri Lanka, India and the Maldives. Even as far away as Somalia, one reporter said, villages had been swept away, fishermen carried out to sea, and swimmers lost. I finally remembered where I'd heard of Banda Aceh, the city on the northern tip of Indonesia, worst hit by the tsunami. It was the town where Rutana's twin sister lived—Rutana, my funny Indonesian beautician back in Munich.

Over the next few days, while the death toll rose from 12,000 to 77,000 amid forecasts of possibly three times that many, my sister's living room transformed from my father's Second World War museum into a tsunami crisis information centre. And then of course there were the survivor stories that we both dreaded and craved. Distraught mothers described not being able to hold on to their children or partners. Hand-held video cameras meant to record summer holidays caught instead terrifying scenes of wild rivers demolishing hotel foyers. Others recorded waves crashing through resorts carrying beach umbrellas, trees and cars. News reports kept showing a white haired man up to his neck in water clinging desperately to a tree trunk, looking helpless and confused as debris sailed past him. Further inland, bodies lay in now drained streets or else floated among reeds in flooded fields. News crews filmed bewildered tourists among distraught villagers, some of them children, searching for their families among makeshift morgues outside overcrowded hospitals. Over the last four weeks we'd nearly lost our father, but in Sri Lanka, a man and his wife waded through knee deep water, each carrying a lifeless child in their arms.

'Where are you going?' I asked Dad, who for the first time in weeks had struggled to his feet without assistance.

'I'm gonna make us all a bloody cuppa tea.'

He who must pay for sex

Having returned to find Munich under three feet of snow, Tom and I agreed to celebrate New Year's Eve quietly at home, and in the German tradition. Around 9 pm therefore, along with half the country, we turned on the television to watch *Dinner for One*, an old British film that had proved so popular when it was first screened in Germany back in 1963, it's been shown every New Year since. In this sketch comedy peformed by two elderly British actors, an aristocratic dowager called Miss Sophie hosts her annual birthday dinner, and is waited upon by her equally ancient manservant James. Having outlived all their usual guests, however, James must now drink the many birthday toasts to Miss Sophie for them, an undertaking that becomes increasingly problematic as they alcohol takes effect, with hilarious consequences.

Once the film was over, Tom and I decided to watch the fireworks from Henry's window, in case the noise woke him. In Germany most people celebrate New Year's Eve by stepping out onto their street at midnight, and lighting fireworks with the friends and family. But the strangest tradition I heard concerning this festive season was the one I discovered a few mornings later.

Usually, when someone rang the bell at our front gate, Tom dropped whatever he was doing and bounded to the window to see who it was. But this cold January morning, he remained mysteriously absent.

'I can't get it!' I called out a second time from our sofa. 'I'm feeding Henry!'

Finally, having lain our sleeping boy down in his cot, I went to deal with this persistent bell-ringer myself. I'd just walked into the kitchen when a voice hissed at me from behind, making me jump three feet in the air.

'GET DOWN!'

I turned to see my tall, athletic husband cowering next to our fridge. Who was he hiding from? I asked. Were we in some kind of trouble? Had we brought MRSA back into the country with us?

'It's the rubbish man,' Tom whispered.

Creeping up behind our toaster, I peeped out the window.

'Don't let him see you!' Tom hissed.

But it was too late. A plump man dressed in a fluorescent orange and yellow uniform with a matching cap stood in the snow at our front gate looking directly at our window. Oh no. Had they discovered poor Pavel's frozen body in the Feldmann's garage?

'Every Christmas the rubbish men go door to door collecting their Christmas tip,' Tom growled, 'and if they don't catch you at home, they keep coming back until they do.'

But demanding a tip to the point of harassment somewhat missed the whole point of Christmas spirit, did it not? Back home such offerings were optional. Mum always left a few bottles of beer on the top step for our rubbish men, but if she forgot there'd be no need to hide in the kitchen for the rest of the holidays.

'I'll tell him to go away,' I said, going to open the window.

'NO!' Tom shouted. 'If you don't give them what they want, they can make you *very* sorry.'

Suddenly we were in an episode of *The Sopranos*. How?

Well, if the alternative was to be left with huge piles of rotting rubbish in our driveway, why not just give the man a fiver? I whispered.

'A fiver? A house this size? We'd be lucky if they emptied the recycling bin!'

Couldn't the Müllers downstairs and dear Gretchen upstairs to put in for it as well?

'What do you think they're doing right now?' Tom asked.

Just at that moment, directly above my head, Gretchen's floorboards creaked. Quietly amused by the image of Germans hiding from their aggressive rubbish men, pretending they were still holidaying on the North Sea, I left Tom crouched in our kitchen, and returned to my book.

'Oh, it was gorgeous!' my mother cried down the phone from Hobart. 'Like flying in the Hilton, and all thanks to your extra-ordinary sister.'

In one breath, Rox told me about their luxurious business class trip home, their happy reunion with Ella the dog who was now as big as a camel, the new 'bridle' called a 'halti' they'd bought for her, how my father had already reviewed two musicals since landing, how wonderful everyone said he looked, and finally how busy she was preparing for her French conversation class, her German for beginners course, the Hamilton Literary Society and their book club meeting this Friday.

'But never mind thirteenth century Flemish feminist poets, Honeybee, how are you?'

We were all fine, I told her, but Munich was in mourning.

'Over the tsunami?' my father asked.

No, over Moshammer.

A pause.

'Is that a volcano?'

No, I told them, Moshammer was not a volcano. 'You remember the local celebrity fashion designer I told you about? The old guy who dresses up as Ludwig II, wears make-up and a big black wig and owns a fancy tie shop down in Maximilianstrasse?'

Another pause.

'The one who was rude to me when I went into his shop wearing maternity leisure pants?'

'Oh *him*?' snapped my mother, furious all over again.

But before she could speak ill of the dead, I quickly told both my parents that Tom and I had been woken up this cold January morning to a phone call from a breathless Tante Ilsa, telling us that Moshammer had been found murdered on the floor of his mansion with a telephone cable around his neck.

'Oh dear . . .'

According to the news, Moshammer was last seen the night before driving his Rolls Royce very slowly around Hauptbahnhof, until he stopped at some traffic lights to chat to a young man who then climbed inside.

'Oh dear . . .'

Moshammer had only recently told a journalist, *Wer für Sex bezahlen müsse, der ist am Ende,* which meant, 'For him who has to pay for sex—it's over.'

'Sadly prophetic, wouldn't you say?'

I listened to the sound of my parents breathing.

'Was he a homosexual, love?' my father finally asked.

'Well, of course he's a homosexual!' Rox cried. 'Haven't you been listening? The fellow went around impersonating a gay king, for God's sake. Even wore a wig and carried a small dog!'

'Well, Churchill had a poodle and he wasn't gay!'

'Yes, but he didn't *carry* it everywhere, did he?'

'Queen Victoria carried a dachshund, does that make her a lesbian?'

'God no! She didn't even think lesbians existed, remember? Poor, unimaginative dimwit . . .'

Having finally established that a man, with or without a small dog, who drove slowly around train stations late at night most probably wasn't picking up dry cleaning, my parents went into another thoughtful silence.

'You know who he sounds like?' my father said at last. 'That poor wretch from *Death in Venice*.'

My mother agreed. My descriptions of Moshammer were indeed reminiscent of Thomas Mann's desperate and aging Baron von Aschenbach with his dyed black hair and rouged cheeks, being rowed along the Venetian canals in hopeless search of the beautiful youth and object of his desire, Tadziu. Well, that's funny, I told them. Moshammer had called his boutique Carnival de Venise.

'Oh, Honeybee,' Rox sighed. 'You can almost hear Mahler's Fifth swelling in the background.'

At midday on Sunday, two days after Andreas the chauffeur had found his master lying dead on the floor outside his grand bedroom, the television stations paused in their nonstop tributes for a special news conference. It was good to hear they'd already made an arrest. I'd had enough of headlines like *Nur Daisy kennt den Täter—Kann sie ihn überführen?* ('Only Daisy Knows the Murderer—Can she convict him?') The twenty-five year old Iraqi asylum seeker had even confessed that he and Moshammer had fought over payment of two thousand euros for sexual favours.

'Two thousand euros?' I cried.

Tom scoffed. 'What would *you* know?'

What would I know? I pointed to my book on our top shelf, a book I'd written about my year's experience working in a Sydney brothel and escort agency (as the receptionist).

'Even Genevieve didn't earn that much money for a three hour booking at the Westin!'

But Tom shooshed me so we could hear the final statement of the live broadcast. To answer the thousands of calls coming in from all over Germany, Bavaria's Chief of Police said with great solemnity that Daisy the dog was doing fine and was being looked after by the chauffeur.

Perhaps he'd caught it from me, but the following Friday morning Henry seemed to be in a state of euphoria also, as we made our way through the sleet and the snow down Schellingstrasse. I don't know what I expected might have happened to our *Mutterzentrum* after so many weeks, but when we turned around Schraudolphstrasse to see all the *Kinderwagen* parked outside, I could have wept for joy. And entering the warm room full of familiar smells, sights and sounds of burnt coffee, tracksuit pants, and pure unrestrained enthusiasm, even before Rowena called out to me, I felt as if I'd come home.

'They say there's going to be a state funeral,' Dagmar said, as she passed around the biscuits. 'And it'll be televised, live.'

Had anyone else seen the piles of flowers, candles, cards and letters, Heidi asked, that spread from his famous boutique shop window, right across the footpath? 'It's like Princess Di all over again.'

'What about the headlines?' Jane cried. '*Schneewittchen! Wird Mosi im Gläs-Sagt Beigesetzt?*', meaning 'Snow White! Might Mosi's body really be carried in a glass coffin?'

'Or Daisy darf zur Beerdigung!' Lara added, referring to the headline rejoicing that the small dog would be attending her master's funeral after all.

But the one that summed up this city's infatuation with its favourite eccentric the most for me was '*Mosi starb in Lackschuhe!*' Who needed to know that the poor man had died wearing his patent leather shoes?

'I guess it's comforting,' Rowena explained, 'like the wig being in place too. The chauffeur said that would have been important to him.'

For a moment we all looked at our dribbling, panting, masticating offspring, crawling around the toys on the floor. With the headlines outside about dying with wigs in place and the attendance of dogs at funerals, our little ones helped us keep things in perspective.

Although I had the most dramatic news to share, having nearly lost my dear dad in London on his way home from meeting his grandson, life had not been dull for my new friends back here in Munich either. Due to the lack of bilingual kindergartens and childcare facilities in the area, they had decided to create their own, right here in Schwabing. They'd already formed an 'e.V', a registered association, voted for a *Vorstand* or board, opened a bank account, and had even found a potential location around the corner in Leopoldstrasse.

'Behind the Indian restaurant,' said Lara.

Although setting up a Parents Initiative Kindergarten in Germany was a notoriously complicated endeavour, Rowena said, full of bureaucratic hoops to jump through and a trail of failed attempts by other expat groups, 'We have a secret weapon.'

What?

'Hello!' said Christine, an attractive woman with mashed banana in her hair, baby vomit on her shoulder, and a vigorous handshake. 'I don't think we've met.'

Although she swore she was German, having worked for a law firm in London for several years Christine wouldn't have sounded out of place in the middle of *Brideshead Revisited*. But when she began talking about the legal procedures of starting a kindergarten in Germany, she sounded more like Rumpole of the Bailey, and I knew what Rowena meant by weapon.

'I've already spoken with the Kleinkindertagesstätten and Frau Schiermeyer from the Stadtjugendamt,' Christine told the others, handing Rowena a crying baby while she strapped her toddler into a highchair, 'and she said that due to the new law on funding applying to all Eltern-Kind Initiativen, we need both the Betriebserlaubnis and the Nutzungsänderung if we want to apply for funding from the Ministry. So I'll do that tomorrow.'

'You see?' said Heidi. 'We haven't got a clue what she's talking about, but isn't she fabulous?'

'Oh well,' laughed Christine, pulling the top off a jar of baby food, 'I don't quite know about that!'

I did. And I wanted to be a part of it too. Even if all I could do was make the tea.

'Good,' Christine said, grinning at me, 'we could do with a writer for the website.'

Excellent!

'And we need an urgent meeting to discuss the costings for the Vereinsgründung, the Rechtsanwalt, the Notargebühr für Anmeldungsschreiben für das Registergericht,' she yelled over the protests from her hungry child, 'the Anmietung von Leopoldstrasse, an Anzeige in Saturday's paper for other properties, the Kaution—'

I didn't know what was more impressive: Christine, or the others, who could understand her.

'—and of course, the Maklergebühren!' she concluded.

Yes indeed, the *Maklergebühren.* I'd bring a plate of those too.

The following day, while Tom hid in our kitchen from the garbage man below, I turned on the TV just in time to catch the stately cortege of a dozen black cars as they drove slowly down Maximilianstrasse. Heidi was right. It was like a Bavarian sequel to *Death of a Princess.* The grand street was lined with mourners, between ten and twenty thousand the commentator estimated, who'd braved the snow to come and say farewell. Escorted by a handsome band of soldiers dressed in red uniforms with blue and white feathers in their hats, the procession stopped outside Moshammer's famous shop for a few minutes' silence.

I sat on the couch feeding Henry, riveted to the theatrical scene played before the cameras for millions of German viewers. In a touching twist, someone else opened the passenger door of the Rolls Royce for Andreas the chauffeur who, having now acquired celebrity status of his own, stepped out clutching the famous little dog, today wearing a black bow in her hair instead of her usual pink ribbon. Waiting for both of them were some of Moshammer's closest celebrity friends, including Roberto Blanco, a sort of German/Tunisian version of Kamahl, and the three remaining Jacob Sisters. These stout, aging, Bavarian women never left home without their white miniature poodles, or their blond ringleted wigs to match. Today, however, they'd swapped their poodles for small bouquets of white lilies and red carnations. Although once famous for hits such as 'Adelbert the gnome', 'Heidi', and a refreshing cover of Bob Dylan's 'Blowing In Ze Vind', these days the Jacob Sisters were better known for their appearances on home shopping networks, and for their recent single, 'Hamsterdance'.

Moshammer's large mahogany coffin was finally laid to rest in his family's mausoleum at Ostfriedhof. I was fascinated by this famous cemetery just up the road from where we lived. Apart from being the final resting place for Tom's grandparents, it also housed the cremated remains of various Nazis convicted at Nuremburg, and was where Leni Riefenstahl had been buried too. Jane confessed to me that she'd accidentally discovered the latter when she used to live near Ostfriedhof herself. While walking home from the tram stop, she'd seen a group of neo-Nazi skinheads hanging around the cemetery entrance. Curious to know why, she wandered inside to investigate and ended up attending the funeral of the infamous Nazi propagandist and film maker, while holding a bag of bananas and a large salami.

Despite the inevitable revelations in the tabloids about his private life, Rudolph Moshammer's lavish funeral proved that the people of Munich chose to remember him not as a sex scandal, but fondly and respectfully as *ein gutes Mensch*. He may have been eccentric enough to leave his enormous mansion to his little dog Daisy, but he'd also stipulated that all the money raised from the sale of his boutique, cars, jewellery and other possessions go toward charities for the homeless. And he might have preferred that Australians wearing stretchy mauve pregnancy pants refrain from entering his elegant shop in Maximilianstrasse, but under the bridges of Munich where it really counted, Mosi had proven himself a compassionate, generous and active member of his community. And then there was simply the colour and theatrical glamour that he brought to this somewhat straight-laced Bavarian city. Having left a void no one else could possibly fill, Moshammer would be missed.

Nudity in Germany

Although I now knew Tom's Tuesday night volleyball team well, especially as Christian was Tom's accountant, Wolfgang his lawyer and Veit his urologist, a year after I'd arrived in Munich I still hadn't met their wives. But all that changed when we gathered for Veit's birthday party in the rather posh suburb of Soln. As Henry was now six months old, Tom and I travelled everywhere with his Maxi-Cosi and a large green backpack full of nappies, wipes and towels. Henry always drew a crowd, not just because he was a fairly gorgeous baby but because he seemed to genuinely love meeting people. The only time he hadn't done a little dance of happiness when greeted by a perfect stranger was at my sister's recent birthday drinks in London, when Henry met Vanessa.

Now a struggling actress in LA, Vanessa first met Georgina at drama school back in the eighties, and to say she'd had 'a bit of work done' was a bit like saying the Sistine Chapel ceiling had once had a lick of paint. Waving at our son with her French polished fingernails, Vanessa opened her blue eyes wide, peered into Henry's Maxi-Cosi and, with the parts of her face that still moved, smiled. For a moment Henry stopped babbling. Even his active little hands froze in the air as he took in the face in front of him before letting out a bloodcurdling scream, as if we'd delivered him to the gates of Luna Park.

'And are we women allowed to play volleyball too?' I asked Veit, the birthday boy, winking at the other volleyball wives gathered around our Maxi-Cosi.

'Of course,' Veit answered defensively. 'That is how Florian met Bertha.'

Following Veit's gaze, we all looked to the couch opposite where a large woman with wild hair sat breastfeeding.

'Bertha was the best player on our team until Flo married her,' Veit said, laughing.

Having given birth to three children in the last five years, Bertha didn't look like she was about to bound onto a court in runners any time soon. And to be honest, I knew that once Henry was asleep, it was all I could manage to pour myself a glass of wine and pick up the remote control, never mind leaping around a room yelling 'Aus!'

'And now we've got Isabella!' Veit declared triumphantly before skolling his beer. 'See? She's a woman!'

Isabella? I looked at the other wives. Isabella? Tom hadn't mentioned an Isabella.

Isabella was a friend of Detlef's sister, Veit explained, and had been playing with them for weeks now.

Really? I looked from Petra to Trudl to Ines. For weeks? How many weeks?

Petra leant in close. 'Some of us are hoping that she might pair up with Christian.'

We all looked over at Christian, whose wife had recently left him, now sitting in the corner patting the children's Labrador.

'They're the same age,' Ines added with a twinkle in her eye, 'and both accountants.'

Weeks passed, the days grew longer, every Friday I saw my friends at the *Mutterzentrum*, Henry was crawling and, unbelievably, Bertha was pregnant again. As the snow began to melt on the distant glassy Alps, new leaves appeared on the large chestnut trees in the *Biergarten*, while our own garden showed small signs of life with a bird here, a squirrel there, and even an occasional bud. As our now-mobile son had discovered every lethal thing up to thirty centimetres off the ground, safety locks had been purchased, power points had been sealed, and the fire poker had been placed somewhere Henry could never, ever find it again. When he was awake I showed him picture books, sang songs, explored our house and garden and took things out of his mouth, and when he slept I either pushed him in the pram along the Isar, or else wrote on my laptop at home. And while I continued finishing my second book, Tom continued building his digital printing business, occasionally looking in on his parents, and every Tuesday night he played volleyball.

It was our first beautiful spring day, and as I sat on our bed writing on my laptop I could hear Henry lying on his little rug next door making happy sounds from under his favourite animal mobile, while Tom sat at his computer at the dining table nearby, laughing his head off. Tom was the only man I knew whose laughter often turned to tears. Some of my favourite moments in our married life so far weren't of romantic dinners, but of both of us doubled over in the kitchen with Tom wiping tears from his face.

'What's so funny?' I called out.

'Another email from Detlef!' Tom cried, barely able to speak.

Detlef might have been one of Munich's most senior public prosecutors, not to mention incompetent volleyball players, but judging by the sniffing and high pitched giggling coming from the dinner table he'd once again scoured the web for the latest funny video and had pressed 'send'. This one, featuring a ferret, so tickled Tom he rang his friend immediately to congratulate him. Although I was proud that I could now understand fifty percent of Tom's telephone conversations, it could also be terribly distracting.

'Wirklich? Noch keine Antwort von Isabella? Kommt sie nicht mehr?'

For some weeks, apparently, Isabella had gone AWOL from volleyball. I tried to focus on the paragraph I was writing, but it was useless. Five games in a row Isabella had missed, and not answered one call, Tom said. It was a mystery. As the two men competed to come up with the funniest explanation for their female team mate's absence, I felt relieved I couldn't understand fluent German, until Tom said something I understood only too well.

'Sie darf mit uns dann nicht mehr duschen!'

I looked up from my screen. *She may with us then not more shower.* I took off my glasses. *Isabella may with us then not more shower?* I slid my computer off my lap. *With us?* Since when did my husband with another woman at all shower? And curse these Germans with their verbs always at the end of their sentences putting. Having left my work on the bed, I now stood in our bedroom doorway looking directly at Tom, who although still in paroxysms of laughter managed to wink at me.

'Ok, Detlef,' he wrapped up his call. 'Bis acht dann, ohne Isabella!'

'We were just saying,' Tom answered my question, wiping his eyes, 'that if Isabella keeps missing volleyball, we'll tell her she's not allowed to shower with us any more.'

I now found Tom's tears of laughter extremely irritating.

'You won't let her *shower* with you any more?'

Tom nodded. 'It will be her punishment.'

There must be so many ways for a man to confess to his wife he's been taking showers with another woman once a week, but to do so while laughing his head off, I felt sure, was not one of them.

'Normally she showers with you?' I asked. 'All *six* of you?'

Tom nodded.

'So when you've played volleyball in the school sports hall, you, Detlef, Wolfgang, Christian, Veit, Florian and Isabella, you take off all your clothes and take a *shower* together?'

Still smiling, Tom nodded.

'Why doesn't Isabella go to the *girls'* shower to shower?' I cried.

'Why would there be a *girls'* shower in a *boys'* school?' Tom shot back at me.

So did these boys' showers have cubicles at least?

Tom squinted as if to say 'What's a cubicle?' And then I remembered how shocked I was last summer when he'd taken me to the popular Nordbad swimming pool. As the ladies' showers had no dividing screens whatsoever between the showerheads, I had to bathe with five other women, including one young girl who stared at my pregnant stomach as if I'd swallowed her beachball.

'There are no cubicles,' Tom finally said.

I blinked at my husband. The next question would be tough, but I was going in.

'How many showerheads?'

Tom seemed to find the question amusing.

'Oh God,' I groaned. 'Don't tell me.'

For some reason Tom found my panic even funnier than one of Detlef's viral emails.

'Stop laughing!' I shouted.

He stopped.

'Six men and one woman,' I cried, 'under *one* showerhead?'

'We take turns to jump under!' my German husband protested. 'And it's *five* men, not six. Florian showers at home.'

I remembered the last time I'd seen Florian's wife, Bertha, now visibly pregnant, wrangling two active toddlers and a baby. It made sense. The woman could crush a man's skull between her knees.

'I couldn't do it,' Tom confessed.

Couldn't do what exactly? Couldn't join in? Couldn't be unfaithful? Couldn't have sex in front of his urologist?

'I couldn't get in the car all hot and sweaty after volleyball and drive all the way to Starnbergersee without a shower.'

Clearly.

Over the next few days I made discreet, urgent phone calls to women all over the world.

'Question for you,' I said to Lee, who was just beginning her dawn workout on her StepMaster in Manly. 'One evening a week your husband plays volleyball with five guys down the road at the local boys' school, and once a week they all shower together, and I mean together, in the one and only shower.'

'Go on,' Lee panted, already intrigued.

'A seventh member joins the team. Goes by the name of Isabella. That's right. *Isabella.* Tall chap with breasts.'

There was a long hissing sound as Lee's StepMaster began its descent.

'Guess where Isabella showers when the game's over?' I asked my friend.

The StepMaster finally came to a stop.

'Oh no . . .' Lee groaned.

'Can you believe it?'

'They shower together—with *a transsexual*?'

'Not a transsexual!' I shouted down the phone to Sydney. 'Isabella's a woman!'

'Oh God, that's even worse!'

'Tom says in Germany this is quite normal!' I babbled to my lifeline. 'He says they're not as hung up about nudity in Europe as we are in Australia, in the UK, and that Americans are the worst. He says over here it's considered healthy and natural to be naked, especially in the context of sports or bathing.'

'Oh, that's a good one. And I suppose orgies open the sinuses.'

'He says they're even less prudish about bathing together in Sweden, and don't even ask about Finland, he says, or the Netherlands.'

'Well, let's see how free and easy they are about showering together when you turn up to watch the game next Tuesday night,' Lee declared. 'See which one's first to get their kit off then!'

Next Tuesday night? I hadn't thought about next Tuesday night. Or all the Tuesday nights I had in front of me, week after week, month after month. How would I ever get a single thing done on a Tuesday night again?

At three o'clock in the morning, with Tom's steady breathing in my ear, my imagination was going walkabout. I remembered the Tuesday night only three of the team had turned up to play volleyball, and they'd played as usual. What would happen if only Tom and Isabella turned up? Two could play volleyball. Would they then have a shower together? I imagined Tom and an attractive, sporty woman having a shower together on their own in an abandoned school changing room at night. As soon as the soap came out, neither of them stood a chance. Then I wondered how many of the team went home and had sex with their wives on Tuesday nights, including Tom, while fantasising about soapy Isabella.

If they travelled together to compete in some beach volleyball championship on an exotic island, my imagination galloped onward, which one of the volleyball team would inevitably make a pass at Isabella first? And if due to a tsunami they found themselves stranded there, which ones might inevitably fight over her? I imagined them all sitting around a campfire, unshaven, tearing the heads off fish, leering at Isabella like a pack of savages. Just before dawn I tapped Tom on the shoulder to ask what Isabella looked like.

'Blond . . . tall . . . slim . . .' he mumbled.

I nearly threw up on the pillow.

'You'd like her very mush . . .'

Ten minutes later, his deep voice rose from the other side of the bed. 'Crooked nose.'

Oh, I hoped it was crooked. I hoped it was so crooked you had to tilt your head to look at her.

When the following Tuesday night came, I was watching a story on the bird flu pandemic on CNN trying not to think of people showering together when the phone rang.

'Morning, Honeybee!' my mother sang in my ear from Hobart. 'The dog's just taken your father for a walk, so I thought I'd ring the Pearl of the Southern Seas.'

My sister was the Star of Egypt. I was the Pearl. My brother was Gork the Stork. We never asked why. We just accepted it, like we each accepted being described as 'phosphorous', 'nacreous', and sometimes 'velvety'. Rox asked the usual questions. How was I? How was Henry? And lastly, how was Tommy? Imagining my husband with five other men and one woman soaping each other under one showerhead in a boys' school down the road, I told my mother it was Tom's volleyball night.

'How wonderful for him to have such an outlet,' Rox cried with her usual enthusiasm. 'I'm sure it'll be your turn when Henry's a little less dependent on you.'

Hardly. I was just about to tell my mum about certain challenging European attitudes towards bathing when she interrupted me.

'Oh, I'll have to call you back, Honeybee! Exquisite Robert Dessaix's on Radio National talking to Romana about Turgenev, and I simply have to hear that.'

I sat on the couch staring out the window, wishing I could just forget my worries and immerse myself in Russian literature too. I was imagining Turgenev sitting at his desk in his villa in France, when unexpectedly he put down his pencil, took off his smock frock and stepped into his bathroom where a naked Tolstoy, Dostoyevsky and Gogol were all waiting for him under the shower. Not knowing any famous Russian women writers, I sent in Anna Pavlova.

Desperate to hear a German woman's perspective on communal showering after playing sport, I asked Tom's friend Betty to meet me for a coffee as soon as she could. I liked Betty, and didn't mind at all that she'd invited her psychologist friend Claudia along, even if they did choose one of the noisiest cafés in Schwabing.

'Well, this is something you need to try to understand,' Claudia shouted across the table. 'Have you heard of Heinrich Pudor?'

I shook my head.

'He was er—*Soziologe*?'

Sociologist, Betty translated for her friend.

'Who wrote the famous—*Abhandlung*?'

Essay, Betty said.

'On the Culture of Nudism over a hundred years ago, and we have been taking our clothes off together ever since. Not absolutely all Germans do it, but no one is shocked by it either.'

'It started the FKK movement,' Betty continued, pronouncing it *Eff-Ka-Ka*. 'You heard of FKK?'

I shook my head.

'FKK stands for Freikörperkultur, or free body culture, the celebration of nudity without shame, especially while enjoying nature, sport or outdoor activities—or anything to do with water.'

Leaning forward, I cut to the chase. Heinrich Pudor and designated FKK areas aside, would either of them jump in a shower with six men after a game of volleyball?

The two women considered the question for some time. While Betty lit up another of her exotic brown *zigarillos* and Claudia fed her large golden retriever a *Brezn* under the table, I waited. No, they finally agreed, but Betty might if the school had more showers, and Claudia possibly would have if there were other women on the team.

'Eier im Glass,' our waiter interrupted, placing a tall glass with a soft boiled egg sitting in the bottom in front of Betty. 'Und Schnittlauchbrote,' he said, presenting Claudia with her slice of wholemeal bread covered with chopped-up chives. 'Und für Sie,' he said leaning in front of me, 'ein Croissant.'

And as I waved the cigar smoke away from Henry's Maxi-Cosi

on the seat next to me and watched them begin their unusual breakfasts, I was reminded again how far I was from home.

'Any other questions?' Betty asked just as a truly terrible smell rose from under the table.

'Oh, Pippi!' Claudia cried. 'Hast du gepupst?'

She sure had. *Gepoopst* so bad I felt *gesick*.

After our Friday morning get-together, I sat in the warm sunshine with my favourite expat mothers on the benches at the Alte Pinakothek *Spielplatz* rocking our *Kinderwagen*, deep in thought. Having lived in Munich more than ten years, Rowena, Jane, Dagmar, Lara and Heidi were wonderfully helpful when it came to cultural differences and, sure enough, had been confronted with a bit of *Freikörperkultur* themselves. Ten years ago, Rowena's first German boyfriend, Lukas, had taken her to the sumptuous Romanesque sauna in the city called Müller'sches Volksbad. Having changed into her bathers, Rowena went in search of Lukas only to realise that everyone around her—young, old, thin, fat, male or female—was completely starkers.

'And then one of them, an old biddy with her husband, began shouting at me as if I'd done something to upset her.'

Jane agreed with me. Cantankerous, naked old ladies emerging from the steam sounded like the first scene of Polanski's *Macbeth*.

'It was *nicht hygienisch,* she was shouting, to wear bathers in a sauna, and demanded I take mine off before she went and got the manager.'

'And did you?' Lara asked.

''course I did. You think I'm going to argue with a naked old lady in a room full of naked Germans?'

For a moment we sat there in silence behind Munich's Alte Pinakothek, inside of which hung some of Europe's finest paintings from the fourteenth to eighteenth centuries, considering what each of us would have done.

'Nothing shocks me any more,' Dagmar sighed, looking across the vast green lawn. 'And I don't just mean inside the saunas and swimming pools either.'

'Just go for a walk in summer,' said Jane, 'and you'll find them lying naked on the banks of the Isar.'

Really?

'Or else letting it all hang out at the Englischer Garten,' added Rowena.

The English Gardens? Were they serious? Back home that would be like taking our clothes off in the Botanical Gardens! I'd never seen naked people at the English Gardens!

Lara nodded. 'Just avoid the FKK area behind the Haus der Kunst.'

But just as I found it within me to finally accept that I was now living in a country with different sensibilities to mine, with people who had challenging but refreshing ideas about their own bodies, about nature and health, who'd come up with outdoor kindergartens, river surfing, nudist areas in the middle of the city, just when I was feeling almost ok about my husband and his male friends showering with a woman once a week, with absolutely no interference from me whatsoever Isabella disappeared off the face of the planet.

'I think it was because we played so badly,' the men agreed, looking somewhat dejected in our kitchen one summer afternoon.

'Or maybe it was Wolfgang's terrible jokes,' Tom suggested, kicking his friend lightly with his foot.

'Or Detlef's emails . . .'

As Henry and I left them grieving over the loss of their star player they switched immediately back to German, and despite their low voices, from the other end of our apartment I could easily translate the conversation that followed.

'Well, it definitely wasn't the showers.'

'Isabella loved showering with us, don't you think?'

'Of course she did!'

'Who wouldn't?'

'I didn't mind!'

They roared laughing.

'Who else does your sister know, Detlef?'

Their laughter could have been heard two blocks away.

•

On a snowy Saturday morning the following winter, we were in the car park outside Aldi's at Taufkirchen and had just finished packing the Volvo.

'She seemed nice,' I said to Tom, strapping Henry's Maxi-Cosi into the back seat. I was referring to another acquaintance of Tom's we'd just bumped into, this time at the entrance to the supermarket. 'Yet another old school friend?'

'That was Isabella,' Tom said, smiling as he closed the back door. 'Isabella Moll from volleyball.'

Almost giving myself whiplash, I looked back towards the entrance, desperately searching the crowd of coats and beanies for the tall blond woman who'd just shaken my hand. Damn! Tom could laugh at me all he liked, but I wished I hadn't been in such a hurry to get Henry into our warm car. I'd just wanted to see one thing and that was all. I just wanted to see how crooked her nose really was.

Enjoying the company of women

The end of 2005 was literally capped off by the mother of all winters, covering Bavaria with so much snow that rooftops began collapsing including that of the Bad Reichenhall Ice Rink, sixty miles south of Munich, tragically killing fifteen people. And while Europe's winter was making headlines so was summer in Australia, but in a way that did not make me homesick at all. Maybe it was the books I'd been reading from the tower beside my bed, but sitting with Tom on our blue sofa as we watched footage from the Cronulla riots on television, I couldn't help but think of *Kristallnacht*, an event that had taken place in Munich and in other cities all over Germany nearly seventy years earlier when angry citizens took to the streets with bats and bottles. Here in Germany they'd targeted the Jewish community, shouting 'Jude raus!' In Cronulla the crowd pursued anyone of middle eastern appearance chanting, 'We grew here, you flew here!' The two events might have differed in scale and circumstance, but each sprang from the same cankered seed of fear and intolerance.

Despite depressing news stories on BBC World and four feet of snow, the new year began with a promise of great things to come, especially to München. Not only were people still celebrating the fact that a German cardinal, Munich's own Joseph Ratzinger, had recently been made Pope, and that Christian Democrats leader Angela Merkel had been elected the first female Chancellor, but come summer Germany would be hosting the World Cup. In the lead up to this much anticipated event even Henry seemed to have caught cup fever and, at the age of fourteen months, took his first steps.

As usual, every Friday morning Henry and I caught our two trains across Munich until we'd reached the U-Bahn at Universität. There the lift would deliver us up onto the footpath on Ludwigstrasse, and if it was raining or snowing I'd pull the plastic cover down over Henry's *Kinderwagen* and push his pram down Schellingstrasse for several blocks until finally, forty minutes after we'd left home, we'd reach our destination.

Inside the cosy *Mutterzentrum* in Schraudolphstrasse, while toddlers and babies played happily at our feet, I got to chat with other women adjusting to motherhood and life in Germany. Many had put their own careers on hold to follow partners who worked for one of the big German car companies, or Siemens, or perhaps one of the universities, only to decide this was as good a time as any to start a family. Although most were here for a short time only, it was the small group of stayers I felt most drawn to. It wasn't just that I admired Rowena, Lara, Jane, Dagmar and Heidi for their ability to speak German, for finding work in Munich and for having made this Bavarian city their home, these five funny, smart women gave me the confidence to realise that I too could carve out an existence for myself, at least for a while, and that I didn't have to wear a *Dirndl*, eat *Schweinshaxe*, convert to Catholicism or learn the *Schuhplattler* dance to do so.

And so in this little room at number 10 Schraudolphstrasse, for a couple of hours every Friday morning, forty or so of us expats would cram in as much conversation as our little ones permitted, occasionally pausing to sniff the air before swooping down to examine a small rear end and, if necessary, carry the suspect to the change table next to the toilets. But at the ringing of the little bell, all conversation stopped as we grabbed our children and made our way to the end of the room for Circle Time. Ignoring his violent wriggles and angry protests, I'd hold Henry in my lap and sing nursery rhymes about Little Miss Muffet, Humpty Dumpty and the Grand Old Duke of York until I gave up and let him return to his broken fire engine or headless Barbie. The fact that mine was the only child who steadfastly refused to show any interest in a sing-a-long somewhat deflated my pride in being a former *Playschool* presenter, but such are the levelling lessons our children teach us.

'Were you on *Playschool*?'

I felt so old. Not only had my young audience grown into young adults, they now had toddlers of their own.

'Oh, my God!' cried Denise from Cairns, just passing through. 'I called my cabbage patch doll after you!'

What was truly levelling, however, was when our eighteen month old son began to speak back to me in German.

'NEIN!'

I shouldn't have been so surprised. After all, Henry's very first word was in German.

'AUTO!'

He shouted it whenever he saw anything with wheels. 'AUTO!' he'd yell, pointing at the shopping trolley. 'AUTO!' he'd cry at the sight of a skateboard, and 'AUTO!' leaning out of his pram as we passed people in wheelchairs. 'BRRMM, BRRMM!'

Following the advice of various multilingual experts, Tom and I consistently spoke to Henry in our native tongues, sometimes with curious results. Although he could name his farmyard animals in English, they all bleated, barked or clucked in German. Instead of cock-a-doodle-doo, Henry's roosters went *Kikeriki*. His frogs *quacked*, his bees *summed*, his chickens *tocked*. But that was nothing. His fire engine went *Ta-too-Ta-ta*.

'Well, what do *your* fire engines say?' Tom asked defensively.

'Na-na-na-na-na-na,' I sang, doing my best siren impersonation.

The way Tom looked at me, you'd think I'd said *Ta-too-Ta-ta*.

Not satisfied catching up just one morning a week in our noisy *Mutterzentrum*, Rowena, Heidi, Lara, Dagmar, Jane and I occasionally met for a special brunch at Tambosi, an old *Kaffeehaus* situated in one corner of Odeonsplatz, next to the Hofgarten. In summer the patrons of Tambosi often sat in rows outside on the terrace enjoying the view of the majestic Feldherrenhalle and the baroque Theatinerkirche opposite, but for us the charm of this two hundred year old Viennese style café, no matter what the season, was its neoclassical interior complete with Venetian glass chandeliers, elegant tables and chairs and a theatrical upstairs balcony.

No doubt we weren't exactly the clientele the management preferred to see parking our *Kinderwagen*, bicycles and trailers outside their front door, and then carrying our warmly wrapped offspring up to our favourite nook upstairs. Perhaps they would have preferred us to choose Starbucks next door, or the San Francisco Coffee Company across the square that even had a *Spielecke* with toys and a changing table. Not that they were ever rude to us at Tambosi. The busy staff tolerated us with a cool professionalism I had to admire, and we in turn never changed our little ones on their antique chaise longue, or asked them to heat up a bottle. Nor did we request the manager to turn down Andrea Bocelli singing 'Nessun Dorma', which by the end of winter we could have sung with our eyes closed too. And then, like so many of these old buildings in Munich, there was the history.

'Did you know this was one of Hitler's favourite haunts?' I whispered to Dagmar the first time I admired the view from the balcony.

'Oh gawd,' Dagmar groaned, turning to the others sitting in their antique armchairs. 'She's going on about Hitler again.'

'You're like that boy who keeps seeing dead people,' Jane sighed, 'except with you it's Nazis.'

Sitting upstairs at Tambosi's, or Thrombosis as we affectionately called it, my new friends and I would share stories about our daily trials and celebrations of motherhood and life in Germany. I was glad to discover that I wasn't the only one who found it odd to be randomly confronted by elderly German women, especially since I'd become a mum. One old biddy had recently stopped me on the street near our place, I thought to ask the time, but soon realised it was to express her intense disapproval of my baby sling, the long strip of blanket that wraps around both mother and child, despite how popular the *Babytragetuch* was in Germany.

I'd found myself similarly speechless during the next two confrontations as well, both of which had taken place on the U-Bahn. Concerned by the crying coming from Henry's *Kinderwagen*, a sweet little old lady standing near us on the platform had crept up to take a peek under his canopy, only to stand bolt upright and declare accusingly, '*Das Kind hat Hunger!*' And just a few days later, a wizened creature sitting by the doors inside a carriage had pointed at Henry's socked feet sticking out the bottom of his blanket.

'Kalte Füsse!' she shouted, and everyone peered over their newspapers and laptops to look at my son's apparently cold feet.

My friends nodded knowingly and smiled as if they'd heard it all before. Since becoming a mum, Rowena had been told by complete strangers in pleated skirts that her daughter wasn't comfortable, wasn't warm enough, wasn't cool enough, was in the sun or was in the wind. Dagmar's two year old had nearly caused a mutiny on the U2 when he stood on a train seat without taking his shoes off, and just that morning Jane had been shouted at by an elderly woman as she sailed past on her vintage bicycle.

'I knew my son had my keys in his mouth,' Jane protested. 'I bloody gave them to him, didn't I?'

So as integrated expatriates, how did they explain this phenomenon on the streets of Munich? Heidi put it down to the frustration of a generation of German women who once got medals for being good housewives or having large families, and who possibly now felt redundant or unappreciated. Lara thought it was due more to *Sozialcourage*, or the social responsibility so many

Germans couldn't resist acting upon when they saw something amiss, to keep everying *in Ordnung.* I thought this a good time to put forward Tom's friend Alex's theory, that many of the women of this generation were possibly the *Trümmerfrauen,* still bitter from their years of having to clean up after a war that left them widowed, hungry and devastated.

'Off she goes again with the Nazis . . .' Dagmar sighed.

'Next time it happens,' Jane said, wrestling with her hungry infant and the clip on her maternity bra, 'you just say Das ist nicht dein Bier.'

I was delighted to add another funny German expression to my repertoire. I much preferred saying 'That's not your beer' to 'Mind your own business.' I'd already picked up a few others from Tom, including *Ich verstehe nur Bahnhof,* meaning 'All I understood was train station.' Or *Das sind mir spanische Dörfer,* meaning 'It's all Spanish villages to me.' And I knew from his arguments with bad drivers that *Jemandem einen Vogel zeigen* while tapping one's temple indicated that someone had bats (or in this case a bird) in his belfry. And rather than accuse someone of farting, one could tactfully ask, *Hat jemand einen Koffer stehen lassen?*, or 'Did someone abandon a suitcase?' But my favourite expression by far was the one Germans used to describe a lifeless venue or boring event: How was the party? *Tote Hose.* Meaning 'dead pants'.

And of course, while reclining on the elegant lounge furniture at Tambosi's, perhaps because spring was approaching, our minds turned to more personal things, such as our relationships with our German in-laws or, more importantly, their sons.

'I know he's absolutely right, but does he have to be so—'

'—direct?'

'—confrontational?'

'—brutal?'

Clearly I wasn't the only one adjusting to life with a man, a gorgeous, funny and loving man, who also called a spade *ein Spaten.* But the German flair for directness and straightforwardness was a double edged sword, Lara reminded us. On the one hand, it might hurt to hear the honest reply to 'Does my bum look big in this?' But on the other, at least one finally knew not to wear one's high-waisted burgundy angora pants ever again, certainly not without a jacket.

Before we lived together I'd caught glimpses of Tom's inherited direct and sometimes authoritative manner, but it wasn't until we began sharing a kitchen that I found myself on the receiving end of it. 'Turn that tap off—shut that fridge door—turn that hotplate down!' And of course, 'Will you stop putting the sharp knives in the dishwasher? It makes them blunt!' So shocked was I the first time I experienced my German fiancé's occasional brusque manner with me, I responded with the first thing that came into my head.

'You didn't!' the girls cried.

Oh, but I did. Although I knew it was illegal to do the Hitler salute in public, I had no idea what a bad idea it was to *Heil* one's German boyfriend in his kitchen, saying, *Jawohl, mein Führer!*

And while Andrea Bocelli once again fervently resolved through Tambosi's stereo speakers to win his Turandot, the girls offered me advice on other, less important issues, such as where to find an affordable but decent hairdresser in Munich. Unused to being financially dependent on a man, it had been hard enough to allow Tom to pay for my new wardrobe, let alone a good colourist as well. And having only dated women with luxurious hair that swung from side to side, Tom had no idea how expensive it was to maintain the tousled, pixie style with warm highlights. Consequently, I'd spent the last two years in Munich visiting salons that had *Schneiden und Föhnen €20* painted on their windows. Getting a cut and blowdry back home for under forty dollars usually meant getting my hair cut by an Irish or Scottish backpacker from one of those no-frills salons in a shopping mall, the sort with names like Quickuts or Snip. The German equivalent seemed to be salons run by friendly Eastern Europeans who all looked like Eurovision song contestants and hadn't a clue what to do with a woman with short hair.

'Vasylina!'

Coming out from a tiny kitchen, a young woman with blond hair extensions and a heavily jewelled belt would try to smile with a mouthful of food as she wiped her hands on her tight hipster jeans. And as she'd show me to the chair, I'd sometimes catch her pitying smile in the mirror, as if my short hair meant I possibly worked on a farm and slept with the horses. Running her fingers through my overgrown bob, she'd ask my reflection what I had in mind.

'Was wollen Sie heute?'

As much as I was tempted to ask Vasylina if she could remember Madonna's gamine cut for the *Rain* album, faced with my tired eyes under the fluorescent lights, I thought better. And now feeling sorry for interrupting Vasylina's lunch, I'd suggest she do whatever she wanted.

'Ah, machen was Sie wollen.'

Although it seemed we had little in common, me and my Turkish, Croatian, Hungarian or Romanian hairdresser always ended up sharing stories about being an *Ausländerin* in *Deutschland*. Although it went without saying that the German transport system was the best in the world, and Bayern's soccer team was magnificent, we always agreed in a whisper that the biggest challenge, apart from the language, was that the Germans weren't exactly the most *Freundliche Menschen*. And the more we talked, the more I surrendered to Vasylina, Bohuslava or Shakira's comb, scissors and, finally, turbo hairdryer. And here was the rub. To create a voluminous, messy look, my hair needed to be lightly tousled dry, not brushed, and definitely not brushed into submission. But time and time again I'd watch with sad resignation as my bodacious hairdresser grabbed her brush and blowdryer and deliberately, fervently even, curled my hair under before sending me forth into the world looking like an Albanian librarian.

But thanks to some excellent advice from my girlfriends, things were about to change. Having promised to return the following Friday to show them the result, I left them at Tambosi's and pushed Henry's pram just two doors further down Ludwigstrasse to the majestic Vidal Sassoon-Friseur. Having battled my way through their enormous, heavy glass doors with a baby's pram, I finally found myself facing an immaculately dressed receptionist wearing a name-tag.

'Kann ich Ihnen helfen?'

A tall, slender, graceful chap, Blas looked as if any second he might leap over the enormous granite top counter and perform Prince Siegfried's solo from *Swan Lake*.

'Ich würde gerne einen Modelle Termin, bitte,' I told him, carefully repeating the words the girls had taught me, 'für schneiden und Farbe.'

According to Lara, a *Modelle Termin* at Vidal Sassoon meant my hair would be cut and coloured by a trainee under the supervision of a senior stylist and colourist. And even though it might take hours, between three and five Dagmar warned, I would be charged no more than Vasylina charged for turning me into a Ukranian potato farmer. No doubt this was what Blas was explaining in fluent German when Henry began howling for his next feed. And so hastily agreeing to whatever time he was offering, I gave Blas my name and number, waited for him to give me an appointment card, and then raced out the door while a supermodel held it open for me.

'Danke!'

'Gerne!'

The following Thursday morning at 10 am, while Tom stayed at home minding Henry, I sat like a queen in a comfortable black leather chair in front of a full length mirror, looking out on Odeonsplatz, having my hair cut by Karla. Not many girls could have carried off a cubist haircut like Karla's, and not many could have worked with just one eye either, the other hidden under her immaculate, oblong fringe. But Karla had a deft way with a comb and scissors that put one immediately at ease, and contrary to Dagmar's warning it took the trainee just one hour to not only restyle my hair, but take ten years off my life. Having delivered me downstairs, I took a seat and waited for my young colourist to finish putting foils into the hair of an elderly dowager with two enormous Great Danes entwined at her feet. I'd seen dogs on trains and buses, in restaurants and cafes, but this was a first.

An hour later, I began to pray for my colourist's supervisor to appear, because even I could deduce that if it took Johan this long to foil the left side of my head, by the time he did the right the other half would have turned yellow or, worse, died. I tried to read an article about George Michael in German, but all I could think about was my foils falling to the floor, taking my broken hair with them, and going home to Tom half bald.

'Kommt gleich,' Johan said, waking me with a gentle touch to the shoulder.

Speaking German, Johan pointed to his empty hair colour bowl, his watch, my foils, and even to the dowager's two Great Danes, making me wonder if one of the dogs was going to rinse me off while Johan went next door for tapas. But soon he was back, and even humming along to Amy Winehouse as he continued combing, painting and foiling. An hour later I was sitting upstairs as Karla admired the warm coppers, golden blonds and chocolate browns in my hair. We both agreed that despite his young years and my misgivings, Johan certainly knew a thing or two about colour, especially for a student.

'*Student?*' Karla yelped. 'Johan ist kein Student! Johan ist unser Meister Farbenkünstler!'

Get out of town! Their master colourist? Young Johan? He looked barely old enough to leave home on his own. But if Johan wasn't a student, I thought to myself, feeling sicker by the second, what was Karla?

'Ich bin Top Stylist.'

Really? Top? As in—*Gott in Himmel!*

'Two hundred and fifty-five euros?' Tom roared as he followed me out of our kitchen. 'Do you know how much money that is?'

A bit over three hundred dollars?

'Try three hundred and fifty-seven dollars!'

Normally I found Tom's ability to convert currency impressive, but today it just seemed anal.

'We could have gone on a holiday to Spain for less money than you paid for that haircut!'

And colour.

'What colour?'

'You can see it better in daylight,' I mumbled.

'In *daylight*? Verdammte Hacke!'

And then he did it.

'Did what?' asked the girls at Tambosi's the following Friday, sitting on the edge of their antique lounge chairs, already horrified at whatever Tom did next.

'He rang them.'

No! Not Vidal Sassoon!

All'alba vinceró! Vinceró! sang Andrea Bocelli in disbelief.

I nodded. My husband rang Vidal Sassoon, one of the classiest hairdressing salons in the world, to give them a piece of his mind about their Top Stylists, their *Meister Farbenkünstler*, and their pricelist.

Vinceeeeeerooooooó!

'So,' I told the girls back at Tambosi, 'until they've all forgotten me at Vidal's, it's back to Vasylina for me.'

'That's ok,' said Dagmar, patting my leg consolingly. 'Just take your beanie.'

The elephant in the room

It's one of my favourite cartoons: lying down on a couch, an anxious elephant complains to his psychiatrist, 'I'm right there in the room, and no one even acknowledges me.'

At first I tried to ignore him too, but just recently I could hear him munching apples on our balcony, and once caught a glimpse of his flapping grey ear as he lumbered out of our bathroom. By late April, the anniversary of my second year in Bavaria, I knew that if Tom and I didn't discuss our future in Munich soon, the elephant would be sitting between us on the sofa, helping himself to our Ritter Sport Schokolade. I'd done it, hadn't I? I'd 'given Munich a go for a couple of years' as promised, and now it was time to discuss how we both felt about staying on, was it not?

So why was it so difficult for either of us to raise this subject? Could it have been because both the elephant and I knew that Tom didn't want to? Why would he? Munich was his home, where he'd lived all his life, near his family and friends, where he'd worked hard to start a business and create a warm and loving home for his wife and child. Yes, he'd made a vague promise a couple of years earlier, but who remembered that now? Apart from me, Tom, and Jumbo.

'You're not going to stay in Munich, are you?' Rowena asked point blank as we drank our tea in her Schellingstrasse apartment.

Not even waiting for the answer, she sighed. Due to the number of expats like me who'd arrived in Munich only to leave a couple of years later, she'd deliberately cultivated most of her friendships with Germans.

'It hurts less,' she said. 'They stay.'

I felt terrible. After all, with friends like Rowena and the girls from the *Mutterzentrum*, Europe on my doorstep, Tom and Henry by my side, I knew I could stay in Munich, keep learning German, write more books, raise our beautiful boy with Tom and live a full and happy life.

'Is it the weather?' she asked, smiling. 'Dour Germans? In-laws? Or are you just homesick?'

I had to admit, although I loved my in-laws, whenever Tom's well-meaning mother complained that Henry spoke too much English, or asked which local school we'd be sending him to (that would then send him home by midday for the next six years), or how many more words I still had to write, as if I was encumbered by being an author, I did catch myself longing for a departures screen and a boarding pass. But it was also the disapproving looks Henry and I received on public transport for being too animated, too loud, or too silly. And just recently, it was how despondent I felt standing on the footpath with the other pedestrians, waiting for the lights to give us permission to cross a totally empty street. For a spirited bounder like me, this was almost as sad an outcome as Randle McMurphy's at the end of *One Flew Over the Cuckoo's Nest*. But most of all, it was the thought of my parents, ten thousand miles away, rummaging around in our big old family house in Hobart, being pulled around Sandy Bay beach by their increasingly large dog, while their three children plus their only grandson lived on the other side of the planet. I was waiting for the right moment, I told Rowena, to remind Tom, like Rumpelstiltskin, about a promise he once made, even if it was just to make me spin more gold.

But if ever there was a wrong moment to discuss leaving Germany, it was between 9 June and 9 July 2006. Even during the weeks leading up to the World Cup, the sense of pride and excitement on the streets was contagious. Not only had Munich been chosen as one of the twelve German cities to hold cup tournaments, it was home to the nation's most popular football team, FC Bayern München, many of whose players would be representing Germany. And as if this wasn't rousing enough, when thousands of revellers from all over the world began pouring in to support their country, the noise and colour they brought with them created a carnival atmosphere, even on the underground.

'Party!' Henry shouted from his *Kinderwagen* as we stepped out onto the usually drab, subdued platform at Sendlinger Tor, now crammed with visitors draped in the colours of Poland, Costa Rica, Ecuador, England, Paraguay, Trinidad and Tobago, Argentina, Netherlands, Serbia and Montenegro, Ivory Coast, Mexico, Iran, Angola, Ghana, Switzerland, South Korea, Togo, Ukraine, Spain, Tunisia, Saudi Arabia, the Czech Republic, the US, Italy, Croatia, Japan, Sweden, Portugal, France, Brazil and even Australia. And they all seemed to be boarding our train. Up until now I hadn't realised that the U6 that always delivered Henry and me to our *Mutterzentrum* in Schwabing then continued north to Fröttmaning, home to the Allianz Arena soccer stadium.

Although the Australians wore the same colours as the Brazilians, it was never difficult to tell them apart. I knew we had our fair share of beautiful young women back home, but Brazil seemed to have a factory. Never had I seen so much tumbling hair, tanned stomachs and stunning white teeth en masse. Nor had Henry. 'Look, Mama!' he'd shout, violently pushing me to face the back of our carriage where a row of women who all looked like Penelope Cruz waved back at him, making him dive for cover.

But there was no doubt about the middle-aged couple who sat opposite us on our way back from the *Mutterzentrum* as I held a sleeping Henry in my arms. They might have been dressed from head to toe in green and yellow, but even before they opened their mouths I knew they weren't from Brazil.

'Don't look now,' the male muttered to his partner out the side of his mouth, 'but don't ya reckon she looks like whatsername from *Playschool*?'

Following her partner's unsubtle nod in my direction, the woman studied my face, while I watched their reflections in my window.

'Oh yeah . . .' she whispered back. '. . . that one who was on *The Grass is Greener*.'

Dressed in my tracksuit pants, wearing no make-up and carrying a sleeping toddler in my arms, I guess it was safe to assume I was just another German *Hausfrau* going about her daily chores and not an Australian actress who now lived in Germany. For one cheeky moment I considered revealing the truth, just so we could share a laugh together.

'I hated her in that.'

'Me too.'

Perhaps not.

'. . . such an idiot.'

'Who was the guy that played her hubby?' the man continued as I rose to my feet with Henry and my backpack. 'He was great in *Snowy River*.'

'Andrew MacFarlane,' she answered with certainty.

'Andrew Clarke,' I corrected her politely. 'And it was *Always Greener*.'

It wasn't my fault I always got cast as comical idiots, I thought as I queued at the door. Someone had to play them . . .

As cup fever took over Germany, people everywhere seemed to be talking about the same thing, either the match of the day, or else the flags. No one could remember seeing this many Germans waving their flag with pride. Small flags poked out of backpacks and bicycle seats or flapped from car windows, and large ones hung from windows and balconies or were draped over shoulders and worn as cloaks. Young people especially wore red, black and yellow wrist bands, head bands, face paintings and, to Henry's delight, the occasional afro wig.

'Normally we don't dare express such patriotism,' Alex explained to me, always happy to offer the German perspective. 'Since the war we haven't allowed ourselves the same display of national pride other countries enjoy. There is still too much shame, too much guilt, you understand. But the pride of hosting these games, and in our German team, has made something shift. Whether it's permanent, we shall have to see.'

Permanent or not, the positive press about Germany's 2006 FIFA World Cup had spread throughout the world. Even the British tabloids dropped their old clichés resorting to wartime rivalry in favour of compliments to the host country and its impressive team. And the good feeling extended even into our own lounge room, where Tom could not believe my response to the German national anthem played at the beginning of the game between Germany and Poland.

'Are you *crying*?'

I could not have felt more proud if they'd been my brothers, I told him, even if I was old enough to be their mother. I don't know if it was their handsome, determined but nervous young faces, or whether it was the German anthem, surely the most stirring of them all, but by the time both captains tossed the coin I was a sniffing, dribbling mess.

'Isn't it great about Australia?' my brother shouted down the phone from London just minutes after the game began.

What? Had we finally apologised to the Aborigines? Signed the Kyoto protocol?

'Darl, we beat Japan!'

At ping pong?

'At soccer! Two days ago! It's our first World Cup game in thirty-two years! We're over there where you are, in bloody Germany!'

Oh yes, so we were, but I had to go. My favourite midfielder had just intercepted three Poles.

'Come on, Schweinsteiger!' I yelled at the television. 'Ballack, quit the fancy footwork and kick it, you big girl. Podolski, run, you gorgeous creature—oh, scheisse echt, Frings, what the hell—Lahm! Go, you good thing, go and *oh my God KLOSE* that was close!'

When did this happen? Tom asked putting his arm around me. When exactly had I learnt the names of the entire German football team?

We lived less than one minute's walk from FC Bayern München, I reminded my husband. While Tom was at work, Henry and I had spent many afternoons watching them train. We'd once been the only ones there when Oliver Kahn practised defending goals for over an hour with two other players. Handsome Oliver Kahn who was, by the way, the spitting image of my ex-boy—

'Yes,' Tom rolled his eyes. 'You say it every time we see his photo . . .'

I might have been born in Australia, but when it came to soccer my heart belonged to Germany.

If the 2006 World Cup made Germans feel a little differently about themselves, it made me feel a little differently about Germany. And as Henry and I headed into our third winter together, I had to ask myself, would it really be so hard to stay? Not only had I met these wonderful women from my *Mutterzentrum*, but having completed another three months at Inlingua, my German was good enough to deal with almost any situation. I may not have been able to tell jokes at a dinner party, but I could almost understand one. More importantly, I could now have conversations with Henry's doctor, chat with the other mums at our local *Spielplatz*, and ask a sales assistant where I might find patterned tights.

It wasn't until my sister George flew in for another of her

entertaining weekend stopovers that my inner compass changed direction yet again.

'Well, darls, I can see you staying here forever, can't you? And I just think it's fab. Speaking Deutsch with your family, seeing young Hen off to school, popping home once a year to see the folks. You mustn't worry about them by the way. They just adore that dog, even if she does eat everything in sight, ha! Did you hear she ate last week's washing off the line? Amazing! Mum's best nightie, completely shredded. God, we laughed. But washing aside, and Diedre's banana lounge, and the back door, Ella brings them a *lot* of happiness. As does Henry. They show everyone the birthday card he made for his grandad, you know. Absolutely everyone. And they've got photos of that child everywhere, just everywhere . . .'

And how would we support ourselves if and when we went back to Australia? Tom asked as soon as my sister had gone. Did I think I'd just walk into another role in a television series? And what about him? What would he do?

I had no answers to these questions, but could only assure Tom that three years ago I didn't believe it possible to relocate to Munich, have a baby, write a book, make new friends and help set up a bilingual kindergarten either. If the last three years had taught us one lesson, surely it was that anything was possible. For a long time, Tom stared out into space, as if imagining breaking the news to his family, dismantling his groovy digital printing showroom, packing up forty-five years of belongings, photo albums and sports equipment, renting out his apartment, selling his Volvos and saying goodbye to all his friends. I didn't need to go right away, I said, gently touching his arm. I just wanted to remind him, I never promised to live in Germany for the rest of my life, that's all.

Waking from his trance, Tom pulled me into a very reassuring hug. 'We'll see,' he said, kissing my hair. 'We'll see.'

Although the elephant hadn't left our house, he was no longer in the room. Perhaps he'd gone to see his psychiatrist.

Treehouse

If anyone had told that core group of women from the *Mutterzentrum*, Christine, Debbie, Rowena, Lara and Meredith, just how much of their time and energy it would take to set up a parent-initiative-bilingual-kindergarten, I wonder if they'd have continued with their plans, meetings, paperwork, organising, designing and hard slog, or if they'd have just enrolled their children in German kindergartens instead. If so, what a huge loss it would have been to our little family, and to the wider international community in Munich.

By the end of winter 2007, Christine the lawyer, our intrepid leader and administrator, had already found the perfect 140 square metres space, Rowena our interior architect had begun designing the rooms within, Debbie our treasurer and communications leader had prepared the funding proposals and operational budget, Meredith and Lara had interviewed potential staff, and Sinead, Lisa and various other women were giving up their valuable time as well. By early spring there was a team of twenty to thirty parents, expats and nationals including Tom who all shared the same vision, busily fundraising, training, interviewing, accounting, gardening, buying, selling, haggling, painting, rostering and cleaning. As a writer, I was delegated the job of coming up with text for the website for the parents' handbook, and a list of potential names for our English/German kindergarten in Schwabing.

'And so that's twenty-two votes for Treehouse, three for Pooh's Corner, and we all agree that a kindergarten in Germany called Goose Steps is just not funny.'

Finally, with Treehouse up and running, and Henry attending with his friends from the *Mutterzentrum* every morning, I was beginning to realise the enormity of the task ahead of me. I may have attempted a couple of humorous memoirs, I grumbled to Tom in our kitchen one morning, but I was no more capable of putting together a kindergarten and day care parents handbook than I was of writing a user's manual for a combine harvester with a hydraulic hillside levelling system. Until I'd begun my research into early childhood education, I thought Steiner made pianos, Waldorf was a salad and Montessori was somewhere in Italy. But as I trawled through various kindergarten websites, I learnt so much about these three innovative educators I almost considered becoming a teacher myself. Instead of getting on with the book I was writing, I spent my mornings sitting in our garden with my laptop investigating other kindergartens policies regarding immunisation, children with mumps, measles, rashes and nits, plus nut and bee allergies. When Henry and Tom were both asleep, I stayed up studying third-party pick-ups, complaint procedures and behavioural codes (for children *and* parents). But when I started having dreams about catering, clothes labelling and circle time, I began to wish I'd just offered to do Purchasing, Cleaning and Kitchen Supplies, like Petra.

And then there were other challenges we had to face during those early days of Treehouse, such as the plagues our children circulated on a weekly basis. No one had warned me what a Petri dish of bacteria and viral lurgies a kindergarten could be until the autumn of 2007, when I figured it out for myself.

Having picked him up from Treehouse, Henry and I were sitting opposite each other on a very full Number 27 tram as it made its way down Barerstrasse, past the Neue Pinakothek, then the Pinakothek der Moderne, before snaking its way around Karolinenplatz. Wanting to enjoy the late afternoon sun before heading for home, I suggested we get off at Karlsplatz for a stroll through the ancient city, maybe even buy a Hot Wheels car at Kaufhof. Henry agreed, and I was still smiling out my window as we passed the Staatsministerium der Justiz, one of my favourite buildings, when I heard him calling me.

'Yes, Hen?'

My three year old boy looked at me with such sweet helplessness, it reminded of the heartbreaking look Fay Dunaway gives Warren Beatty in the final scene of *Bonnie and Clyde*, just before they're both shot to pieces.

'What?'

And just like Warren Beatty, I guessed too late that my son

was trying to warn me of some imminent danger with terrible consequences. Sure enough:

Brrruuhhllaah . . .

'Urgh . . .' went the cry from everyone around us as Henry vomited all over my lap, shoes, and onto the floor.

'Mein Gott . . .' passengers cursed, parting like the Red Sea so I could reverse through them while catching the continuous spray of Alphabet Noodles with Mozzarella in Tomato Sauce in my two cupped hands, as only a mother can.

'Igitt!' someone said as the tram reached its stop.

'Pfui!' a few gasped as the doors opened.

And 'Bäh!' cried a couple from the footpath before circumnavigating us to get on.

As I stood in the corner of the empty tram shelter next to my poor vomiting son, flicking my wet, putrid hands at the ground, I didn't know what was worse, the fact that Henry had picked up yet another viral bug from one of his kindy classmates, or the unspeakable mess we'd just left behind on a Number 27 tram, now packed with nauseous Bavarians.

'You ok, Hen?' I asked, feeling my son's hot forehead with the dry back of my hand.

No sooner had Henry nodded when he let out another jet, I guessed by the smell this morning's banana and yoghurt. I was still searching in my bag for my Wet Ones when an angry finger poked my back like a jackhammer, and I turned to find an immaculately dressed elderly woman glowering over me. Oh no, I thought. Not now. I'd had such a good run lately. Nothing but sweet old ladies!

'Schau!' she shouted, pointing to a tiny noodle on her perfectly creased pants. 'Schau mal was ihr Sohn gemacht hat!'

As she seemed to be waiting for an answer, I squinted at the speck on her knee and told her I couldn't be sure, but it looked like an F to me.

Although all the other parent initiative kindergartens that I knew of held their meetings once a quarter, until Treehouse was running more smoothly we had to hold ours once a week. But uncomfortable as it was to sit for two hours on bonsai wooden chairs made for smaller bottoms than ours, the meetings were never dull. Christine was the only person any of us knew who could whip through an agenda in two languages, solve three disputes with good humour and announce a fundraising barbecue, all while nursing her new baby girl in her arms. And by the beginning of winter, thanks to a massive group effort and the total devotion of our founding members and team leaders, Treehouse was no longer just a daycare and kindergarten with a waiting list. It was a close knit community of nationals and expats offering support and friendship to all its members. Our diaries were permanently full of birthday parties, picnics, brunches, various outings and family dinners, and we were only too happy to swap valuable information with each other, be it recipes, resorts with kids clubs, speech therapists, advice about returning to work and, if required, the phone numbers of good marriage guidance counsellors.

The arrival of December's snow brought with it a new routine. Having picked up our children from Treehouse, zipped them up in their lined, waterproof coats and boots, wrapped them in scarves, and put their beanies and gloves on, a dozen of us would spend the rest of the afternoon pushing them down the snowy banks of Massmanpark on their 32 euro wooden sleds from OBI. Hours later, as the sun was setting, Henry and I would sit on the heavenly warm Strassenbahn together as it made its way through the city. At the same time, having locked up his shop in the Glockenbachviertel, Tom would be making his way on foot to meet us in Marienplatz. And there, by the glittering Christmas tree, after greeting each other with hugs and kisses, Tom would put Henry on his shoulders, I'd put the sled in the *Kinderwagen*, and together we'd stroll through the Christkindlmarkt with a thousand others before making our way to Karlsplatz. Once there, joining the other spectators on the side of the rink, I'd sip hot *Glühwein* while watching Tom give our laughing boy a quick ice-skating lesson. Sometimes, there was nowhere in the world I'd rather be than here in Munich.

•

'Now, we don't want to worry you, Honeybee,' my mother's voice croaked down the line one frosty January morning, 'but it would seem your precious dad is once again trying to get everyone's attention. Last night he had to review the Huon Valley Players' production of the *Kiss of the Spiderwoman* and despite dear old Maura Hooper driving us home in torrential rain in less than forty minutes, your father got so worked up trying to get his review in to the paper by midnight that when the computer deleted the whole thing for the second time and his arm went numb, I just cut to the chase and called the ambulance.'

'What happened?' I asked her.

'We don't know! Every time we try to "save" something on Word, it just bloody disappears! I wrote a poem for the Hammos about the pigface growing outside our—'

'Not the computer, you silly woman! Dad! What happened to Dad?'

'Oh, he's fine, Honeybee. Happily tucked up in hospital, chatting up all the nurses, until they're sure everything's ticking normally again. But I've told him, next time the Huon Valley Players put on a musical, he's to send someone else. Ella for all I care, 'cause he's staying home watching *Midsomer Murders* with me.'

As I lay in his arms that night, Tom told me that he now knew what to give me for my upcoming birthday.

'But can we please, please live in Sydney?' he asked. 'I just can't live in Hobart until it's got central heating.'

Auf wiedersehen

Now that I knew I wasn't staying, I saw the beauty everywhere. I even enjoyed the smooth wooden panelling and rustic deer antlers in the traditional Bavarian restaurants, although when Tom offered me some of his *Semmelknödel* I told him not to push it. Henry saw the beauty everywhere too. I didn't give him any choice. He may have been only four, but whenever we passed through the city I parked his *Kinderwagen* in front of every historical building as if he was on some kind of educational excursion and only had months to learn about his cultural heritage. It wasn't until he held my hand in Odeonsplatz, mesmerised by the buskers as they performed scenes from Mozart operas, accompanied by four fellows on strings and a clarinet, that I realised I didn't have to try so hard. There were so many things we would miss about our life here in Munich. I even bought myself some *Stubenmusik*. Originally heard in the *Stuben* or parlour, the warmest room of the house, after people had eaten their meals, this lyrical music was played on zither, hammered dulcimer, guitar and harp. Listening to it on my ipod as I travelled on the U-Bahn into the city to meet the girls, I fancied that I'd finally unlocked the secret to my silent fellow commuters, as if this gentle and tender music was a part of the Bavarians I'd never understood until now.

At our next Easter weekend family reunion in Marquartstein, my fifth since arriving in Germany, I gathered by my in-laws' slightly nervous smiles that Tom had already broken the news, and it was still being digested. But even before Wilhelm had begun showing signs of Alzheimer's, I seldom knew what my dear old father-in-law was feeling. Our news may have been big, but expressing big emotions was not the Bavarian way, at least not the way of this stoic and quiet family. Equally subdued was Tom's mother, Friedl, although her smile, and warm hand presses, assured me that she at least understood. After all, not one meeting with my mother-in-law over the last five years had passed without her asking after both my parents, living on the other side of the world, seemingly abandoned by all three of their children. Even before they met, Rox and Friedl had regularly exchanged cards, butterflies and brooches to convey their mutual regard for one another and so I trusted they'd continue their touching dialogue, like two gracious tennis players after swapping places at half-time. There was only one family member who dared mention out loud Tom's and my recent decision to relocate to Sydney.

Despite his initial suggestion, in this very room, that from the moment I arrived I be spoken to only in German, for the last few years my brother-in-law had only ever spoken to me in English, even when I'd address him in German. I always liked to interpret this gesture, accompanied by his more genial manner with me, as a hint of an olive branch.

'What's the matter, Merridy?' Horst asked with a glint in his eye, while the others were busy in the kitchen. 'Isn't our family good enough for you?'

It was an audacious question, even with the glint. But the more I looked at my conventional, proud police commissioner brother-in-law, the more I wondered what Horst would have made of a family like mine: a brother who slept with a black sock over his eyes and did morris dancing at parties; a sister who began her day by reversing her Blue Fairy at high speed out of her cul-de-sac while applying make-up as she talked on her mobile phone; a father, local theatre critic and ex-ABC news reader, who wore ski pants held together with gaffer tape; and a feminist mother who fed her dog cheese, and whenever her husband drove navigated from the passenger seat via her make-up mirror. And then there was me. Not so long ago, I'd sat on a tube in London dressed up as a giant mouse on my way to my clown workshop. If he'd seen us all in our eccentric glory, Horst would never have asked such a question. No matter how 'good enough' Tom's kind and generous family definitely were, no one did barking like my own.

By the time our last summer arrived, I wasn't going to leave Munich or attend my fifth Oktoberfest in a row without one. It was black with a tight bodice and a full skirt covered in pink flowers, and when I put it on over the puffy-sleeved blouse and tied the matching pink apron around my waist, I felt like Miss Bavaria. My mother would have jumped for joy. And although Tom grumbled about it being a 'tourist Dirndl', he had to agree it looked very pretty on, and when we met his parents at the entrance to the Oktoberfest, Friedl expressed her warm approval too. After walking around the enormous Augustiner-Festhalle tent searching for a table, we finally asked a solitary fellow whose *Lederhosen* and feathered hat had all seen better days if he would mind us joining him. Lifting his hat, he kindly moved over, and soon we were salivating over our plates of succulent roast chicken and potato salad.

'Schön,' the man said, gesturing towards Henry as I cut up his food.

'Danke,' I said.

'Und Sie auch,' he said, gesturing to me in my *Dirndl.*

'Danke noch mal!' I said, thanking him for the compliment.

'See?' said Tom, leaning over to plant a kiss on my cheek. 'I told you you looked lovely.'

'Sind Sie die Oma?' the old man asked.

'Bitte?' I asked, the smile frozen on my face.

'Sind Sie die Oma?' he called across the table.

Was I the grandmother? *Was he kidding?*

'Da ist die Oma!' I said, pathetically pointing at Friedl, sitting next to him. 'Ich bin die Mutter.'

The man shrugged, smiled, and took another gulp of his *Weissbier.*

'Be-trunk-en,' my kind mother in-law whispered behind her hand.

Was he? Was he really *betrunken*? I hoped so, I told Friedl. I hoped he was as *betrunken* as a newt.

But apart from being asked if I was a grandmother the first day I ever wore my *Dirndl* to the Oktoberfest, I still believed it was the best seventy euros I'd ever spent, even if my sister's reaction to the photo Tom took of me wasn't quite what I was after either.

'Ha!' said her email. 'Hysterical, darls!'

Hysterical? You don't put on a full skirt, bustier and peasant blouse to look hysterical!

Far more reassuring was the response from our mother.

'Oh, Honeybee. I can't figure out whether you look more like Giselle or Coppelia. You're in the Bolshoi Ballet anyway . . .'

•

The end of 2008 was not a good time to try to sell a business, anywhere. As governments trembled at the approach of the global financial crisis, and stock markets began crashing left, right and centre, Germany was reeling with shock that its own bank, KfW, had lent Lehman Brothers 300 million euros just hours before the US investment bank filed for bankruptcy. Against this foreboding backdrop, and angry newspaper headlines such as '*Deutschlands Dümmste Bank!*', somewhat miraculously Tom sold his digital printing business to a paper wholesale company. And for a good price too, I reported to my Schwabing girlfriends as we huddled on a bench, warming our gloved hands on our takeaway cups of hot chocolate and latte macchiato, watching our children play in subzero temperatures at St Joseph's *Spielplatz*. It was hard to believe that just months earlier we'd sat on these same benches watching them build dams and bridges, wearing nothing but their hats as they played in the sun.

'Looks like young Henry's dividing up his estate too,' Jane said, nodding towards our lanky blond boy who, crouching in the slush, carefully distributed his favourite marbles, the big ones with trapped swirls of red, blue, green and gold that he'd spent so much time choosing at the Christkindlmarkt, to each of his grateful friends.

Still, despite the towers of boxes that now touched the ceiling of our dining room like cardboard skyscrapers, I don't think Tom or I really believed we were leaving until Henry woke us one morning, yelling from the kitchen.

'Look! It's bigger dan a house!'

A few moments later, we stood at the window too, staring at the shipping container that had been parked out the front of our building during the night. It was only just smaller than my one bedroom flat in Paddington, where we would land in another few weeks. Refusing any help, Tom immediately began the gruelling job of transporting every box full of clothes, cutlery, lamps, books, and memories downstairs, and without slipping on the ice outside into our container bound for Sydney. You'd think, by the way he leapt back up those steps three at a time, singing to himself, kissing Henry and I as he passed, that this move had been his idea all along.

In fact I sometimes wondered if relocating to the Antipodes hadn't circumnavigated some sort of midlife crisis. Not that I believed all men reached their mid-forties and automatically bought a sports car, got hair transplants and began dating cheer leaders. But nor had I ever seen my tall German husband so suddenly eager to start all over again, and so far from home. He didn't even seem to miss his beloved showroom, digital wallpaper prints and sound system. Instead, Tom couldn't wait to get to his computer and continue looking up two bedroom apartments in Manly, station wagon cars with roof racks and job vacancies.

'I could be a barrister,' he confidently announced one day, having gone through the positions vacant on seek.com again.

I looked up from my laptop, concerned. Imagining himself striding through Martin Place in a wig and gown was at best a joke, but at worst a sign of a truly disturbing development. It struck me as aiming a little high, I told Tom as gently as I could, given he'd never studied law, let alone had much experience in courtroom advocacy. He'd have to go back to university, possibly for five years or more, I said, and go for his Bachelor of Laws.

'Rubbish,' Tom cried. 'All you need to know is how to operate a coffee machine.'

'Oh!' I cried, flooded with relief. 'You mean a barista!'

'Why not?' he asked. After working in tourism, advertising, banking and digital printing, why not a café at the beach somewhere? So long as they played good music, and the people were friendly?

'Why not indeed,' I said, hugging him. And he wouldn't have to wear the wig either.

Just days before our departure and here we were again, the three of us, looking out our kitchen window. The enormous dark patch of road left by the container that had disappeared as mysteriously as it had appeared in the first place was now covered with snow. Watching him kiss his son's golden hair, it occurred to me that my Bavarian was standing at the same window he had as a child, through which he'd possibly even seen his first snow. Cradled in his father's arms, Henry was a picture of contemplation too, as if remembering trips to the Deutches Museum, the zoo, the Alps, or afternoons spent with his Munich friends as they explored pirate ships, castles and planets together. Or perhaps he was already swimming at Camp Cove with stingrays, turtles and dolphins. I too had been visited by a constant procession of people, places and musings, like random postcards from Bavaria, demanding to be remembered.

Making toast that morning I'd thought of Pavel, our handyman from Warsaw, and hoped he'd get enough work without us next spring. For no reason in particular I thought of José, my Brazilian fellow student from my German class, and wondered if he was still in Munich, with cotton wool stuffed in his ears. Packing up my clothes, I'd thought of the elderly ladies in cardigans who'd demanded to see our tickets on the train; the goth all in black at the neo-Nazi march who'd asked me for a match; and the woman who'd struggled to pull on my *Stützstrumpfhosen* in the geriatric underwear shop. I recollected the first time I'd seen Tom in *Lederhosen*; the first time I'd heard of *Föhn*, the dry air that had sent Tante Ilsa packing from Marquartstein; and the last time I'd sat next to Tante Zelda and had wanted to hug her. Cleaning our bath, I'd wondered what group of men Isabella now showered with, or if perhaps she'd taken up scrapbooking instead. And going through our bathroom cabinet, I'd recalled my royal dentist, our long-necked Bulgarian princess, and my rear molars enlarged in technicolour on her enormous screen. I remembered the Rotkreuz Klinik with its formidable Professor Herr Doktor Borg, the breast pump room in the *Kinderzimmer*, and Schwester Sabine with her frozen peas. Sorting through my jewellery box, I saw myself walking through the glittering rooms of the Rezidenz, into Moshammer's famous boutique, and then through the ancient streets of the Old City. And while pulling out my summer clothes, I'd thought of five Oktoberfests in a row, of riding our bicycles to the Waldwirtschaft Biergarten, and of watching the river surfers until they were interrupted by a log raft carrying revellers swaying to the beat of a five piece *Blas* band. Collecting our washing from the machine downstairs in our freezing basement, I'd remembered the bitterly cold day I'd spent on my own at the concentration camp in Dachau, struggling to imagine the cruel suffering of so many, and my subsequent immersion into the Holocaust. And as I hung out our washing on the clothes horse upstairs in our toasty apartment, I'd thought with gratitude of my favourite warm interior and salvation for lonely mothers, the *Mutterzentrum* in Schraudolphstrasse.

I was still standing at the window with Henry and Tom, smiling at the memory of our small wedding party's arrival nearly five years earlier, their loud voices terrifying the whole neighbourhood when, spookily, our doorbell rang. Waking from our snow reverie, the three of us looked down to the footpath below where a large man in a fluorescent orange uniform waved up at us from our front gate, grinning from ear to ear.

'Frohe Weinachten!' the garbageman shouted.

Scheisse!

'Quick!' Henry cried, jumping down from his father's arms. 'Hide!'

As expected, the hardest people to say goodbye to, for Tom and Henry as much as for me, were our family within the Treehouse community, especially Christine, Harald, Debbie, Michael, our wonderful teacher and child whisperer Shoma, Valerie, and our dear friends Lisa and John, the smart, funny American couple, both writers themselves, who ran my favourite bookshop, The Munich Readery. And all their children. I would especially miss Kara, intelligent observer and secret narrator of all our lives, whose articulate explanations, even at the age of four, often helped me to a better understanding of our own boy's sometimes baffling behaviour.

'Henry didn't have a good morning. He didn't eat his lunch, Felix told him there's no volcanoes in Australia, and his butterfly fell off the wall.'

But I had deliberately left the toughest goodbye until last. We'd met as regularly as ever during those last increasingly cold months in Munich, either at our theatrical Viennese *Kaffeehaus* in the city, or else at our favourite Thai restaurant, Koriander, in Schwabing, until the inevitable final brunch arrived.

Over a bottle of champagne, the five of us sat upstairs on our favourite antique lounges, dismissing each other's confession of bad mothering, laughing at each other's latest trial and tribulation and reminding one another with glasses raised how wonderful we each were. And even before I pulled the string and tore open their large present wrapped in brown paper, I knew exactly what they'd gone and bought me.

'And it's a real one,' Rowena said as I held the dress up to my shoulders. 'Not a tourist one, so Tom should be pleased.'

I would wear it next Oktoberfest, I cried, when we'd come back for a holiday. We would all go together!'

'Never mind that,' Jane said, who in ten years had refused to buy herself a *Dirndl*. 'We just want you to wear it on the cover of your book.'

I would, I promised them. And for a moment we all blinked at each other, unable to postpone the inevitable. As we hugged each other tight, sobbing into each other's collars and scarves, it occurred to me that in my nearly five years living in Munich I'd made some of the very best friends of my life.

'Wait a minute,' said Dagmar, having blown her nose into her napkin. 'Just in case it's the wrong size, run downstairs and try it on.'

I was already on my way.

'Then come back,' Rowena called over the balcony, 'and give us a look at you!'

As I twirled like a teenage girl in front of the large mirrors in the basement toilets at Tambosi's in my dark green *Dirndl* with matching white blouse and red apron, I couldn't have felt happier, prettier, or more Bavarian. Although I wasn't quite able to fill the bodice at the front, there were certain bras that could help me out there.

'Schön,' said the cleaning lady, smiling as she leant forward in her chair by the door.

'Ein Geschenk,' I told her, my eyes brimming with tears as I pointed upstairs, 'von meinen Freundinnen.'

What good friends they were, she said, to have bought something so meaningful, so authentic and beautiful. I'd be sure to think of them, she said, whenever I wore it. I agreed. It would also remind me of my *Heimat*. My home. Our other home, München.

Acknowledgments

A huge thanks to the wonderful, wise and patient women at Allen & Unwin, Sue Hines, Rebecca Kaiser and Jo Jarrah for putting this book so beautifully together. And to Fiona Inglis for all the support.

Thanks to my loving, barking family, especially good sport and generous sister who, no matter how much I exaggerate 'George' for comic effect, always says 'it's your book, darls!'

Thanks to my mate Simon Hughes for all the hilarious emails, especially the one in which he asked, *How Now Brown Frau?*

Thanks to dear Deb Lanser and Ashley Johnson for hair and make up for Lisa White's fabulous cover.

And finally thanks to Tom for putting up with me and this book, for the best hugs ever, for being a secret brilliant slapstick comedian, and for driving really fast around the sleepy Taufkirchen roundabout on our way to Aldi every Saturday morning until Henry and I screamed with laughter.